TEACHING
WITH
CASES

A Practical Guide

ESPEN ANDERSEN + BILL SCHIANO

TEACHING WITH CASES

A Practical Guide

HARVARD BUSINESS SCHOOL PUBLISHING

Boston, Massachusetts

10 9 8 7 6 5 4 3 2 1

The web addresses referenced in this book were live and correct at the time of the
book's publication but may be subject to change.

Library of Congress Cataloging-in-Publication Data

Andersen, Espen.
Teaching with cases : a practical guide / Espen Andersen and Bill Schiano.
    pages cm
ISBN 978-1-62527-626-1 (alk. paper)
1. Management—Study and teaching. 2. Case method. 3. Business education.
I. Schiano, Bill. II. Title.
HD30.4.S329 2014
658.0071'1—dc23

                                                            2014009959

The paper used in this publication meets the requirements of the American
National Standard for Permanence of Paper for Publications and Documents in
Libraries and Archives Z39.48-1992.

Contents

Preface

This book got its start when Espen sat down to explain how to do case teaching to his colleagues at BI Norwegian Business School in Oslo. Faculty at BI, as at most business schools, use case teaching sporadically, at their own initiative. Espen loves case teaching, uses it for most of his classes, and would like to see more of it, so he set out to write a short and punchy "Top Ten Tip List for Case Teachers." Before he knew it, the document had expanded to ten pages, then to twenty, and eventually to an eighty-page print-on-demand book in Norwegian.

Bill teaches in the United States, at Bentley University in Waltham, Massachusetts, and, like Espen, is a proponent of cases and discussion-based teaching. We have known each other since our doctoral student days and even taught courses together via video-conferencing across the Atlantic. When Espen spent sabbatical time at Bentley in 2009, the little Norwegian case teaching book became a subject for discussion. Bill liked it but had lots of suggestions (Bill always has lots of suggestions), and the idea of writing a real book on the practice of case teaching was born.

And here is the result: approximately 90,000 words of practical advice on how to do case teaching in—and this is a key point—a setting where case teaching is not the norm. We intend the book to be easy reading, with a relentless focus on the practical. We do not expect you to absorb and implement all of the ideas at once—and while we certainly encourage reading the book chapter by chapter, we hope you will find it useful as a reference when specific issues come up and as a periodic refresher. Each chapter can be read independently and is divided into subsections to facilitate searching.

As in a good case discussion, most of the content of the book is not about right and wrong answers. The two of us often approach teaching differently, and we share our contrasting perspectives throughout the text. Even when we agree, many of our suggestions are appropriate only in some situations. Throughout the book, we discuss various ways context can differ and how you might adapt to it. We hope the book sparks ideas for how you can improve your own teaching, and we encourage you to adapt our ideas to your unique situation—and to share your insights and experiences with us.

The website associated with this book (teachingwithcases. hbsp.harvard.edu), includes all of the online resources referred to throughout the text. As we develop and find other materials that support case teaching, we will provide links to them there. Please make use of the materials in your courses, and join us in creating new and better ones!

Case teaching can be challenging and even scary at times, and it certainly is more work than regular lectures, at least until your skills are fully developed. But it is also more rewarding for you. Every discussion is different, ensuring that you will never again feel like a video player, rattling off lectures on the repeat setting. And it is more rewarding for your students, who experience being placed in situations where they are allowed to learn not just from you, but also from each other. And in a technologically changing marketplace for learning, the intense case discussion is more resistant to automation and commoditization than any other form of teaching.

Did we mention that it's also fun?

Acknowledgments

Espen would like to thank his colleagues at BI Norwegian Business School: Øystein Fjeldstad, Lars Huemer, Hermann Kopp, Mark Kriger, Randi Lunnan, Idoia Olazar, Hanno Roberts, Ragnvald Sannes, Amir Sasson, and Erik Wilberg, for their tips on case teaching; for their emotional and, in some cases, organizational support; for their immense patience in the face of his tiresome rants; and for discreetly pointing him in less damaging directions. He would also like to thank his daughters, Julie, Helene, and Jenny Marie, for their tolerance of his prolonged mental absences and their skill in bringing him down to earth. Most of all he would like to thank his wife Lena for sticking with him all these years.

Bill would like to thank Bentley colleagues too numerous to name for actively engaging in discussions about teaching (even if many of them haven't succumbed to Bill's incessant pitches for the case method). He would also like to thank his many great teachers, particularly Professors Geoffrey Jehle and Robert Jackall, whose infectious enthusiasm for what they did and the ideas they discussed inspired Bill to implement the techniques in this book, and Grandmaster Robert Moran for teaching him to think deeply about adapting approaches for individual students. Most of all, Bill would like to thank Jen, who remained unfailingly supportive and a delight to be around throughout the project, even when Bill was unreasonably absorbed in the work.

We would both like to thank our students—those we have taught separately and those we have taught together, including participants in Harvard Business Publishing's Case Method Teaching seminars— for all the experiences that informed this book. We owe particular thanks to our fellow case-method seminar facilitators, Bob Austin, Bill Bruns, Jim Heskett, and Dorothy Leonard, for their mentorship, and to Jackie White, Paul Sluk, and Amanda Boomhower, who helped us become better, more deliberate case teachers.

We had each heard countless tales of woe from book authors about the harrowing process of finishing a book. While the workload has been everything we were warned it would be, not only has our friendship survived intact, but we have greatly enjoyed the opportunity to work with so many wonderful, dedicated professionals.

Nick Morgan believed in us and in the project from the outset, taught us what a book treatment is and how to write one, and helped us develop our voices. Ellen Gandt and Allison Monro at Harvard Business Publishing saw value in the book and helped give it shape. We are particularly grateful to Allison for her determination and support in shepherding the project through to its completion and for matching us with our developmental editor, Bill Ellet, who provided invaluable insights and perspective and was a pleasure to work with.

We are indebted to many others who helped guide us in the development of this book. Bob Kelley and Denis Saulnier generously shared their wisdom on online case teaching. We were honored that our reviewers, Cynthia Ingols, Ann Mirabito, Hanno Roberts, Haowen Wu, and Kelly Zellars, read the manuscript with remarkable care and depth and provided thorough, thoughtful feedback. Though we don't know who wrote which reviews, all of the input helped considerably. Beyond serving as a reviewer, Cynthia Ingols was incredibly generous with her time, provided vital insights and guidance, and introduced Bill to Debbie Ettington and Anne Lawrence, who were also generous with their time and perspective. Jane Schiano, Sam Wigutow, and Peter Schiano patiently, enthusiastically, and with great humor provided invaluable edits and generally helped us write something readable. Last but certainly not least, the meticulous work of our copy editor, Jane Gebhart dramatically improved the text and made us better writers.

1

INTRODUCTION

Why You Should Read This Book

This book is about how to teach cases, especially in environments where case teaching is not the norm. We intend this book for anyone interested in case teaching, whether basing a whole course on cases, using cases as a supplement, or just using some discussion facilitation techniques employed in case teaching. Though we base our discussion on business schools, the techniques here can be used both outside business schools and outside the academic setting altogether.

A wide range of teachers seeks help teaching cases. We think you would benefit from reading this book if you are:

- An experienced teacher planning to teach cases for the first time.

- A new teacher teaching for the first time in a course with cases.

- An instructor new to teaching executives who wants to engage them through discussion, because executives like to talk.

- An experienced case teacher hoping to refresh and deepen your facilitation skills and perhaps pick up a few pointers.

- An administrator or academic leader wanting to understand what case teaching is about and how to support someone doing it.

Most business schools are not set up with the classrooms, culture, and course structure for case teaching as the preferred or even common way of teaching. We have taught cases in many schools and many countries and do not routinely encounter students experienced in the method. Most of our colleagues do not use case teaching at all. An evaluation system with up to 50 percent of the grade based on class participation is anathema in many schools and, in fact, is outlawed in some countries. And few schools take teaching seriously enough to make it a basis for promotion.

So why teach cases in such an environment in the first place? Is it really worth it?

Why Case Teaching?

We call our primary form of teaching "case teaching." Many descriptive terms are floating around—"discussion-based teaching," "participant-centered learning," "problem-centered teaching," "the Socratic method"—and we choose not to differentiate them. For instance, case teaching does not necessarily mean using a purpose-written business case as the basis for a class. You might use a chapter of a book, a newspaper article, a film, or just a question.

Case teaching is an underused, but very effective way of teaching in a number of contexts, but especially so in business schools. Understanding the problems of business is more a question of pattern recognition than use of precise diagnostic tools or scientific hypothesis testing (Christensen & Raynor, 2003). To recognize patterns, you need experience. Case discussion transfers experience-based knowledge, so the students learn not only from the teacher but from each other by bringing their collective experience to bear on the problem. To develop judgment, you need to not only read theory but also apply it, and discussion-based or case-based teaching is a way to simulate business situations and have students ask themselves, "What would I do if I were in this specific situation?"

Case teaching is unevenly applied. A number of business schools, such as Harvard, Ivey, Darden, IESE, Haas, Tuck, Stanford, and Wharton, use cases as their primary teaching method (Byrne, 2012), but most use it occasionally. More should do it, if for no other reason than that the good students like it, even though they have to work more than with the regular lecture-based teaching. Case teaching makes the knowledge of the whole class, not just the instructor, available to the student. Students can teach and learn from each other. Done well, it can provide a simulated business environment, allowing students to learn by trying things out. It trains the student not just for finding a solution, but also for arguing for it and shaping it to fit to a context. And most importantly, case teaching surfaces the depth of problems and many alternative perspectives and solutions, more deeply and more extensively than can be done by a single instructor.

The main benefit of case teaching to the instructor is that you have a more interesting time doing the classes, rather than feeling that you are repeatedly performing the same lectures, which could just as well be videotaped. In chapter 10, we will make the case that most noninteractive lecture material will be moving online. Case teaching also helps ensure that the students learn what is relevant and practical and that you learn from your students, especially at the executive level. We have also found that case teaching increases your speaking and consulting marketability.

Central to case teaching is a problem of some sort, presented in a way that students can discuss, which normally means that there are several alternative legitimate solutions with good arguments for each. As any decision maker has to do in real life, the point of the discussion is to understand the problem, identify solutions, and choose among them. Case teaching has a long tradition in law schools—hence the term "case"—where students discuss court cases and sometimes even simulate the actual proceedings of a courtroom in order to prepare themselves for the real thing. In a less stylized format in medical studies, professors give students medical cases with complicated symptoms and ask them for a diagnosis and proposed treatment.

Classic case teaching in business schools means having students read and analyze a business case—a one- to forty-page description of a business, organizational, or leadership problem, normally presented from the viewpoint of top management—and then discussing it in class with their peers (see online resource 1 for an example of a short business case and online resource 2 for the accompanying teaching note).* The discussion lasts for 1 to 1.5 hours and takes the students through the background of the case, possible solutions to the problem, each solution's pros and cons, and perhaps, but not always, a conclusion. The role of the teacher is to facilitate the discussion, capturing key points on the blackboard and perhaps rounding off the class with a few concluding comments.

The main idea is that the students are the primary participants. In the discussion, which the instructor facilitates, they use their experience and relevant theory to understand the case and its place in the curriculum. It need not be, as some teachers think, an inquisitorial interrogation of high-strung and fearsomely competitive students who have prepared through the night to the point where they can recite case and theory verbatim, as portrayed in such films as *Paper Chase* and *Legally Blond*. In practice, there is room for a wide range of teaching styles. Throughout the book, we advocate that you find and use your authentic voice and resist the temptation to exercise undue influence over the discussion.

How Case Classes and Students Vary

A standard case class—the base case, if you will—has full-time students meeting regularly over a semester in a classroom. Most of the advice in this book takes this as a starting point. For most of us, teaching well requires adapting to a myriad of challenges. Case classes are no different. They vary on many dimensions, and cases are used in an ever-widening array of contexts. Throughout the book, we will be discussing these variables and how to adapt your teaching to them.

---

* To see this and other online resources for the book,
visit the web site: teachingwithcases.hbsp.harvard.edu.

Class Size

Case teaching can be done effectively in courses ranging from small seminars to groups larger than a hundred, and online, potentially in the hundreds or more. But the nature of the discussions and the facilitation required vary dramatically according to the number of students, as do many of the goals for the course and for individual students.

Core versus Elective

Instructors need to develop and teach core and elective courses differently. Students in core courses show greater diversity of interest and background in the topic. The variance in interest calls for case selection and class management with emphasis on motivating and engaging students. Maintaining the energy and participation levels in core courses requires more explicit effort to involve all students. Electives offer the great benefit of students who have chosen to be there—as Espen says, "no tourists"—which is fantastic as long as you can keep enough students signing up for your course.

Part-Time versus Full-Time

Most case teaching material is targeted toward full-time students, even though the vast majority of MBA students are now part-time. Faculty have less control over part-time students as they have obligations at work that often supersede those for class. Part-time students also tend to be less connected to one another and are usually less invested in class dynamics and interaction than their full-time counterparts.

Gender

Gender differences surface in all facets of case courses among and between students and faculty. The case method amplifies the issues by changing the power dynamics and requiring far more interaction. By paying explicit attention to the issues and managing them overtly, faculty can improve the learning and experience for all students. One gender, typically the males (though in some academic settings, it can go the other way), can dominate the other, ignoring comments, interrupting, or simply being more assertive and shaping the discussion. We will discuss this issue more in chapter 3, but you can counter this even at the course-preparation stage if you choose reading materials carefully, are explicit about how you want to conduct the discussions, and set up side communication channels such as written summary assignments.

Weekly versus Modular Courses

Many courses are now delivered in intensive weeks or weekends, requiring different approaches for design, preparation, and teaching. Modular courses that meet for long periods of time with gaps between them raise issues of preparation, retention, and focus. In a weekly course, you have more control over the students and get to know them better, and it is easier to adjust the content and process of the course during the semester.

Domestic versus International

Many programs now have a substantial international contingent. The diversity can greatly enhance discussions but also introduce many challenges. Many students are educated in cultures that do not support speaking in class, much less being responsible for the discussion.

The language and pacing of a diverse class may challenge some students. This requires explicit management by the teacher. See chapter 7 for a more thorough treatment of this topic.

Single versus Multisection

Coordinating courses that are taught to more than one group in the same semester, often by different faculty, requires more of instructors. Courses with only one section afford freedom, but require more effort from the instructor to develop and teach.

Executive versus Graduate versus Undergraduate

These three audiences vary widely in their maturity, experience, learning goals, facility with the material, knowledge of the domain, and diligence in preparation and the instructor must treat them differently.

One of Many Case Classes versus One of Few

Teaching with cases in a school or program where most of the other classes are lecture-based introduces myriad challenges for the faculty and students, including variances in student expectations, infrastructure, student behavior, and pressure from other faculty. If there are many case classes at the school, the main issue is coordinating the use of cases, so that the same case is not used, at least not inadvertently, in several courses.

In School versus Other Locations

Many courses are taught off campus. Teaching in a hotel, resort, conference center, or company office presents unique problems. Instructors of a class where everyone comes from the same company can also encounter problems created by differences in the students' positions in the company hierarchy. Not that on-campus classes are necessarily utopia; many classrooms are not designed for cases, and norms for students set by other courses can make case teaching more difficult.

Practical Guidance for All Case-Teaching Faculty

We focus on practical issues and advice for faculty that they can easily implement. We consider the full range of students and environments, not limiting ourselves to the traditional focus on a full-time MBA class of experienced, domestic students in institutions dedicated to case teaching.

We see teaching not as a science, but a craft, and a practical one at that. You learn a craft by listening to people with experience, trying out their practices, then changing or discarding them to suit your own situation, knowledge, and personality. Much teaching knowledge is implicit, learned from experience, gut feel, experimentation, mistakes, and imitation. Observation and reflection are important. In the absence of the former, we will have to start with the latter.

Our ambition is therefore to share, in practical detail, how to organize a case course, how to teach it, and how to evaluate it. We express our ideas in language somewhere between that of *The Economist* and Richard Feynman: provocative enough that some will feel a need to argue against it and provide alternative solutions.

We would love that debate, and we invite you to join us at the companion web site to this book (teachingwithcases.hbsp.harvard.edu), where you will also find the book's online resources and other useful material. We are most happy when the students are busily discussing what a case protagonist should do, knowing that the whole point of having the discussion is not which solution you choose, but the questions you must ask to uncover the alternatives.

The Central Framework:
Foundations, Flow, and Feedback

The rest of the book is practically oriented, with a very simple central framework consisting of three core elements:

1. *Foundations.* When you teach in a setting where case teaching is not the norm, you need to spend time and energy establishing a contract between the students and you about how the course will unfold, and more specifically, what the students should do and what you will do. This involves planning the course structure carefully, making expectations explicit, and wisely selecting cases and other reading materials. Establishing the foundations is discussed in chapter 2.

2. *Flow.* Before and during the course itself, you can use a number of techniques to make the job easier and more systematic, plan and prepare every class carefully, and work on creating a lively discussion in the classroom. Flow is

discussed in detail in chapter 3 and what to do if problems arise in chapter 5.

3. *Feedback*. Before, during, and after the course, you need to think carefully about student evaluation and how to communicate it to the students. We offer guidance to help you make this part of the job easier and the feedback to the students more actionable. We discuss feedback in chapter 4.

These elements are all you need to do a great case course. But the book doesn't end there. We have also included material on using technology to support in-classroom case teaching, and how to do case teaching online, both synchronously and asynchronously. In addition, we discuss how to take case teaching from something you do in a single course to your normal modus operandi and what it takes to make case teaching—and the ensuing focus on teaching quality—an integral part of the institution in which you teach.

You may think we are belaboring the small stuff, such as what to bring to class and what to wear. However, given the focus on the teacher and the importance of not being derailed by small irritations when you teach, the details matter. How you dress, having fresh whiteboard pens or chalk available, and taking control of the classroom to suit your needs are all examples of small things that, if not thought about beforehand, can lower your self-confidence and the quality of the session. You need to feel sure that everything is taken care of, and having the easy but important details settled before the course starts means you can concentrate on content and impression from the very beginning. The devil, quite literally, is in the details.

It's time to dive into the specifics by, first, preparing.

References

Byrne, J. A. "How the World's Top Business Schools Teach Their MBAs." *Poets & Quants*. November 11, 2012. http://poetsandquants.com/2012/11/18/how-the-worlds-top-business-schools-teach-their-mbas/3/.

Christensen, C. M. and M. E. Raynor (2003). "Why Hard-nosed Executives Should Care about Management Theory." *Harvard Business Review* (September): 67–74.

2

FOUNDATIONS

Preparing for the Course

We believe that at least two-thirds of your success as a case teacher lies in what you do before the course starts: how you prepare yourself, your course, and the contract between you and your students. If case teaching is the exception in your setting, preparation becomes even more important. You quite literally need to build a solid foundation for your course by making everything involved in case preparation and discussion explicit.

Preparing for a case course requires a lot of work, but not necessarily more than for a quality lecture course, and it requires less after you become experienced. For a case class, you need to think more carefully than for a lecture-based class about the classroom environment, the relationship with the students, and the preparation of each case so you understand the case at least well as the students. But once the discussion gets going, you'll learn a lot from the students, enjoy interesting discussions, and increase your legitimacy as a teacher in the process.

In this chapter, we discuss essential issues to consider and act on before the course starts. The amount of preparation may seem a bit intimidating. We are not saying you need to do it all, but whether or

Preparing for Classes

How and how much you prepare is a very personal matter. We are quite different in how we prepare.

Bill prepares extensively and relatively early, even going as far as preparing many cases before the course has started. Espen, on the other hand, prefers to leave gaps in the course setup and almost build the course as it goes forward, leaving room for experimentation and improvisation.

not to do it should be a conscious decision. Some of these points of preparation will become habit. Others you might avoid or cut short.

Taking Ownership

Preparation is not just doing things that are visible and tangible, such as selecting the right cases and creating a detailed syllabus for the course. Especially in a setting where cases are not the norm, it also involves self-preparation, which includes:

- Making the content and message of the course clear to yourself and others.

- Ensuring that you have the authority and self-confidence to take control of the whole student experience.

- Understanding where your support and your opposition will be.

- Setting the students' expectations about the content and conduct of the course, and their own role in it.

Preparation cannot obviate all problems that may arise in a course, but it will help you avoid most of them and position you well to deal with the rest.

When you are about to create a course or assume someone else's course design, remember that *the course is yours*. This is probably our most important piece of advice. Your predecessor may have had a well-defined structure or a textbook that encouraged a specific and detailed design. Your school may have traditions about how courses are designed and taught, or perhaps you are teaching just a small part of a larger course. In any case, you need to take ownership of the course and the class within the parameters over which you have control.

Ownership is often a matter of self-confidence. A well-known study (Ambady & Rosenthal, 1993) has shown that students' opinions of a teacher tend to form during the first thirty seconds when they see or meet him or her. What they are looking for is self-confidence, so spend some time thinking about how you create and maintain a confident impression. Take ownership of the course, and you will bolster your self-confidence and hence the students' first impressions. (In this digital age, the first time the students see you may be in a video presentation of the course or a video conference; the same need for a confident and reassuring presence applies.) Chapter 3 will address the first class meeting in more detail.

Often, if you are new to teaching or in a junior position, taking charge can be difficult. If you are teaching executive audiences, you can be sure that in any class, one or more students will know a lot more about the content than you do. If you are teaching a case course for a single company, you will have a whole classroom of experts, real or self-appointed, on that particular company or industry. For almost all kinds of students, you will probably have to work to make them change their study and classroom habits, particularly if they are part-time students. Reverting back to the safety and comfort of lecturing can be very tempting.

Resist this temptation. You have been appointed to teach the course, which implies that you have some level of expertise in the field—and as such, you are entitled to call the shots. That means you decide what is good and bad, which examples are relevant and which are not, which article or textbook is necessary and which is not. Resist pressure to do things you do not find educationally defensible. This does not mean you should ignore other people's opinions, but if the course is your responsibility, then you have authority to make the calls. You should make them, even if it is difficult.

Making a Contract

Establishing norms and expectations about how you will conduct the course at the outset is crucial, because, once set, they are very difficult to change. We allocate time early in the course to giving clear directions and forging an explicit contract both with the students and, to a lesser extent, with the administration and our peers. Our part of the contract is that we will guide the students through a challenging and important subject at a level comparable to the best universities in the world in ways that rely on and are designed to fit with the students' experience and background. The students commit to prepare for each class and to participate actively. In doing so, they take responsibility not just for their own learning but for that of their classmates.

In practice, this means being explicit about expectations in the course description (see online resource 4 for some sample syllabi),* sending a letter to the students before the course starts explaining the contract and devoting some time in the first class to explain the course structure and, if necessary, how you will conduct case discussions. Sometimes it may be worthwhile to conduct a special class before the course starts to explain case classes and how to prepare a case. If the school already conducts such a course, it may not meet your needs; be sure to adapt as necessary. Online resource 5 includes some examples of explanatory notes distributed to students to guide preparation.

We expect students to come prepared for all classes, including the first one. Most courses have so few class meetings and so much material to cover that one to three hours cannot be wasted on introductory discussions. In many schools, even well-intentioned students might miss the first meeting because they have not yet enrolled in the program, or they are shopping courses during a drop or add period. If you cannot avoid this, give a lecture in the first class meeting and then perhaps use a short case distributed during class to introduce discussion, draw on something that is in the news and can be discussed, or send out an email with attached material. All of these measures underscore that participation and preparation are integral to the course from the very beginning.

---

* To see this and other online resources for the book,
visit the web site: teachingwithcases.hbsp.harvard.edu.

It is crucial to set expectations about office hours. In many schools, faculty are expected to be widely available, while in others, student access to faculty outside class is severely limited. If you are going to schedule office hours, be sure to consider likely timing conflicts for students, such as other courses many of your students may be taking, or full-time jobs students may have, making them unable to meet during workday hours. Be clear, especially if you teach undergraduates, that office hours are not a way to improve a class participation grade.

Getting the contract right with the students has first priority, but you also need to contract with the administration and, to some extent, with your peers. Make clear what you want early so you get priority on resources, such as classrooms that facilitate interaction.

Contracting with peers is less common, unless you are team-teaching a course with parallel sessions, in which case the team needs to discuss and coordinate each session (we discuss team-teaching in chapter 3). You should ensure you are not using the same material as any of your fellow teachers in other courses or at least not in the same way. However, don't overestimate this problem: many cases are rich in detail and with forethought can be taught from several perspectives. You should also find out what other courses the students are taking and know something about what the other teachers say, lest you find yourself embroiled in discussions with students on the topic: "But Professor X said this in his course. Why are you saying something different?" Those discussions can be very fruitful but only if you know what Professor X teaches and really says.

If you become a good case teacher in a noncase setting, students may end up spending more time preparing for your course than for others, partly because you force them to and partly because students often become enthusiastic and interested when challenged with relevant cases. This can sometimes result in professional jealousy from other teachers, who will hear questions about why their courses are not taught the same way your course is. While seemingly a good problem to have, it can be a real issue in program meetings, for instance, where people will complain about unprepared students, with the underlying messages that "your excellent teaching is making the rest of us look bad."

We have dealt with this criticism on the few occasions it has arisen by explaining our teaching strategy, especially how we force students to prepare, and making it clear that everyone else is perfectly free to adopt the same strategies. It is very hard to openly counter that argument. If you are a younger teacher, however, keeping your superiors—that is, program deans—informed and onboard before these issues arise can be a smart move. Assuming that the time you commit to teaching is not having a negative impact on your research productivity, most department chairs and administrators will be delighted that you are engaging and challenging students.

Developing Content

We suggest you create the course content in this order: first line up the issues you want to cover by dividing the course into parts. For example:

- The first three classes explore basic issues.

- The next three focus on planning and analysis.

- The next two, on execution.

- The next three, on handling special cases.

- The final two, on integrating viewpoints and conclusions.

Next, select the cases for each class meeting. Third, select articles and supporting material for each case.

As with any advice we give here, this is not absolute. Perhaps you have a few favorite cases you want in the class; perhaps you let the theory drive the structure of the course. Remember that students tend to retain the cases better than the articles, and course design is primarily about what you want the students to remember.

Structuring the Syllabus

The syllabus is the written contract with students and outlines the structure of the course. Forethought and thoroughness in the syllabus will save time later and enhance the students' experience. We like to be very detailed in our syllabi and to keep them as living documents.

Syllabus structure works best if you can find a logical progression through the topics, from fundamentals to advanced or from general to specific. To the extent you have unifying themes, introduce them early and reinforce them throughout the term. The first case sets the tone for the course; choose one with some twists that is not too easy. If students have a nearly complete analysis of the first case, they may believe the course will be easy and put less effort into preparation or describe the class as easy to others. We like to keep students guessing, especially early in the course. The last case in the course should be as comprehensive as possible, allowing students to apply and integrate much of what they have learned during the course.

Some case teachers never allow a discussion of a case to go beyond a single class meeting, even if key issues are never discussed. This certainly makes pacing the course easier and instills discipline in both students and faculty. We never plan for the discussion of a single

Sharing the Syllabus

Consider having the syllabus as an online, shared, and constantly updated document, perhaps even with editing rights for the students. (There are various ways to do this, such as with Google Docs or Windows Live.) Having the document online gives students one place, and one place only, to look for updates and information. Making it a live document means that you can change the content of the course as you are teaching it. We like to have at least one session open, for instance, to deal with issues the students find interesting. Enabling the students to edit and comment on the page underscores the joint responsibility for the course outcome between teacher and student. It also saves work. We have often found that small errors, such as dead URLs to articles, have been fixed by the first student who found the error directly, without involving us at all.

Questions about the Topics for Class Discussion

When students ask what questions will be discussed in class, Bill retells a Bruce Springsteen story about his band backing up American rock-and-roll legend Chuck Berry. Berry arrived backstage a few minutes before show time, and Springsteen, on behalf of the band, asked Berry what songs they would be playing that night. Berry responded, matter-of-factly, "We are going to play some Chuck Berry songs."

In other words, when students ask what you will discuss in class, simply say "the case."

case to take more than one class period, but are not doctrinaire and will pick up discussion in the next class if there is sufficiently valuable material that was not addressed. Done often, it will frustrate students and reflect poor planning, but occasionally it is entirely reasonable. Building some slack into the syllabus with a case that can be covered in less time if necessary allows for some catch-up around midterm.

We generally include questions in the syllabus to guide case preparation, but make it clear to the students that these questions are for preparation and are unlikely to be discussed in class. Unless this is clear, students—especially those from countries with a tradition for rote learning, such as China—sometimes prepare and read out loud written answers to the preparation questions, but are unable to discuss any other issues in the case or put them in a larger context.

Selecting Cases

Your choice of cases can have a dramatic impact on the quality of your course. You need to consider how effectively the cases will facilitate learning, how they will work together in a course, and how much the cases will appeal to the audience. Here are thirteen basic factors to consider when choosing cases, in no particular order.

Age of the Case

Many, if not most, topics in business courses are perennial, and well-written cases that address such issues can be evergreen. Even in our information technology courses, we regularly use cases that are ten or twenty years old. This sends a powerful message to students about the longevity of issues, and it leverages your preparation from previous terms. When the occasional student complains that the cases are old, we ask the students to take out a pencil and change all the dates in the case twenty years ahead to see if anything else changes, aside from the speed and spread of the technology. Most cases keep surprisingly well.

Unfortunately, no matter how well reasoned your argument, this rationale may not prove compelling to many students. If all of your cases are a decade or more old—and keep in mind that the publication date is often a year or more after the case takes place—you can give the appearance of not being up to date or even that you are choosing cases to minimize your own preparation time. At a minimum, you should pepper the course with some fresh cases, making sure that you do not go more than a few meetings without a relatively recent one. Once or twice, you can also introduce something that is very fresh, even working from newspaper features, magazine articles, or blog posts instead of a teaching case.

Availability of Teaching Notes

Teaching notes help, especially if you are a relatively inexperienced case teacher. It may be tempting to limit yourself to cases for which there is a published teaching note, and some teachers do. However, teaching notes vary widely in structure, focus, completeness, and quality, and so does the amount of preparation time they will save. You should also recognize the likelihood that you will teach this course or case more than once. The best preparation for teaching a case is often to teach it and then modify your preparation notes. Given that you have to do the work anyway, and that preparation notes are highly personal and associative (that is, you build off your own experiences), doing the case preparation from scratch is not that much extra work, especially if you choose companies and industries with which you already are familiar.

Industries

Varying cases across industries gives students wider exposure, and if your students are experienced, you have the opportunity to draw on a broad range of their expertise. We have found that, while students prefer cases from their own industries, having occasional cases from unfamiliar industries is useful, as are cases from different contexts, such as nongovernmental organizations (NGOs), the public sector, or the military. Variation can reinforce the importance of good theory across industries. Moreover, NGO and public-sector cases tend to offer easy access to guest speakers from the case organization, which is always a good thing.

Diversity of Protagonists

While difficult to find in many disciplines, a range of protagonists, varying in age, gender, nationality, organizational level, and so on, is crucial. You will be shortchanging your students and look distinctly passé if all your cases feature middle-aged, white American men in the starring roles. You want students to find role models in the cases, and you owe it to them to offer a range of examples.

Company Size

There is a bias in business school cases toward large organizations. As one veteran faculty member and case writer once said to Bill when presented with an idea for a case study about a company with revenue in the tens of millions of dollars, "This is not interesting. Where are the numbers?" In addition to sheer scale as a sign of importance, large organizations have more explicit (thus, more observable) routines, whereas in small companies, much can be and often is done over a Friday beer.

Many students, however, are planning careers in small organizations or entrepreneurial ventures, and become frustrated if all of the cases are about multidivisional multinationals. Having at least a few cases about smaller organizations addresses this concern and enriches the course. It also helps students who might feel a bit intimidated by large numbers and well-known companies.

Stage of Company

Mature companies are very different from early-stage or high-growth companies and require different ways of managing and perhaps different types of managers as well. By varying the cases, you can draw more directly on the range of your students' backgrounds and interests, whether they aspire to be entrepreneurs or *Fortune* 500 CEOs.

Case Complexity

Cases vary widely in complexity. The business model or processes may be complicated, or the situation may involve a wide array of people, departments, or processes. Case authors vary the depth of information and write cases to work in many teaching situations and, hence, focus on more than one topic. Some authors deliberately hide the key clues in a dense cloud of descriptive verbiage and extraneous data.

If you choose complex cases, be sure the complexity is not beyond the reach of students. Consider supplemental materials that may help students understand the terminology, technology, or processes. If you plan to teach complex cases in relatively short class periods, let students know that the discussions will not be exhaustive. If you have students for whom English is not their first language, you need to avoid cases with dense jargon and lots of verbiage. More and more cases have been translated, particularly into Chinese and Spanish. Providing those translations mitigates the language problem for preparation, but does not help with English proficiency, if that is an issue.

Case Length

Some faculty rule out brief or long cases without considering the content and fit with the course. We have had productive eighty-minute discussions of cases as short as one page and found cases as long as fifty pages manageable in the same time period. The discussions may vary according to the English proficiency of the students. You might have to break up longer cases over several classes, or you can give detailed instructions on which parts to focus on.

One of the most important things a student—and a manager—must learn is how to absorb much information quickly, developing an ability to wade through lots of material and decide what is relevant. This requires practice and lots of reading. Inundating students with reading material can be useful, but this sink-or-swim strategy needs to be judiciously applied to ensure students end up swimming.

This strategy can backfire badly. For instance, complex cases may be a bad fit with students in their first or one of their few case courses, undergraduates already adjusting to a different way of learning, or overtaxed part-time students. Many students ignore the bulk of the exhibits or become frustrated by them, and you will need to spend a good deal of time and effort remediating the issues. See chapter 3 for suggestions on how to do this.

Cases Used in Other Courses

In most schools, the choice of cases is not formally coordinated across courses. Communicate with those colleagues who teach courses in or related to your discipline to ensure you are not inadvertently using the same case. However, you should not automatically exclude a case used in another course. You might choose to use the same case because relatively few students will take both courses, or the two courses can use the case quite differently.

Multipart Cases

Cases with parts B, C, or more offer an opportunity to develop the discussion and analysis over time, and novice case teachers often find them helpful because they provide an additional element of structure in the discussion. If the later parts are distributed and read during class, it helps students develop skills in thinking and analyzing on the fly. However, students may see the later parts as answers to the earlier parts, so you may need to reinforce the message that what the company did was not necessarily the best choice.

Multipart cases can offer some logistical issues: most often, the students buy a case package (electronically or on paper) directly from a case clearinghouse. The students will prepare the A case they have purchased, but should not have access to the B and C cases until the appropriate point in the discussion. You can ensure this by paying for the B and C cases yourself (if your department has a budget) or having students pay for them, and then distribute them in class. Electronic solutions (where you can make the cases available electronically at a certain time or directly) will be available in the future, but we still prefer handing out paper copies in class. With paper, you can see when the students are finished reading, and you avoid having them dive into their laptops and be distracted during class.

Multiple Cases about One Company

You might have opportunities to teach more than one case about a given company in a single course. Sometimes, these cases are intended to be taught in sequence, but are not multipart cases. In other instances, if you choose to round up the usual suspects (for example, General Electric, Nike, Dell, or Google), you could teach an entire course on a single company.

We have found that fatigue sets in quickly, however, particularly for inexperienced students. On the other hand, having at least one instance of multiple one-company cases can be helpful in allowing students to gain different perspectives.

Geography

In countries where there are few business teaching materials focused on that country, students appreciate the inclusion of any local material, even if the local aspect is not salient. If you are teaching basic business issues, you might choose a local case or other materials to show respect to students, since demands for local content tends to be pedagogically insignificant but a recurring issue in course evaluations.

Field-Based, Anonymous, and Library Cases

A field-based case is about a real, identified company; contains material from the company; and has been signed off as correct by the company. Information might have been changed, and if this has been done, it is usually noted clearly, at least by the larger case clearinghouses. An anonymous case typically deals with a real company, but the company's name (and often data) has been changed. A library case is based on previously published information only and does not need a release from the company.

Students tend to prefer undisguised cases with proprietary data, but the anonymous format allows information to be published that companies don't want revealed, and you tend to learn more from failures than successes. We select cases based on the relevance and quality of the case alone, but we ensure that every course contains at least some cases from well-known companies, simply because students like to learn some real context in addition to the core issue of the case.

Selecting Readings and Textbooks

Supplementing cases with readings and audiovisual material helps introduce frameworks and analytical tools, provides context by explaining industries and technologies, and gives students an understanding of related academic business research. The material need not be directly linked to the case, but should enhance the students' understanding or their preparation of it. A good rule of thumb is to ask, "Would a case protagonist benefit from seeing this material?"

To find supporting material, begin with the case publisher or clearinghouse. Often, cases or teaching notes suggest accompanying notes, articles, or other material to assign to students. Practitioner-focused management journals are also an excellent source; we draw heavily from *Harvard Business Review, Sloan Management Review,* and *California Management Review,* for instance. More academic-focused journals may also be useful, but you need to calibrate carefully for your program and audience. Many MBA programs are intended to skew toward practice, and articles laden with academic jargon and methodological minutiae may not be appropriate; some undergraduate and Master of Science programs are intended to develop participants' academic research skills, and deep academic pieces are integral. Be sure to consider the students' research and statistics background when choosing academic articles. You would choose differently if you are offering a course for an engineering company than for a public relations audience, as Espen has found, when teaching a course to an audience composed fifty-fifty of each.

Consider casting a wider net beyond these sources. Over the term, try to draw from an array of sources to teach the students that they can find pertinent information in many places and that finding these resources is an important skill for their careers. Consulting reports, industry white papers, quality newspapers, trade magazines, and blogs can be fruitful. Also, don't limit yourself to text. We regularly assign videos from TED, MIT and other universities, and YouTube. Be careful about copyright issues. We have also used movies, TV, and radio shows. Do not assign nontext media just to be different. Use them when they are the best content you can get, not to increase the entertainment factor of the course, a ploy that backfires with the best students and in the long run.

Approach textbooks with caution. There is often pressure, particularly from students and sometimes from accreditation procedures, to use a textbook. Students and accreditors find comfort in the relatively definitive presentation of ideas and the linear structure. Neither of us has used textbooks as a central element in our case-based courses in more than a decade, opting instead for articles and trade books written for practitioners.

We do this for several reasons. It sends a clear message that the cases are at the heart of the course and the other materials are meant to supplement them. It takes students out of the rote, linear thinking that textbooks can foster. Omitting or deemphasizing a textbook also forces students to learn to cope with greater ambiguity and to integrate material themselves rather than consume it already highly structured. This improves students' understanding and retention of the material.

When we use textbooks, we do not teach to them. Instead we might use the textbook as additional material, included as a regular part of the course. For example, an exam can ask questions from cases, from anything discussed in class, and from chapters in a textbook. Since we both teach courses with technical components, we sometimes also use basic textbooks as recommended reading for students who need an introduction to the technology (or its vocabulary) itself.

Using Teaching Groups

Many programs include team-taught classes, with either multiple faculty teaching the same course to different students or multiple faculty teaching a single course to several sections of students. To achieve the benefits of working with other faculty without incurring enormous cost requires forethought and explicit management.

If you are teaching a course with multiple sections and faculty, coordinating efforts can be valuable. For case teaching, you can exchange ideas for questions and exercises and identify likely pitfalls. If you are trying to give students a similar experience (perhaps enforced through a common exam) across the multiple sections, you might also share the most important discussion topics and takeaways. Even though the discussions are likely to vary dramatically across the sections, the learning, particularly when averaged across a semester, can be quite consistent. At some schools, the teaching groups meet before each case is delivered. They also debrief the results of the previous case. You can use metrics we describe in chapter 8 to provide more in-depth analysis of the consistency and effectiveness across multiple classrooms.

If meetings before each class are infeasible or too expensive, formalizing exchange of some information can be useful, as can facilitating informal exchange. The formal exchange could involve a site on the learning management system, a wiki, or, for the technically phobic, email exchanges where faculty share notes on the cases, supporting materials, and discussion of teaching issues. Online resource 6 shows a form used at Harvard Business School to summarize information about a case for case teachers.

Using Guest Speakers

Guest speakers such as representatives from companies that are the subject of case studies can be a valuable addition to a course. They bring different perspectives and offer students an often welcome change of pace; they can strengthen your legitimacy as a teacher; and they can be a fruitful way of extending your own network, providing material for your research, and infusing routine classroom sessions with some variety.

Manage guests in the classroom with care. They must know their role in the course and the classroom. We tend to ask guest speakers to be themselves, and only that. We have consistently found that both the students and the guest speaker have the best experience when the guest comes in at the end of a case discussion, primarily responding to students' questions. This also means the guest has to do less preparation.

If you want the guest to do a presentation, you should discuss the content beforehand. Many businesspeople are used to doing sales or investor presentations, and some think that they won't have anything to say unless they bring some material. We explicitly discourage sales pitches and standard corporate presentations in the classroom. This can be a fine line and a difficult one for many speakers to tread, so be explicit about it. Some businesspeople might feel they have to behave like a lecturing academic. This seldom works well.

If the guest brings a presentation, consider asking for a quick look at it, at least if you have not heard the person speak before. You should also provide the guest with the class materials and syllabus, but be sure to summarize the relevant background in a short email to increase the chances that he or she reads and considers it in his or her talk. Because introductions are crucial, give thought to how you are going to introduce the speaker. Ask the guests if there is anything they would like you to emphasize.

The charisma or gravitas of the speaker is at least as important as the person's formal role in the organization. We have each seen senior executives fall completely flat, and junior people light up the room and generate discussion. While having the CEO or another top management member talk to the class is great, it doesn't hurt to have some variety, as long as the guest is able to speak at the appropriate level for the class and the case. Former students of your courses are an excellent resource, as they are more likely to understand what you and the course are about and what role they should play—and they have legitimacy with the class, since they have been in the same boat as your current students.

Good speakers are scarce. Cultivate them and bring them back in subsequent terms while being careful they don't burn out. Over time, they become an organic part of the course, as they improve their understanding of their role and contribution. Incidentally, students can bring guests to class, too. Introduce any guests to the class and explain why they are there, even if a student is just bringing in a friend or a potential student wanting to check out the class. This underscores the community feel of the classroom; if you are holding students responsible for their peers' learning, you need to make them aware of all context. It also ensures that you don't mistakenly invite someone to speak who does not belong in the class, which tends to break the flow of the discussion.

Using Assignments

Smaller assignments throughout the course can increase participation and preparation. If you teach relatively small classes, consider using short writing assignments (two to four hundred words) before each class, submitted electronically the night before. This has many advantages: First, it forces every student to prepare. Second, it gives you a check on how much the students have understood each case. Third, it energizes the discussion; if the students have answered a basic question the day before class, you can go faster into the deeper and more interesting issues. Last, written assignments give an additional basis for grading, especially for good but quiet students. The downside is that you need to read those hand-ins, and there is a risk that the students will limit their preparation to answering the question(s) in the assignment and not consider the whole range of issues in the case.

You can also use longer assignments to help students develop research skills or to apply frameworks and models discussed in class. These assignments may be more quantitative in nature or be proper term papers; they can be done individually or in groups. Also, assignments do not need to be limited to one class, but can stretch over the whole course: Espen has one exercise on the topic of online work in which he requires students to write for Wikipedia from the beginning of the course, in whatever language and on whatever topics they feel comfortable with. The hand-in and discussion is a list of what each student worked on and a short reflection on what they learned from doing it. This ensures that students get practice in contributing to a shared, electronic work setting and also helps make Wikipedia better, which is a good thing. In this class, the teacher needs to do very little preparation; the students all have experiences to share and formulate their thoughts before the class. The discussion generally starts with a listing of the students' individual experiences and then a comparison to theory about norms and cultures in social media settings.

If you are doing research in an area pertinent to the course, consider having the students be research assistants, for instance, by writing term papers that may end up as teaching or research cases themselves. For more on this topic, see chapter 4, as well as Christensen and Carlisle (2009).

Working with Students

If there is one question we get from budding case teachers, it is, "How do you get students to prepare before class?" The answer is that it is complicated and will take time, and involves setting course-level expectations, helping students understand what preparation means, and placing the same demands on yourself as you do on your students.

Let's start with expectations: most business schools want to attract excellent students, educate "tomorrow's leaders," and describe themselves as leading in some (frequently not very specific) direction. We think this is an admirable ambition, but it means that the students' workload and the quality and level of the material taught should be comparable not to local schools—that would be too easy—but to schools such as London Business School, Sloan, Harvard, Wharton, and INSEAD. Standard fare at an MBA program at one of these places is two or three case discussions per day, five days a week. We recommend a preparation time for each case of three to four hours, including discussions in student groups before class. Do the math, and you will arrive at a figure far higher than most students are used to. In fact, according to most studies [for example, Pryor et al. (2012);

Franke et al. (2010), and Arnesen et al. (2011)], the average "full-time" student reports spending less than thirty hours per week studying, including class time.

We also recommend that cases should be a common and integral part of your courses, rather than used a few times merely as examples (a practice one professor referred to as "case snacking.") To get deep discussion and high engagement, both you and the students need to push past the sense of cases as a novelty and an exception, and see them as business as usual and a way to learn, which requires that students arrive prepared and ready to talk, no (or at least, very few) excuses accepted.

So how do you get the students to work that hard? Surprising them definitely will not do it, so make a comprehensive syllabus in which you specify what they should prepare for each class and how

What to Include in a Syllabus

Here's what you should include in the syllabus to help students prepare for cases:

- Information about case teaching and expected preparation

- Description of course

- Information about grading, including how participation is graded

- Outline of classes, with the following (for each class):

  — Case to be discussed

  — Supporting literature (articles or book chapters)

  — Preparation questions

  — Audiovisual material, if relevant

  — Assignments, if relevant

  — Further, nonrequired literature

well prepared you expect them to be. For an eighty-minute class, we normally schedule one to three articles and/or book chapters and a case. We expect that every student should be able to give a five-to ten-minute introduction to the company, explain the central case problems, and give her or his view of what the case protagonist should do.

We like to give lots of additional reading, for those students who are especially interested, in the form of links to articles or books that delve deeper into the topics covered. This has two benefits. First, it points the diligent and interested student to more material, not necessarily for reading during the course, but useful if the topic should come up later. Second, giving more than the compulsory reading reduces the howls of horror at the workload: it subtly suggests that the required reading is not that much after all. In effect, we are applying our version of Goldilocks pricing (Shapiro & Varian, 1999); that is, we introduce a more expensive offering to make the regular offering look cheap or, in this situation, easier.

To most students, this looks like a lot, and perhaps it is. It tends to be more than what our colleagues demand. We do this on purpose, because being slightly tougher than your colleagues has benefits. If your course requires more work than others, you will meet resistance in the beginning, definitely from the students and perhaps from the

Students' Complaints about Workload

In his first few years of teaching, Espen regularly had a small delegation of students in his office about two weeks into the course, who pointed out that they had five courses per semester and spent half their time preparing for his course. His well-honed counterargument included some ambitious course descriptions from well-known business schools. He pointed out that his courses, in that context, were significantly less demanding. He then asked whether they considered themselves less capable, in terms of percentage, than a first-tier business school student. After three years, the delegation visits ceased. At that point, the reading levels had been institutionalized.

administration, which is concerned with average workloads or student admissions.

However, in our experience, perseverance pays off. After two decades of teaching, we have earned reputations as very demanding professors. After the first couple of years, the students were forewarned by student advisers and course alumni. We get few protests and see fewer tourists in our electives. Instead, we get the students who are interested and prepared to work hard.

Being the toughest professor or burying students in work is not a goal in itself, but there is no point in designing courses at a comfortable level. A good course gives the best students something to reach for and takes the weaker students further than they thought possible.

Don't give up; demand much from your students. It works! We are very proud that one of the most common comments from our student evaluations is, "I have never worked so hard in any course before, but I learned much more than I expected." If 20 percent to 30 percent of your students are having trouble keeping up, it is not a problem, but a sign you are doing something right. You do, however, need to calibrate the workload, particularly if the course is new. Consider how many hours per week you expect students to spend on the course outside of class. Then determine how much work you can expect the average student to accomplish in that much time. As the course progresses, you can test your estimates in discussions with students.

Many students are not used to having demands placed on them. They tend to react first with objections, then resignation, then enthusiasm. If you demand that they be prepared, check that they are, and retain the right to question any student at any time, they will prepare. Then you get better questions and better discussion, can dive deeper into the problems at hand, and create a very positive experience for all involved.

Motivating Students

Some faculty cannot include class participation as a component of students' grades or, in some situations, even mandate attendance in class because of the course, program, school, or legal restrictions. In some countries—such as Denmark, as we have been told by many

Danish case teachers—no student may be required to attend class as part of the grade. So can you motivate students to participate in class if grades are not part of the grade?

Some faculty consider it unseemly or inappropriate for faculty to market their courses in order to attract students, believing that it should succeed on its own merits—by word of mouth and course description only. We believe such promotion is not only appropriate but necessary. We expect students to invest scores of hours in a course; they have the right to know why doing so is worthwhile. And we want to attract good students, because that is the most significant factor in making the course better.

To convince students, focus on five things.

Enthusiasm and Engagement

To capture and hold students' attention, faculty must demonstrate enthusiasm for the material. While we both have extremely high energy in the classroom and use that energy to raise the level of intensity in the classroom, it can be equally effective to show enthusiasm in more subdued ways. Enthusiasm is contagious however it is presented, as long as it is genuine.

Relevance

Students are often hesitant to invest time and energy in a course when they think there will be no valuable payoff to them. We are deeply committed to the value of learning for its own sake, but emphasizing the real-world relevance of case studies need not denigrate the learning experience. You will not discourage students motivated by the joy of learning by emphasizing that the case discussions will teach them about the practical implications of what they are learning. But for those many students motivated by the trade aspects of what we teach, we emphasize how grounded case discussions are in the reality of practice.

Opportunities to Build Valuable Skills

Case discussions present students with the opportunity to improve their ability to speak publicly, think on their feet, and improve their problem-solving and pattern-matching skills. While being forced to use these skills will provoke anxiety for many students, they will also have an opportunity to get past that anxiety and build skills that will help them succeed in both their academic and work careers. It is easy to draw direct parallels for students between the skills employed in a case discussion and those needed in a job interview or in their careers. After all, isn't it better to fail and learn in the simulated environment of a classroom, than make your first fumbling mistakes with real money and your job on the line?

Safe Participation

We have found that most students experience significant anxiety in case discussion classes, particularly in the first half of the semester. This anxiety is amplified for those students whose prior education involved only lectures and often exams with unique correct answers. While their expressions may not reveal this, when you speak with them after the course or read student evaluations, it will become clear. Some of this anxiety is a natural by-product of challenging students in unfamiliar ways. The anxiety can be particularly acute for women and for students culturally accustomed to not speaking in class and not challenging classmates and professors. Acknowledging this anxiety openly and making it clear that causing the anxiety is not your goal can go a long way toward assuring students that your course will be a safe environment in which to overcome this anxiety.

Early on, try to calibrate the difficulty and intensity of questions for students you know are struggling to allow them to build confidence. Keep the environment safe by enforcing norms for patience with students struggling for words (whether due to anxiety or language issues) and prohibiting mockery. However, you do need to make it clear that students need to participate in class in order to get past that anxiety. Handling more severe cases is discussed in chapter 5.

Fun

With all the pedagogical goals involved in a course, it's easy to forget that the class can still be fun. On the first day of class, Bill states, as an explicit goal, that he wants everyone to look forward to coming to class each week. Well-facilitated case discussions are engaging and often punctuated by humor. Even if your personal style is on the somber side, you can still encourage participants to enjoy coming to class and emphasize that you personally look forward to class, too. If you tend to be unexpressive when you speak, then say in words how excited you are to be in this class with this group.

Finding Information about Students' Backgrounds

Always try to get as much information as possible about the students' backgrounds. Knowing something about the students before you meet them will allow you to tailor the course somewhat, if not in content, at least in conduct.

You can get background information in a number of ways. The school supplies some information. For executive classes, there is normally a list of participants with some background, such as age, employers, position, and perhaps education. For graduate or undergraduate students, there tends to be less information, often limited to name, study program (if not the same for all of them), and perhaps education. If at all possible, try to get pictures of the students; tying a name and some background to a picture before starting the class helps memorization.

You can collect additional information yourself, either by having the students provide it on paper or online (see online resource 7 for a sample background form). If you are using an online forum to support the course, filling in some background information can be a requirement of admission to the forum. If you are using a learning management system (LMS) of some sort, it likely has a "personal profile" page that you can ask the students to complete. You can also set up an online form, for instance a Google Doc, to quickly capture something, or set up a group on LinkedIn, if that is popular where you teach. If you have students with an international background, getting them to record audio files pronouncing their names can be particularly helpful. Another choice is to have students introduce themselves in the first meeting, which we discuss in the next chapter.

Having background information makes it easier to select students for opening calls (for instance, you might want a student with industry experience to open a particular case or explain some part of it), for role-plays (picking students with characteristics similar to the people they are going to play, just as casting agents do), and also to identify and assess students who might cause problems later in the course.

Helping the Students Prepare for Case Discussions

While challenging students and encouraging self-discovery is important, if you are assigning types of readings, including cases, that may be entirely unfamiliar to some students, consider offering a brief guide for doing the reading and analysis. For an excellent guide to preparing cases from a student perspective, see Ellet (2007). In online resource 8 we offer Espen's guide to analyzing long and complex cases.

Remind students to dedicate enough time, read the case several times, pay attention to exhibits with numbers, answer any preparation questions, ask what the main challenges are for the case protagonist(s) and what you would do about them, formulate an outline for a strategy, and be ready to talk about it in class.

Explicitly recommending preclass group discussions is particularly important if you teach in noncase institutions. We always encourage students to work together to prepare for class. The students can individually prepare the case(s) and then meet in groups (in person or via teleconferencing) to discuss before class. Even a short meeting helps; the point of the meeting is not to rehearse for the classroom, but to enhance understanding of the case by hearing other people's views. Many students will find their solutions to be only one of several, and perhaps not the best one. That is one of the most important takeaways from any case discussion.

Classroom Participation Requirement

We require participation in our courses and normally include classroom participation as a part of the grade. We fully expect every student, every time, to come to class prepared and ready to discuss the case and make clear that their participation grade will suffer if they don't show up or are unprepared. There are exceptions, of course, such as illness. We are fairly lenient here, as long as it doesn't happen too often and the student informs us before class starts.

We make clear from the very beginning that we reserve the right to call on any student at any time on any question or course material for which we have requested preparation. Classroom participation does not just mean that the student is physically in the classroom, awake, and facing the right direction. The student has to say something. Almost half of the grade depends on the student's discussion contributions, not just saying something to show preparation, but building off the comments from classmates and the teacher to work toward understanding problems and generating alternative solutions. Both quantity and quality count, quality more than quantity. Good participation means moving the discussion forward. Great participation happens when everyone, including the teacher, learns something from the discussion. One rule of thumb we offer students to judge quality: after you have spoken, are your classmates better off because you did so?

To calibrate quantity, in most case discussions we have observed, students speak for an average of one to two minutes, so there are thirty to sixty opportunities for students to raise their hands per hour. You may find it helpful to have someone count the number of opportunities for students to speak in your classes. This will allow you and students to determine how often they should be speaking in each class session. We discuss the grading implications in more detail in chapter 4.

Demanding participation requires professors to have a thick skin, especially in environments without a participative culture. Much depends on your own background and personality. If you are relatively young and new to the job, lack legitimacy from experience, or feel insecure in the teaching situation, getting participation can be difficult. Good preparation helps, as well as being clear and unequivocal about the how and when of participation. It also helps to think through what to answer should students raise objections, which they are apt to do.

Two objections are most common. First, quite a few students think the job of the teacher is to serve up the content in easily digestible form, so they can take notes and not have to crack the books. To us, this sounds a bit like the old definition of a lecture: "A method of transferring the lecturer's notes to the students without passing through the brain of either." The counterargument is, as a colleague of Espen is fond of saying, "A business school is a health club, not a tanning salon." Practice is the thing, and participation the way to do it.

Second, some students also protest that they are grown-ups and want to choose whether or not they should attend classes, or instead read the literature by themselves and just take the exam. The counterargument here is a bit more complicated and personal, not to mention contingent on your subject. We tend to emphasize that business is not something you can learn by merely reading about it. Problem solving in business and public management is a matter of pattern recognition and development of solutions in cooperation with others (Christensen & Raynor, 2003). This is best learned by deep examples, where you distill key problems from fuzzy data, formulate solutions, and advocate for them in dialogue with peers. The classroom then becomes a simulation of the reality students will meet when they graduate. And the only way to learn something in a simulator is to be in it and to use it.

We usually require attendance in our courses, whether they are discussion-based or not. If this is hard to do (if you have a class of 150, for instance, or if you have forgotten to include required attendance in the course description), we make clear to students that the exam may include anything on the literature list, whether it was discussed in class or not, any other current material pertinent to the course such as recent newspaper articles, and *anything discussed in class.* This makes missing class a risky proposition. We also stress that skipping class is insulting to the other students. You are depriving them of the chance to learn from you, and case learning is a responsibility shared among the teacher and the students.

Establishing Infrastructure

Discussion-based teaching needs a supporting infrastructure. Schools dedicated to case teaching have special classrooms designed for discussion and the administrative support necessary for handling the many little details involved in a successful case course. If your school has not been built for case teaching, then you need to adapt both the teaching and the classroom.

Establishing Seating Arrangements

The ideal seating arrangement for case teaching is one in which the students face each other in a horseshoe or, less commonly, a circular pattern. (Circular arrangements make displaying visual aids challenging unless you have a setup with an electronic writing pad and multiple monitors.) Yet most schools are designed like performance halls, with all seats facing the stage and a sarcophagus-sized podium. While great for, and perhaps reflective of, faculty ego, this arrangement sets precisely the wrong tone for discussion, reinforcing students' expectations that faculty will provide all the answers.

If your school has a limited number of horseshoe rooms or "case classrooms," request them early on and be specific about how you intend to use them. In many schools, administrators are flooded with requests for these rooms because they are often the newest, nicest, and most comfortable. If you provide details and even metrics (as we discuss in chapter 3) about why you want the room, you are more likely to be placed at the front of the queue.

If there are no horseshoe-shaped or case rooms available, seek those with movable desks or swivel seating, and rearrange them mercilessly. The flat horseshoe pattern—where you move regular tables to a squarish U—works for up to thirty people, provided that the room is large. For more people than that, or if the room is not wide enough, you may be forced to use a fishbone pattern, but make sure the aisles are broad enough for you and others to move around. (Conference rooms almost always place the speaker at the narrow walls in a rectangle; if you have a choice, insist on being on the wider side.) If you have a choice of round or rectangular tables, go with the round ones, and make sure you have some group exercises that allow discussion across each table. If there is a table between you and the students, move it out of the way, if at all possible. (See figure 2-1 for the variety of seating arrangements.)

FIGURE 2-1

Classroom seating arrangements

Case room

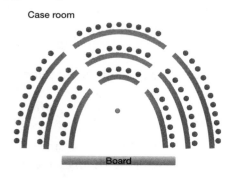

U-shape (horseshoe)

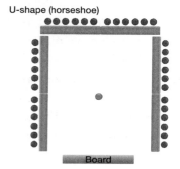

Fishbone

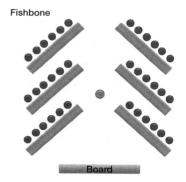

Round tables

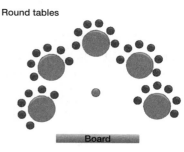

Carrying Your Own Pens

Whiteboard pens normally come in four colors—black, blue, red, and green—and, due to demand, the black, blue, and red tend to be dried out or missing from classrooms, leaving you with the anemic green that students cannot see. Keep your own black and blue pens and perhaps a clean eraser just to be on the safe side.

Lack of board space is a frequent problem with modern classrooms. Many universities have classrooms designed like hotel meeting rooms, with two relatively small whiteboards, sometimes partially obscured by the projection screen. The assumption is that the lecturer will make an electronic presentation and that one or maybe two boards are sufficient. Case teaching, however, is all about exploring a myriad of complicated and interrelated issues, meaning that you need adequate space to write down issues, do calculations, and draw figures and arrows. Therefore—whatever you do—do not start a case-teaching class without complete familiarity with the classroom and confidence that you have all the things you need. If board space is lacking, get an extra rolling board or some flipchart easels, or use a tablet computer and take notes directly on the projection screen (more about this in chapter 10 on technology).

Case teachers commonly experience frustrations with classrooms, but we have found that as long as the cases are interesting and the students engaged, the layout and quality of the classroom fade to the background. The important thing is that you familiarize yourself with the room before the class starts, so that you don't organize your teaching in ways that the room cannot support; for instance, using role-play in situations where the students can't quite see each other, or having a board plan that requires frequent switching between computer use and board writing when the projector screen obscures the board.

Using Name Cards and Seating Charts

Evaluating students' performance requires a way to recognize and remember them. To help you do this, every student should have a name card legible from across the room. The students also need to sit in the same seat in the classroom throughout the course. The spatial reference will help you remember who they are and what they say. This relatively minor detail really helps memorization. We can meet students many years after a class, recognize their face but not their name, but remember that this person sat in the third seat on the second row to the right and had a really good comment on the Johnson & Johnson case.

The administration sometimes makes the name cards, but you can easily make them yourself. Online resource 9 shows examples of name cards. You can download templates for printing on letter- and A4-size paper from the book's web site and feed in the names from a

---

Seating Students

One option is to seat the students alphabetically, which is easy to do if you can get to the classroom early and place the name cards in advance. This makes it much easier to remember each student. Look at his or her last name and figure out where in the classroom each sits. That is often all that is necessary to fire up the requisite synapses. The disadvantage is that students Aachen and Zoroaster might be a bit miffed to always end up in the end seats, out of your normal field of view.

Incidentally, if you allow the students to seat themselves, a mythology of which seats are the most advantageous will spring up, no doubt helped by Internet lore and business school memoirs. Also, the quiet and unassuming students will tend to float to the far sides, right where they are hardest to spot and help participate. One colleague who teaches in rooms with extra capacity solves this by waiting until all students are seated and then having the students in the back row move to the invariably empty seats in the front.

---

class list. If special name cards are not available, preprint the cards using a standard letter or A4 paper; folded once lengthwise, it will stand up by itself. Make sure the name is printed on both front and back, so the students in the back rows can see the names. Facilitating the learning of names is important for students as well as faculty. In classrooms with flat floors, the name cards are not easy to see. One alternative is to have the students hang their name cards from their laptop screens; another is to make conference-like name cards with first names printed in a large font, to be fastened onto clothing.

Students tend to forget or lose their name cards. If you make the electronic name-card template available, they can recreate them. Emphasize that it is the student's responsibility to have a name card; if you don't know his or her name, you cannot reward contributions. When you have made name cards, hand them out at the first class and explain that the students have to sit in the same seat for every class.

You will need a seating chart with pictures of the students laid out according to where they sit. The ideal is to have a constructed seating chart with individual pictures of each student; this is standard issue for all courses in case-focused institutions. If the administration does not provide one, you might have to make one yourself. Take pictures of the classroom with the students holding their name cards in front of them. Clip the pictures together using software or scissors,

FIGURE 2-2

Take a picture of students holding their name cards

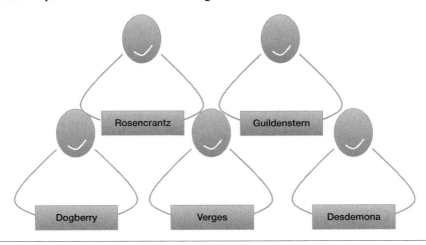

and you have a recognizable seating chart without much work. We have found such pictures are just as good as a seating chart built from individual student ID pictures, mainly because the individual ID pictures tend to be rather flattering and do not reflect how the students look in the classroom setting.

The seating photos are also great for keeping track of classroom participation, as discussed in chapter 5. Photocopy the classroom pictures or print them out in weak grayscale, one for each class. After each class, write down notes about the students' performance directly on one of these copies. As a mnemonic device, this is very effective, provided you do it as soon as possible after every class. Do not take notes during class; this breaks the discussion flow and overly focuses the students on participating for points rather than content. For large groups, you might be able to get an assistant to take notes, but hide this person unobtrusively in a corner toward the back and don't rely completely on him or her. You still have to do the after-class review.

Some argue that case teaching can only be done in small groups. We disagree. With the right infrastructure, including name cards, a photographic classroom map, fixed seating, short compulsory submissions, and simplified grading, it is possible to teach up to a hundred students effectively. Case-centric schools routinely have class sizes up to ninety, drawing on their heavily optimized infrastructure.

Setting Length and Frequency of Class Sessions

Most faculty do not get to choose the timing of their courses. Many teaching notes and other guides for case teaching assume eighty-minute regularly scheduled classes, with time between each session, for example, two times per week. The variety in session length and meeting frequency has important implications for course design.

Deciding how long to discuss a single case when most teaching notes are tailored to seventy-five to eighty minutes is a major challenge. If you are meeting students for a day or two on a weekend and assigning a case for every hour and a quarter, busy, largely part-time students would have to prepare many hours and might confuse the cases during discussion.

Session Length

Most schools have a set timetable (that is, forty-five minutes with a fifteen-minute break), often defined out of some idea that forty-five minutes is as much presentation time as students can endure. Forty-five minutes is very short for a case discussion; for most cases, you will need at least one hour and longer for inexperienced students. We recommend longer blocks of time, up to eighty minutes. For longer sessions, you need to have a break in the discussion—group work or a guest speaker, for instance—to maintain energy. Case discussion is (and should be) intense, and it can be a real problem to maintain student attention, especially for as long as eighty minutes. People's attention time seems to be shortening, perhaps due in part to increased multitasking with laptops and smartphones in the classroom.

Taking a break during the discussion of a single case disrupts the momentum. If you choose to use one case for more than eighty minutes, you must carefully consider the timing of the break, coming to closure on a topic and resuming with a strong topic. Using only one case for a 2.5- or 3-hour session allows a great deal more flexibility during the class. There is time for meaningful small-group or individual exercises, or exploration of elements of the case beyond core questions. You might also choose longer or more complex cases. If the case is multipart (that is, there is a B case and possibly additional parts), you can distribute the next part before the break and give the students some extra time to read it.

Session Frequency

Teaching full-time students for relatively short classes one or several times per week is increasingly a luxury. When you see the students for two or three eighty-minute sessions per week, you learn their names and can keep the energy level very high during the whole session, and they only need to prepare one case for each session. However, fewer and fewer MBA programs are full-time. Executive MBA programs, where "executive" is a euphemism for part-time, are becoming the norm. An international dimension and the pressures of work as well as the cost of travel mean having module-based programs, often wholly or partially done on weekends.

Module-based programs are harder to teach: you have less time to get to know the students, less ability to get the infrastructure just right (for instance, you may not have access to a decent classroom), and less ability to set up the contract between you and the students to make them come prepared. Because students are working, they have less time to prepare than a full-time student does. In fact, you sometimes encounter students who think that an executive course or even a degree program is nothing more than a welcome break from their jobs, and they need to be disabused of that notion.

In terms of preparation, you need to be extremely specific about the contract ahead of time, investigate the use of electronic or other tools to keep the students charged up between modules, and consider a mix of straight case teaching and regular presentations during the day. You need to limit the amount of material per time unit; trying to do four cases in one day just isn't going to work and will only damage your legitimacy.

As the amount of time between class meetings increases, student retention erodes, and it becomes more important to remind them of links to earlier material. But there is greater opportunity to require more extensive assignments between class meetings, which can offset the drop in retention.

Wrapping Up

Preparation is not just about the structure, content, and context of the course, but also about what comes after it—evaluation and feedback for both the student and the teacher.

Preparing for evaluation in a case setting primarily means setting up a structure for capturing information about student performance and satisfaction before the course starts. We will not go into detail about that here—see chapter 4—but just highlight that it pays to think about and set up the infrastructure (grading spreadsheets, student feedback forms, configuration of learning management systems) before the course starts. Preparing in advance means less work during the course period (when the pressure is most intense) and increases the likelihood that you actually will capture the necessary information. Trust us, when the students come back to you after the course and ask why their participation grade was not what they were expecting, you want to be able to pull out structured notes on their participation in class, from the very first day. Nothing settles discussions like data.

If you will teach the course again, it is important that when you produce syllabi, content, and administrative communications, you prepare them so they are repeatable the next time you teach the course. Both of us have lots of collected advice, old syllabi, instructions on how to do things, and spreadsheets for keeping track of progress—material that has been created over years of teaching. Little things, such as archiving this material in an easy-to-find way, not writing course names and dates in documents (save that for the cover email or learning management system post) so you don't have to edit and don't have to save a copy for each course, mean that next time you teach the course, you can reuse documents, course system setups, and large parts of your syllabi from year to year. It also helps to change documents as issues come up and not wait until the next course begins and you have forgotten the details.

Loving to teach does not mean you have to redo the course every time. Save that sense of a new start for the classroom. That is where your effort and energy should go.

We are now ready for the most exciting part of a course—going to the first class and actually teaching it.

References

Ambady, N., and R. Rosenthal. "Half a Minute: Predicting Teacher Evaluations from Thin Slices of Nonverbal Behavior and Physical Attractiveness." *Journal of Personality and Social Psychology* 64, no. 3 (1993): 431–441.

Arnesen, C. Å., E. Hovdhaugen, J. Wiers-Jenssen, and P. O. Aamodt. *Studiesituasjon og studentøkonomi: Norske resultater fra den europeiske studentundersøkelsen Eurostudent IV,* NIFU Report 33, 2011. http://www.nifu.no/Norway/Publications/2011/NIFU%20Webrapport%2033-2011.pdf.

Christensen, C. M., and P. R. Carlisle. "Course Research, Using the Case Method to Build and Teach Management Theory." *Academy of Management Learning and Education* 8, no. 2 (2009): 240–251.

Christensen, C. M., and M. E. Raynor. "Why Hard-nosed Executives Should Care about Management Theory." *Harvard Business Review,* September 2003, 67–74.

Ellet, W. *The Case Study Handbook: How to Read, Discuss, and Write Persuasively About Cases*. Boston: Harvard Business School Press, 2007.

Franke, R., S. Ruiz, J. Sharkness, L. DeAngelo, and J. Pryor. *Findings from the 2009 Administration of the College Senior Survey (CSS): National Aggregates*. Higher Education Research Institute, Graduate School of Education & Information Studies. Los Angeles: University of California, 2010. http://www.heri.ucla.edu/PDFs/pubs/Reports/2009_CSS_Report.pdf.

Garvin, D. A. "Making the Case: Professional Education for the World of Practice." *Harvard Magazine* 106, no. 1 (2003): 56ff. http://www.harvardmagazine.com/2003/09/making-the-case-html.

Pryor, J. H., K. Eagan, L. P. Blake, S. Hurtado, J. Berdan, and M. H. Case. *The American Freshman: National Norms Fall 2012*. Higher Education Research Institute, Graduate School of Education & Information Studies. Los Angeles: University of California, 2012. http://www.heri.ucla.edu/monographs/TheAmericanFreshman2012.pdf.

Shapiro, C., and H. R. Varian. *Information Rules: A Strategic Guide to the Network Economy*. Boston: Harvard Business School Press, 1999.

3

FLOW DURING THE
CLASS SESSION

The ideal in case-based teaching is a teacher who does not say much, but instead gently guides the discussion like a comfortable, benevolent, and slightly distant Socrates. Practicing this is simple, in principle: you ask a student to open the discussion and gently but firmly steer the students' discussion through the case and the topics by posing questions and signaling who should speak next, while capturing notes on the boards.

Despite this apparent simplicity, we have found that when we talk to prospective case teachers, almost all of their questions and worries relate to running the class. These worries may be the chief impediment to the adoption of case teaching.

The worries are many: Will the students be prepared? Will they be willing to discuss the topics, or discuss at all? Will the discussion become a shouting match? Will some students Google their way to instant contradiction of the teacher? Will a student become tearful, angry, or hurt? Will a student know more about the case company and industry than you? Will you run out of material? Will there be a mysterious super-student who "cracks the case" in the first five minutes, leaving everyone with nothing to say? Will the stress of managing both content and process cause you to say or do something stupid?

After two decades of teaching, we could easily be flippant about the attendant anxiety of case teaching. We have had most of these problems and consistently find that the process of case teaching itself provides the means to deal with them all. Giving up the comfort, predictability, and control of the lecture format can be terrifying. In choosing not to lecture, we partially relinquish control of when things are discussed, what conclusions will be reached, and perhaps what topics will be covered. You may not cover everything you planned to, but that can happen in lectures, too. As students work out and evaluate solutions for themselves, they engage more and gain a much deeper understanding of their learning.

In this chapter, we will talk about how to prepare for and conduct the class itself, focusing on many small details that together will help you not only survive, but enjoy a case class. (In chapter 5, we cover what to do if things *don't* go according to plan.) We share what has worked for us. Take everything in this chapter with a healthy dose of skepticism; filter it through your own preferences and experiences. What's important is not that you do what we say, but that you think through in detail what you are going to do once teaching starts.

Unless you specifically tell the students otherwise, case discussions should only be based on the facts that are in the case, not other information the students can find by searching the web or otherwise dig up. The cases are designed to be self-contained, and the depth of analysis and quality of the discussion will be better if everyone starts from the same base. Be explicit here; Espen once learned that a student group showed up at the door of one of the case protagonists (the CIO of Norway's largest company) on a Sunday afternoon to gain some insider knowledge. You should also stick to the time period of the case as much as possible. If students introduce anachronisms, point them out, but explore them if you think they are instructive.

Teaching is a very personal matter, and how you choose to teach is up to you. You can learn from others, but merely imitating another teacher, however excellent, never works. You will have to develop your own style based on who you are. You will be effective in the classroom and enjoy it if you can make it your own, not solely play a role. An honest self-assessment is a critical starting point. If you are nervous, acknowledge and accept that you may be for a while (or, indeed, forever, as some well-known case teachers insist). You may need to play the role of a confident discussion leader for a while, but over time, your confidence will become genuine.

Preparing Yourself

Preparing the course is a scene-setting exercise, expressed in documents such as the syllabus. But you also need to prepare for each case you are going to teach: understand the content of the case and how it relates to other topics and cases in the course; decide on a teaching plan, most likely including a board plan; and plan how you are going to run the discussion. Preparing yourself also has a psychological dimension. You need to think about your impression on the students.

If you are teaching a case for the first time, you need to read it carefully, along with any published teaching notes. Even if you read most of the cases when you assembled the syllabus, you need to at least refresh your memory by carefully going through it the day before class. Take notes, use a highlighter, or scratch comments in the margin, as you prefer.

The difference between preparing a case as a student and preparing it as an instructor is similar to the difference between reading a book as a reader and as a film director: The reader will focus on the content and understanding the characters. The film director must do both of these things and consider how the material will play as a film: Where are the dramatic points I must underscore? Where can I put in references to literature or other ideas? How can I make the material come alive through dialogue? How much time should I spend on each part?

If you are pressed for time, you can base your teaching solely on the case summary in the teaching note that accompanies many cases, but this is akin to reading a Wikipedia entry in lieu of the real book. However, it will give you the case author's main teaching points as well as the keys to the domain-specific analysis of the case.

We recommend you read the case first without looking at the teaching note. This lets you see things in the case that you might miss otherwise and allows you to make the case your own. The teaching note typically presents only the case author's view of the case. Avoiding the spoilers contained in the teaching note as well as the author's biased perspective allows you to see the case as the students will see it. You will gain insight into the difficulties, as well as potentially interesting fodder for discussion, that the author may not have intended or may have omitted from the teaching note.

Crafting a Teaching Plan

Your preparation as an instructor should result in a *teaching plan* for the case. Having a plan might seem contradictory to the idea of a free flow of a discussion; after all, a well-taught case session can look to the uninitiated like it just happens spontaneously. This is, however, carefully planned improvisation, and the plan is more like a framework giving some milestones you want to reach than a detailed script.

The plan should contain:

- The *main points* you want the students to take away from the class. It is easy to be too ambitious here. Two or three points should be considered a maximum for seventy-five minutes. It's better to learn one or two important things well than four or five lightly.

- *Links* to other cases and topics in the course.

- The *topics* to be discussed, in which *order* you want to discuss them, and how much *time* you want to devote to each. We have found it useful to write down the desired starting time for each topic, rather than writing "ten minutes" or whatever next to it. You need your notes to be quickly understandable as you are teaching; ideally, students shouldn't be aware that you are using notes at all.

- The *opening question*, who should answer it, and if necessary, a few follow-up questions. You pick the students to answer based on a number of attributes (more about this later), and always have a reserve candidate in case your first choice fumbles or doesn't show up.

- A rough *board plan,* that is, how you will structure what you write on the board(s).

- Frameworks, models, theories, presentations, videos, and other *supporting material* you are going to use.

- A *concluding point* or two and a possible transition to the next class, such as questions for the students to ponder, or an anecdote or other pearl of wisdom to send them off with.

Write the plan down before class, in as concentrated a format as possible. Bring it to class along with the case and any other materials you need and leave it in front of you (but not so the students can see it) while you run the discussion.

We deal with each of the points the plan addresses in the rest of the chapter. See online resource 3 for an example of our teaching plans for the same case.* They are very different. Be sure to read "Class Plan Notes" before looking at the plans.

As any entrepreneur knows, a business plan is a great tool, but as the company starts to grow, it will deviate more and more from the

---

Class Plan Notes

Everyone has a personal way of preparing before class. Bill's and Espen's notes don't resemble each other. You can see this in online resource 3 where we have each prepared the Catatech Industries case. Bill uses Word documents with detailed outlines for teaching plans and highlights each of the blocks and marks the starting times in large lettering with red ink on his hard copy for reference at a glance. He doesn't always use the notes, but he has them. Espen uses a single sheet handwritten in pencil with a few key words, sometimes a mind map, a miniature board plan, and three or four class milestones with times attached to them. He rewrites this single sheet almost every time he teaches the case, as part of his preparation.

---

* To see this and other online resources for the book, visit the web site: teachingwithcases.hbsp.harvard.edu.

plan. It is the same with teaching plans; you may want to plan out the class in great detail, but as soon as the discussion starts, you will want to follow it where the participants take it. The notes and support material are valuable as a foundation for what you want to do, and, like Dumbo's magical feather, are perhaps more a tool for allowing you the self-confidence to take off and less important once you are airborne.

Demeanor in Class

We know many great teachers, and every one is great in his or her own way. Common to them all, however, is that they have their own style and let their personality show through their teaching.

We are both tall, suit-clad, middle-aged white men—attributes that are great for projecting authority in a classroom. A former colleague of ours, with a long career as a university professor, consultant, textbook writer, and excellent case teacher, is an unassuming woman, about five feet tall. She thinks a lot about how to teach well and once observed that our teaching styles are very different: we can signal authority in the classroom just by body language and movement and at times must dampen our authoritarian signals to foster discussion. Our colleague needs to underscore her authority in different ways, using strong argumentation skills, a somewhat stricter class structure, and deep examples. She has lots of authority.

Case teachers vary widely in how much structure they impose on the class. Some eschew explicit guidance and simply wait for the discussion to start, writing things on the board and very occasionally asking simple questions. Others run a very tight ship: a well-known and extremely good case teacher once went through his preparation for a class with Espen, a class where he had not met the students before. He showed how he planned the discussion to progress and at one point said, "When we get to this part of the case, some student, *generally in the top right row*, will take issue with me and make a rather irritated comment." Then Espen observed him teach the case twice the same day to two different student groups, and the comments came in right on time and from the top right row, just as he said they would.

You can become *too* structured. We have seen stellar case teachers who script their class to the point where the students are reduced to mere bit players, delivering lines when they are supposed to, leading to the professor's predetermined destination. This makes a fantastic impression in the beginning, but as the course progresses, the students, especially those with extensive work experience, grow restless. Students like to talk. They like to discover new things during class and like to think that they are smart and can come up with hitherto unknown perspectives. Once, after teaching the same small case for more than ten years, Espen encountered a student who offered a completely new and very imaginative solution.

Our main advice, which runs counter to what we see many of our colleagues doing, is that in an environment unaccustomed to case teaching, it is much better to start the course in a very disciplined and structured manner, with lots of authority, and then gradually reveal yourself to be not just human, but actually quite friendly, relaxed, and likable. This approach might differ by subject and personal style, but certainly has worked for us and many others. One colleague takes this quite far, telling the students after the first class that "this is the way the course will be; if you don't like it, it is better you drop out now rather than complain later."

We have seen too many faculty try to be friendly with the students in the beginning, then lose control and struggle to rein things in when it turns out that not everyone can or will take responsibility for their own learning. In the end, students (especially younger ones) want a professor and not a superannuated buddy, even though they might say otherwise at the start of the course.

Dressing for Class and Impression Management

Clothes make more of you than most people like to think. What you wear signals who you are, so your wardrobe is not something you should be indifferent about. Yet many teachers do not think about clothes.

We almost always teach wearing a suit or suitlike coat and pants, with a dress shirt (ironed, of course) and a tie (in Espen's case, a bow tie). We do this because we think being dressed somewhat formally for classes is important. It shows the students you take them seriously and sends a message about what you demand of them, in particular, that you are discussing things from a top management viewpoint.

So, how formally should you dress? In general (and this applies as much in teaching as in presentations to companies or speeches at conferences), we think you should dress *slightly more formally than the audience expects and does themselves.* How formal this is depends on the culture in which you are teaching. You want to be above the median for formality among faculty. (We enjoy being at the highest end of the scale, but that's us.) Many female faculty we spoke with felt that this issue is, unfortunately, even greater for women, who often must work harder to establish their credibility with the audience and can lose it more quickly. The easiest way to achieve and sustain your chosen level of formality is to dress classically and not too fashion-forward unless you absolutely know what you are doing. Slightly formal, classic, and discreet elegance, easily carried, suggests that you are a *primus inter pares,* comfortable but authoritative. One colleague suggests thinking of teaching as a job interview. Younger faculty members should be careful not to look too old-fashioned; too much borrowed authority looks, well, borrowed. An added bonus is that classic clothes are comfortable, and you don't have to buy new stuff when fashion changes.

Correct, balanced clothing signals seriousness: in return for a very small investment of time and money, you can buy yourself authority and a good first impression. Quite a few of our colleagues go entirely in the other direction, as if almost to underscore their academic aloofness. This can work—after all, personality trumps most of our advice here—but normally only if you are world famous or teach very technical subjects. A messy exterior tells your audience that this instructor, of whom they have never heard, does not care about the class and, by extension, does not care about them.

You need not obsess over your appearance, but think about what you wear. Go with something that feels comfortable (you will be moving around a lot) and fits well. Your clothing and appearance is not something that you should have to even think about after the class starts.

Don't make the obvious mistakes, such as forgetting to silence your cellphone or leaving change or keys in your pockets. Any little mannerism you display as a teacher is immediately magnified and very visible to the students, and if you do some small thing (such as toying with coins in your pockets), the students will notice that and little else.

Managing Your Anxiety

The unknowns of a case discussion cause faculty a great deal of anxiety. Bill still gets anxious before class. (Espen pretends he doesn't by resorting to various schemes, such as torturing Bill.) You can use your nervousness before class to keep you focused; it is when you are complacent that the real blowups happen. But nervousness can also be detrimental, both to your teaching (trust us, experience helps) and to your life outside the classroom. Try to remember that you can never be completely prepared for a case discussion. Be facile with the case facts and frameworks, know but don't obsess over your teaching plan, and then accept whatever anxiety you have and try to enjoy yourself.

When it comes to managing nervousness, teaching is a lot like acting, and actors have many tricks to combat anxiety. They tend to fall into the categories of preparation, exercises, and rituals.

Preparation

Preparation is, of course, preparing yourself to teach the class: the content, the process, and your mind. Chance favors the prepared mind, and you can do a lot by thinking through what is going to happen and how you will respond to it. If you are new or in unfamiliar surroundings, try to visit the classroom and have a good look at it beforehand. Stand up in front of the empty room; imagine what it looks like with students. Fiddle with the controls for screens, boards, lights, and computers. If you are giving a talk to a large audience, have a chat with the technical people and make sure you understand each other. Locate whiteboard pens or chalk, where to hang your coat, where you want to put your notes. Change something in the room to suit you.

The whole idea with this kind of activity is to *take ownership of the location*, to make it yours. If you are going to use a computer and feel insecure about it, for instance, make sure you can use *your* computer, not some leftover that is already in the room and with which you are unfamiliar. In a similar sense, make the classroom yours. A little rebellion feels good. For example, Espen often bemoans the lack of a table tall enough so that he can put his computer or notes on it and not have to stoop; to get one, he repurposes a wastebasket or box of copier paper to put on a regular table as a computer stand, less because it really is necessary than because he likes to assert control of the room.

Exercises

There are a number of exercises actors use to prepare for a performance and teachers use before a class. Primarily, they prime the voice and breathing. When you are speaking to a class, you will find that you need to speak louder than you usually do. Actors need to do this regularly and prepare by doing voice exercises, such as finding a place where they are alone (the bathroom is good), standing in front of a mirror, and doing things such as holding their arms straight out, opening their mouths wide, emitting a long, loud "aaaaahhhh" sound (similar to a loud yawn) while slowly moving their straight arms together in front of them.

Teachers are often nervous about how they sound and how they look. That is a pretty bad combination, for they are related. Almost every teacher can sound great in front of a class—without a microphone—and keep the volume and diction going throughout a whole day. The key is to breathe with your stomach, not your chest. Breathing with your stomach means letting your stomach out (not sucking it in to hide that embarrassing little paunch) and taking deep breaths, speaking with your whole voice. If you suck your stomach in and don't breathe any further than your sternum, your voice will take on a stressed tone (often going up half an octave). In order to get enough volume, you need to tighten your vocal chords, and as a result, you will be hoarse after a day. The breathing exercises in the bathroom (at least in the beginning; after a while you can learn to do them silently and in public with nobody noticing) serve to open you up, to make you feel large, and to make your voice strong. (And if you are unsure about how to do this, see a vocal coach; just an hour of two can be a really good investment.) As a teacher, you live by your voice. Taking care of it will reduce your nervousness, and reducing your nervousness is good for your voice.

Rituals

Rituals are little things we do to reduce stress, for practical purposes or because we just like to. Many teachers (and actors, of course) use rituals to control their nervousness. Bill always tries to block out a couple of minutes before class to take a few deep breaths and focus himself. When logistics prevent this, he will still take a moment to pause before entering a classroom. One well-known professor used a cup of coffee, holding it in his hand to pace himself. If he got a difficult question, he could slow himself down by taking a sip and thinking for a bit. Taking a favorite piece of clothing or jewelry, visible or not, to class can help or rewarding yourself with a piece of chocolate before or after class.

Nervousness can be beneficial. It keeps you awake and ensures that you approach every class as if it were new and not just routine. See it as a resource, but a resource to be harnessed and used in your service, not an obstacle that gets in your way.

Starting to Teach

Every class needs to be explicitly started, and so does the course itself. We will deal with the first class first and then the generic strategies for starting classes.

The First Class

Students need to learn the mechanics of discussions in your class, particularly if yours is their first case class. When to explain the dynamics of discussions in your class to students presents a challenge. We have found that including rules or guidelines in the written syllabus, available to students well in advance of the course, is often insufficient. Many students do not read the syllabus carefully, particularly in advance of the course. This is especially true when students are "shopping" courses during the drop or add period.

If, like us, you are not afforded the luxury of "preconditioned" students, then you will need to explain case teaching to them. Ideally, you should have a separate session with the students, in person or online, before the course starts. Sending an email to the group with a brief description of how the course will run can also be helpful, although we have not found that to be sufficient.

So how should you start a case course with inexperienced students? After years of opening his first class session with an orientation to case discussion, Bill began opening the first class directly with a case discussion question. He then leaves time at the end of class to discuss the mechanics of class discussion and any administrative issues, including discussion of the syllabus and grading. This sets a much more constructive and collaborative tone than entering the room and essentially lecturing on "how things will be."

A case discussion should be cumulative; as far as possible, each comment should build on the preceding one (except when you change a topic, of course). In order to do that, students need to listen to each comment, rather than sit and wait to chime in with their own, independent of the preceding one. A way to signal this is to have a rule that you should put your hand up when you want to say something, but that you can only do that after someone else has finished what she or he has to say. As soon as someone has gotten the floor, you immediately take your hand down again. In well-run case classes, this is quite noticeable and a very good way to underscore the mechanics of the discussion and the role the students have in giving and receiving learning to and from each other. You may choose to allow an exception for students who want to challenge directly what someone is saying. This creates a more intense, competitive atmosphere.

There are various ways of illustrating this. Bill recounts for his students an illustrative scene from Quentin Tarantino's *Pulp Fiction* (being careful to warn students that the film is quite violent, should they choose to see it). In one scene, Mia Wallace, played by Uma Thurman, is interviewing Vincent Vega, played by John Travolta. She asks him whether he listens or waits to talk. He responds that he waits to talk but is trying to learn to listen. Bill uses this to drive home the point that simply politely waiting to talk is not sufficient; students must listen and make the class a continuous conversation.

A second aspect is how to create a sense of community out of the group—get them to know each other so they can learn from each other. In a traditional class with undergraduate or graduate students who already know each other, you are the new element and need to introduce yourself. If you are teaching an executive class, where the students typically come together for only a few, sometimes quite intensive days, you will need to get to know them and they need to get to know each other. Spend some time and ask the participants what their concerns and expectations are. A rather hackneyed, but still effective technique is to go around the room (depending on the size of the audience, of course), write down their answers on a whiteboard or flipchart for each person, and then revisit the list later to check that you addressed at least most of the expectations. Done well, this can also make it clear that the learning outcome of a seminar or a session is a joint responsibility of the audience and the discussion leader.

If you have time, the students have never met before, and the group has an eclectic background, you can go around the room and have each student introduce him- or herself. This has risks, however; some people see this as an opportunity to present their complete CVs and views of the world. You can humorously set a thirty-second time limit or request that they only state their name, title, and answer to one or two questions ("Why I am taking this course?" "What is my favorite non-work activity?" "Whom would I most like to spend a day with?") Be careful to keep the tempo high when doing this and watch for students who are gregarious, malcontent, shy, and so on, so you know whom to call on when you need a joke, a critical voice, or a carefully prepared answer. But only do this exercise if the students don't know each other beforehand; your need for knowledge about them is not an excuse to take the time for a full introduction. If you find yourself in a situation where you will lead a case discussion in a setting where the students all know each other—an intra-company strategic discussion, for instance—ask if you can sit in on one of the preceding sessions just to get a feel for the group, how members communicate, and what roles they play.

Opening Classes

When it is time to start the discussion, you have a number of ways to do it, and there is much room for individualism, as long as you are consistent. First, you tell the students that the class is about to start, so they quiet down and are ready. How you do that can vary. A facilitator of the participant-centered learning classes at Harvard Business School starts every class by quietly stepping out in the middle of the floor and unbuttoning and rolling up his shirtsleeves. It only takes a session or two before the students understand this signal and immediately quiet down and glance at their case notes. One great professor we know started his classes by barging into the classroom right on the dot, dumping his papers on the dais, barking, "Right, let's get started!" and getting right down to it.

The classic way to start a case is to have a student open the case discussion, and you have three main ways of doing this: a "cold call," a "warm call," and an "open call." Of course, you can make these calls at any point in a case class, not just at the beginning.

- A *cold call* (some teachers refer to this as placing someone in "the hot seat") occurs when an instructor starts by asking a student directly, "Ingrid, what should Dell do about the commoditization of its products?"

- A *warm call* is when you start by naming the student who will open the discussion, but give the person some time to collect his or her thoughts: "Good morning, all. Today I will ask Ingrid to open our discussion, but first I have a few comments to the questions you raised in last week's class." This gives Ingrid a minute or two to get her pulse under 180, check her notes, and decide how to proceed. You can also notify students when and how you plan to call on them further in advance, by email. It may or may not be portrayed as a cold call to the rest of the class.

- An *open call* is when the teacher simply asks for a volunteer to start the discussion: "Today's case is Dell. What should it do about product commoditization?"

You need to decide the depth and breadth of analysis you expect from the first student. You may have a student give a short introduction to the case, focusing on the relevant problems, and start the debate by suggesting a course of action or otherwise respond to your direction. The depth of this introduction needs to be differentiated a bit, depending on the level of the students. In an executive student class, you can assume deep business understanding and start the discussion with less exposition about the details of the company, unless the industry is very different from the students'. In an undergraduate class, you may need to spend more time anchoring the students' understanding of the industry and company—the context—since many of them will have little work experience and tend to base their understanding either in organizational theory or in work life as depicted in TV series or advertisements. More mature students will, on average, be more comfortable speaking and doing so at length.

If you are cold- or warm-calling, you should decide before class which student you will ask to open. This is a choice that has to be made carefully, especially early on. We tend, at least in the beginning, to rely on the biographical information we have collected and choose students with a background indicating a useful perspective on the case. For graduate students, this may be work experience in the industry or role, and for undergraduates or others without work experience, their major, sports, activities, or interests may be useful. Later in the course, as we get to know more about the students' knowledge and abilities, we tend to pick students who are likely to provide good responses (if the case is difficult) or students who need to speak more in class or need to correct a negative impression. It is important not to be too predictable, so sometimes just pick a student at random. Otherwise, many students may conclude they don't need to be prepared to open a case if they don't fall into any of the categories you use for selection. To the extent possible, all students should open the discussion at least once during the course.

These three forms of formalized openings are, of course, not the only way to start a class, but they do have an advantage in that they force the whole class to prepare. You can have the students prepare in groups and ask one group (or a group representative) to open the discussion (see the section on group work later for more detail on this).

A great way to start the class is to have a vote on some question—"How many think EssEmBeeCo should enter the new market?" or poll the students on some numerical point such as the price offered for a company or how much to pay a new employee—graph the distribution, and then query the outliers about why they chose that particular number. Always be careful not to say whether a particular number is correct or not. The point is to find the thinking behind the analysis.

The more senior the students are, the less structure (that is, groups, formalities, grades) is normally required. Senior management seminars, at least in the United States, Scandinavia, and India, tend to turn into quite spirited discussions almost by themselves, at least if the material is engaging. In executive classes, you can rely on people with industry (or even company) experience to share their knowledge, and telling them ahead of time that you will ask them to talk about the conditions in the industry, how their company entered the same market as the case company, or something else can be a great strategy; suddenly you have allies who want the class to succeed as much as you do. This can also be a way to handle people who tend to dominate discussions. Give them some allotted time, with the unspoken agreement that that time is what they get, and not more.

Building Trust in the Class

Compared to traditional lectures, there is considerable personal risk associated with case teaching. Will the students react as you hope and expect? Will they be prepared? Will they have something to say? Will they engage in the discussion? Will you be able to cover the issues you want to teach? No wonder inexperienced case teachers sometimes try to take control of the class by asking very precise questions or answering questions themselves if the students don't.

When we learned case teaching ourselves, the mantra from the master teachers was "trust the class." Have faith in the students. They have knowledge and viewpoints (at least if you give them occasion and incentives to prepare and communicate), and if you can get them engaged, then a lively discussion will ensue. You will have many "hooks" from which to drive the discussion, as long as you dare follow the flow and not lock yourself too much into your planned structure.

Establishing trust in the group is difficult for all participants, particularly the instructor. Good preparation of the course and management of expectations will help, but the crucial first steps in the classroom are yours to take. When you pose questions to the class, you have to be willing to wait for responses. Strategies such as cold calls or polls will not be sufficient if you want to engender discussion and trust in the group. At some point, and we would advocate very early in your first class session, you need to pose an open question to the class. How you handle the pause after that first question and those that follow sets the tenor of your relationship with the class for the rest of the semester. If you do not show faith in the group to be able to answer the questions, they will sense that, and at best you have engendered resentment and you've possibly created a self-fulfilling expectation.

Every year, one legendary professor deliberately enters a class on a case he has taught before, but not recently, without doing any preparation, just to remind himself to listen to students. He starts with an open question and then follows the discussion, trusting the class to provide the analysis.

The dynamics of each group of students can vary wildly. While the students in any course can develop constructive or destructive norms of interaction, those who share multiple classes together are far more prone to developing an ingrained culture. Case discussions accelerate the development of many of these norms not only by the increased amount of communication students are doing, but also by the nature of the communication itself. Setting a positive, constructive, supportive, intellectually curious, and demanding tone is critical. We encourage you to clarify for students that support for one another does not obviate challenging one another's ideas and discussing them openly. Your best efforts at setting and maintaining this tone may be insufficient to prevent a dysfunctional dynamic from developing. In chapter 5, we discuss what to do if counterproductive norms develop.

Building trust lies in how you treat the students. If you micromanage all their work, even how they do assignments outside of class, you run the risk of infantilizing them and you won't see the desired level of maturity in the classroom. We've seen many faculty, even experienced ones, struggle with giving undergraduate students the freedom they need, a problem that is exacerbated when teaching executives or experienced MBA students. But it can also be a factor in teaching less experienced graduate or inexperienced undergraduate students. Many faculty believe that undergraduates need to have their hands held throughout a course. Our experience is that treating students as mature professionals causes most to rise to the occasion. For many students, there is an adjustment period early on, but we have found that if we maintain high expectations, the more mature students who "get it" will bring the rest of the class along with them.

Managing the Discussion

The core of case teaching—and most of its art—lies in managing the students' discussion. This means acting as an emcee; you need to manage who gets to speak, when, and for how long; act as a scribe in using the boards to keep track of the discussion; act like a TV host in asking questions that drive the discussion forward; and not act like a ringmaster in being conscious of your own movement and position in the classroom.

The most important content of case teaching is the student contributions—their suggestions, comments, and questions. Experienced case teachers refer to student contributions, particularly the unexpectedly good ones or those that produce teaching moments, as "gifts" the students offer to the teacher and the class. There is a lot of merit in thinking about student contributions this way. Gift giving is associated with a certain risk. Will the recipient accept the gift, understand why it is given, appreciate its originality, and not suspect a hidden agenda or that the gift really is repurposed from something left over? Being a good case teacher (and participation evaluator) is like being a good gift recipient: you see the students' gifts in the best possible light (don't look a gift horse in the mouth, right?) and try to make sense of even the more awkward presents, all to encourage more gift giving.

The Emcee: Calling on Students and Managing Airtime

Managing who speaks when and for how long—that is, who gets "airtime"—is a crucial part of case discussion leadership, especially when participation accounts for a significant part of the course grade. One of your roles as a case teacher is to make sure that airtime is distributed equitably if not evenly, among the course participants. Allowing a minority of students, even if their contributions are excellent, to dominate the discussion does not achieve your goals and will often lead to resentment among students who feel excluded. The number of times students speak does not need to be equal; some comments are more substantial, make greater contributions to the course, or take more time. For similar reasons, the number of minutes each student speaks during a semester need not be equal. But all students should be given equal opportunity to contribute to the discussions. And, ideally, all students should feel that they have been given an equal opportunity to contribute to the discussions. By being as explicit and transparent as possible from the outset about how and why we call on students, we have found that most students see the system as fair.

Maintaining an equitable distribution of airtime can be quite hard. Not only are all students different (they can be reticent, verbose, competitive, anxious, and sometimes even belligerent, all of which influence their ability to get airtime), but the room itself and your own unconscious behavior can work against you. Be aware that you are normally not a good observer of your own behavior and that having a peer or an assistant observe the patterns in which you assign airtime, if possible with a sheet of paper and some statistics, can be very valuable. We offer specific metrics in chapter 8.

Develop a sense of how many opportunities students have to speak in your classes (our classes tend to have thirty to sixty per hour). If there are not enough opportunities for each student to speak at least once during each class, then you need to be careful to balance who is speaking during any given class. At a minimum, you want to distribute as proportionately as possible for location in the classroom, gender, level of experience, nationality, and any other groups for which bias might be a concern.

Early on, you must explicitly establish your authority to manage airtime, especially the authority to call on any student, at any time. You don't necessarily have to exercise the prerogative to retain it. Bill prefers not to cold-call students (except when nervous students request to be cold-called because they are too hesitant to raise their hands in class), because cold-calling raises anxiety for many students, particularly if they are not cold-called or even required to speak in other classes. But if some students are not preparing sufficiently or are unwilling to raise their hands and Bill exhausts other alternatives, then he will resort to cold-calling.

We tend to run a very tight ship during the first third of a course, striving to have every student in the class contribute to the discussion. After two or three classes in which students understand that they will be asked to comment even if they haven't raised their hand, reality sinks in. The preparation level goes up, even if you haven't scared them into preparing before the course starts. If a student is not prepared, we will not comment on that immediately, but move on and ask another student the same question. We are not saying that getting students to prepare is easy; we address this in chapter 5.

Some instructors take this approach further and employ tricks, such as consistently calling on the person sitting next to the unprepared student. This mobilizes an intense social pressure to prepare. We don't use this approach ourselves; we think it is a bit over the top, as it takes the attention away from the content of the course. Such automatic moves also limit your freedom to pick any student you want. Predictable calling patterns in any form (alphabetical, by seating area, and so on) lower engagement among those students who know they are off the hook.

Transitions from one student to another must be done carefully; it is important to distinguish between students who are prepared, but nervous, and those who are unprepared but try to cover it up with smooth talking and improvisation. With the former, you just wait until they have calmed down and use your body language (nod, smile, wait patiently) to signal that you are listening and have time. With the latter, cut to another student, ask for a volunteer, or, if you suspect lack of preparation and want to make an example of the situation, ask a pointed follow-up question.

We try to give immediate praise if someone is well prepared or has a good piece of analysis, or if she has comments or questions that show she has thought through the case issues. Often the acknowledgment is writing something on the board, perhaps highlighting it in some way, such as circling or underlining it, or putting an asterisk next to it. Other times, we reflect our praise in our body language or physical movement. Sometimes, if the point is particularly strong or we want to single out a student who has been struggling or insecure, we will explicitly and verbally praise the comment. But we don't do this too often, because we want that level of feedback to remain special and we do not want students constantly looking to us for validation.

We try to underscore that students need to do the discussing, not ask questions of the teacher. We allow them to ask questions if they are stuck, and the best questions are those that we don't have a ready answer for. Whenever possible, turn the question back on the student, not as a punishment, but to help students see that they often know more than they think. If that doesn't work or isn't appropriate, open the question to other students. As the course progresses, preparation and discussion become a habit with the students, and we gradually reduce the direct questions and steer the discussion more discreetly.

To encourage students to speak to one another when they are role-playing or disagreeing, deflect attention from yourself. You can do this explicitly by telling the speaker, "don't tell me, tell (the student to whom the speaker is responding)," but we prefer a more subtle technique. Rather than looking at the speaker, look at the student you want to respond. The student you are looking at will take the cue and respond without your intervention. Being able to facilitate student-to-student communication without speaking reinforces that the students own the discussion, so ask questions that will foster this dynamic.

The emcee role is perhaps the most physically demanding aspect of teaching, partly because being on your feet and using the room and your body language consume energy, but also because managing the discussion is cognitively exhausting; you need to do many things at once. It is also, perhaps, the most crucial role of a case teacher. Practice and habits certainly help, but expect to be tired after a class.

The Scribe: Using the Board

The board (or boards, because you'll want to have several) is a vital tool for case teaching; as the students come up with various points about the case, the teacher writes them down (using key words, drawings, tables, or whatever methods he or she can think of to do it fast).

Taking notes in public serves a number of purposes. First, it provides a *shared overview of what students have been discussing,* not just as a list of bullet points in random order. Done well, the teacher will gradually build up an overview of the discussion, posing different topics and solutions against each other. This capturing keeps things on track; if you don't do it, you will quickly find that the discussion becomes repetitive and the number of non sequiturs rises dramatically. Just as your own teaching notes help you focus, well-executed board management—yes, we actually call it that—helps the students remember and understand much more about the case than they would if the discussion were just verbal. You succeed if the students can look at the boards after a class—sometimes, quite a while after—and feel that they have a reasonably complete understanding of what they have discussed.

A second purpose of using the board is to *guide the discussion.* You can do this by signaling to the students what is important in the case; if a student says something and the teacher does not write it down, that is a signal that the comment is inconsequential or repetitive. If you are having problems with students repeating prior comments, highlight the comment on the board and ask how the current student's comment adds to it. If you remember who made the comment, refer back to him or her, which shows you are listening closely and will make the students pay more attention to what is being said. If you are standing at one board, writing down various aspects of the case—say, strategic attributes of the industry the company is in—and one student makes a good comment, but under a different topic, for instance, characteristics of the leadership group or something about the technology the company uses, you can choose to keep the discussion on track, but still capture the point by moving to the next board, writing a new heading (say, "Organization" or "Technology"), capturing the students point, and then saying, "Great point, but let's flesh out the characteristics of the industry a bit more, shall we?" In that way, you keep the discussion on point, but also indicate where to take it next. If you do it well, you steer the discussion and gradually fill up the board with something that looks a bit like what you wanted when you planned the lesson, but it will seem to the students that they themselves created order out of chaos.

You can also use the board to introduce frameworks and models into the discussion. Draw the framework on one of the back boards (that is, a board hidden behind other boards) or use a flipchart and reveal the framework as a natural part of the discussion. It will likely be difficult to use the board this way without students seeing you. Depending upon the intensity in the classroom, students may notice what you have put on the board and frantically prepare to use that during the discussion. If you are not able to get into the classroom before the students to write on the board in advance, a simple request that the students not look while you write the framework on the board will often suffice.

Some faculty want students to take notes; some don't. We are agnostic and think this is firmly within the purview of the students themselves. We certainly don't want students spending all of their time taking notes and not following the discussion, but we have never found this to be a large problem.

Board Plan

A board plan is a simple diagram outlining what you want to be on the boards when you are done and the order in which you want to get there. Some case teachers use the same generic board plan for almost all cases; others vary them based on the case, the audience, and most importantly, the number and configuration of boards in the classroom. Consistency in how you use specific boards can be helpful in developing good habits for you and the students. For instance, you might use the same side board for characters, frameworks, and so on.

Board plans have to be tailored to the classroom, the boards you have, and the case. If you have a classroom designed for case discussions with, say, six boards, three abreast, where the boards in front can be raised to reveal the ones behind, you can draw a board plan that looks something like the one shown in figure 3-1, with the front

FIGURE 3-1

Generic six-board plan

Front board 1 (1)	Front board 2 (2)	Front board 3 (3)
• Case company history and evolution	• Characters in case	• Core issues of case
Back board 1 (4)	**Back board 2 (5)**	**Back board 3 (6)**
• Frameworks	• Strategies • Learnings	• Learnings • B case (if relevant)

FIGURE 3-2

Strategy six-board plan

Front board 1 (1)	Front board 2 (2)	Front board 3 (3)
• History of company • Characteristics of product	• Industry analysis existing market (Porter's 5 forces)	• Industry analysis new market (Porter's 5 forces)
Back board 1 (4)	**Back board 2 (5)**	**Back board 3 (6)**
• Arguments for going into new market	• Arguments for not going into new market	• B case—what happened?

boards initially shielding the back boards (the bold numbers in parentheses signify the order in which you will use them).

Let's look at an example to make it concrete. You are going to teach a case about a midsized manufacturing company called EssEmBeeCo, which is mulling over whether to go into a new market. Your teaching objective is to show the use of a strategic analysis framework, such as Porter's five forces (Porter, 1979). The B case describes what happened when the company entered the market. A board plan for the same six-board setup could then look something like the one in figure 3-2.

A simple way to teach this would be to discuss the issues in the order of the boards, as is consistently done by at least one really good case teacher we know. This is easy and comforting for the students, because they know he will start at board one and end up at board six, and if one of the boards is empty, well, then they have missed something.

An alternative discussion could proceed in the order shown in figure 3-3, which puts the key concept in the middle and allows easier comparison between the old and the new market.

FIGURE 3-3

Alternative strategy board plan

Front board 1 (1)	Front board 2 (2)	Front board 1 (6)
• History of company • Characteristics of product	• Industry analysis existing market (Porter's 5 forces)	• B case—what happened?
Back board 4 (4)	**Back board 2 (3)**	**Back board 3 (5)**
• Arguments for going into new market	• Industry analysis new market (Porter's 5 forces)	• Arguments for not going into new market

If the classroom differs from the one described, especially in terms of board arrangements, create a board plan that reflects that.

Many classrooms have awkward board arrangements, often because architects think classrooms should be designed for business presentations—that is, with a projector and maybe a flipchart or two. Hence, you need to create board plans that reflect the situation in the classroom. Espen frequently teaches in rooms where there are two boards abreast, with two or three boards in front of them, which can be slid to either side (see figure 3-4). This means that at any point you can show only two (albeit large) boards at one time, with the front boards always obscuring some of the back boards. (See figure 3-5 for Espen's board plan.)

Make sure you don't end up with background information or something trivial on the front board, which will be visible throughout the whole session. Since the key to this example is Porter's five-forces framework, a solution could be to save the front board for that (old and new market side-by-side on one board). You would then start with the front board empty to the left, the others to the right, start on the second board, work inward and save the left backboard for the B case. The key is to make sure that your substantial points—what you want the students to be left with—are not blocked by trivial content.

If you have even fewer boards—say, two boards or one board and a few flipcharts—keep in mind what you want to be front and center. Again, for the EssEmBeeCo case, you would want to focus mainly on the Porter analysis, so leave the board for that and use flipcharts, perhaps one on each side of the board, for general discussion points.

You should try to avoid erasing things from the boards, but if you are running out of board space and have to, erase the background

FIGURE 3-4

Sliding front board obscuring back boards

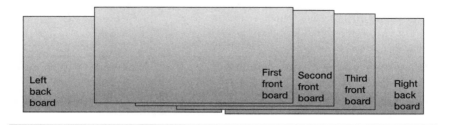

FIGURE 3-5

Plan for sliding boards

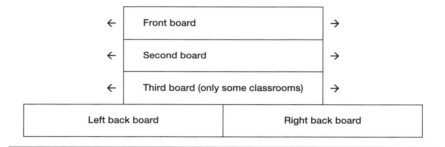

information or other content you will not need to refer back to, and do it during a pause in the discussion, for instance, when you hand out the B case for the students to read. If you have only one board in the room, divide the space in half, thirds, or quarters either in your head or explicitly with lines so that you can erase one part without disrupting the others. Be judicious about what you write on the board rather than writing so small that no one can read it.

What you definitely should avoid is writing with one hand and erasing with the other, in the manner of certain math professors, which turns the class into a note-taking race in which nobody has time to comment.

Writing on the Board

Dexterity with chalk or whiteboard markers is a result of practice. It is normally better to write a few words than whole sentences, better to write large than small, and generally better to write in block letters

Clearing Board Space

If you have limited board space and the structure of the discussion is such that you generate a list of items to discuss, write the list on the board and erase each as it is addressed.

than script, unless your hobby is calligraphy. Use arrows and other symbols to link concepts. Bullet points can give order and formality.

The purpose of using boards is to drive the discussion, not to write official minutes. Don't worry if you miss something; you will; we all do. In subsequent classes, you can come back to things. Also, don't worry about the occasional typo; nobody demands that you write correctly when doing it at speed and in front of people. As a case teaching course attendee once said to us, "There is a general amnesty for spelling mistakes on the board."

If you are doing something that requires a lot of writing—for instance, recording questions for later discussion, or writing down alternative formulations of, say, a company mission statement—consider asking an assistant do the writing, perhaps even one of the students (who should be briefed beforehand and have legible handwriting and at least some spelling skill). Or have students type out their answers and use a computer display to share them. We discuss the use of classroom technology more in chapter 10.

At times, you might want to transcribe the words of the student precisely. Perhaps he or she has turned a particularly clever phrase, done a remarkable job of integrating a concept, or inadvertently communicated something other than what he or she intended. In these situations, take the time to get what he or she said exactly right. Professors who are quick at writing on the board find great power in reproducing a student's exact language. We lean toward summarizing students' points in the interests of expediency, but will go for great precision when there is sufficient value in doing so.

Try to avoid speaking while facing the board. Even if you are able to project your voice sufficiently, some students find it rude. If you have a lot of writing to do, call on two or three students at once ("Alice, then Bob") or pause writing long enough to turn and call on

Keeping the Boards Clean

Keep the board as clean as you can. Writing over erasure marks makes it hard to read. One colleague carries a damp towel to class to get the boards clean. A towel can be particularly helpful if you teach at the end of the day after many other professors. At a minimum, make sure your room is equipped with an effective eraser; getting your own can be good insurance.

Whiteboards can be more difficult to get clean. Even dedicated spray cleaners and wipes don't always work. If the boards are always clean in the mornings, contact your facilities group and get a bottle of whatever it uses.

---

another student before returning to the board. And remember that a few moments of silence is not necessarily a bad thing.

Try not to be anchored to the board, writing all the time. How you move around the classroom is a personal matter, but we advocate that you move quickly out to the middle of the room as often as possible, alternating quickly between the board and the floor. Not only does this give you a better understanding of the dynamics of the class (you see the students from various perspectives), but it also keeps you and the students energized.

The Conductor: Using Body Language, Silence, and Movement

Much of the art of discussion management lies in the use of nonverbal signals. You can direct a discussion well by using body language, and you do not need to be very explicit.

For instance, if a student is a bit fumbling and nervous, lean slightly forward and indicate that you are listening intensely and with interest, perhaps also by nodding and writing something on the board. For students who talk and talk without pause, you can switch over to someone else by walking rapidly toward the talker, especially if she is in one of the two front rows. Normally this will cause her to take a short breather, during which you transfer the discussion to another student. For a droning student in one of the back rows, feign that you are not listening by looking in another direction or stop taking notes. You can, of course, cut the person off by asking him to summarize or saying, "So, I hear you saying [this]. Anyone beg to differ?" but you will be surprised by what you can achieve without words.

Bill once taught a two-hour twenty-minute class entirely mute from throat surgery. He entered the class prepared to type words into a computer to save time instead of writing on the board, but found all of that unnecessary. He was able to run the entire class with hand gestures, aided by a student in class who interpreted some of the less obvious gestures for the rest of the class. He thought it rather humbling that many students later cited that class as the best of the semester. If your mobility is limited, show students your energy through facial and hand gestures and reserve moving around the classroom for particularly dramatic moments. Use your intonation more to change tempo. Use props (Bill extensively used a cane that he had to carry for several months).

As a case instructor, your main job is to generate discussion, not to participate in it. At the same time, the instructor can have opinions and make them known, without striking down those who disagree. We have many times generated discussion by taking more assertive positions than we would outside the classroom. A favorite approach is to assert that a company should be run purely for the benefit of the shareholders, which nearly always produces an irritated and argumentative student or two for the opposition, and off we go. Here we are inspired by the editorial stance of *The Economist*, which has some deeply held convictions but is willing to analyze each issue by itself and always take alternative views seriously.

Sometimes you have very lively, almost acrimonious discussions between groups of students, for instance, in classes discussing various aspects of globalization, where there are deep differences in viewpoints and reaching consensus is hard. If a group of students is overpowering another group or individual, you may move over and stand next to or behind the underdog, tilting the balance. As an instructor, you are the gravitational center of the classroom, and you can use this constructively. If the underdog is still struggling and cannot find any student allies, you can also speak in support. We tend to do this more with less mature students who are often reticent when they find themselves outnumbered.

Being good at reading the body language of others can be invaluable. But so is being aware of what you are signaling. At times, you are likely to have feelings—negative and positive—about students, but you do not want this to show without your knowledge. Bill has studied poker "tells," specific body language that signals useful information (see, for instance, Caro, 2004). When you ask a question, observing students' eye movements, body language, and hand gestures can tell you a great deal about how much they know. This observation can be particularly useful when deciding whether to push with follow-up questions. If you are thinking about a cold call and want the student to be successful, look for signs of sudden interest, such as a change in body position, particularly leaning forward.

Silence is a powerful tool, not to be underestimated. We have seen many presenters pose a question to an audience and when nobody answers, start to rephrase the question or answer it themselves. Don't do it. Instead, wait and keep quiet. You may find it hard to stand there while the seconds tick away and nothing happens, but it is much worse for the audience, whose panic will increase until somebody blurts out something in pure desperation. Then you can let this person start the discussion. You have to adjust this strategy somewhat depending on where you are in the world, however. Espen has experienced long silences in the Netherlands (and lots of discussion during the breaks), and Bill has found that many Finnish students are comfortable with long silences, simply sitting there waiting for the end of class.

Espen experienced the effectiveness of silence very powerfully when he was leading a strategy conference for a major Scandinavian corporation. He had given a short talk on strategy, followed by the division vice presidents presenting the strategies for each of the company's four divisions. The participants had been split into eight tables with eight participants, each table named after a consulting company. (This is, incidentally, a useful trick to get people to step out of their roles and can be used in a classroom as well.) Each "consulting company" consisted of people from divisions other than the one whose strategy it would evaluate. After a discussion break, each of the consulting companies presented its evaluations of the divisional strategies. Toward the end, Espen was going to lead a plenary discussion on the overall strategy of the corporation.

By the final discussion, it had become embarrassingly clear that one of the divisions had a strategy that stood in clear contrast and to a certain extent at cross-purposes to the others. Espen was keenly aware that as an outsider—and a perfidious academic, to boot—he lacked the legitimacy to point this out or suggest solutions. So when it was his turn, he made a few remarks about the importance of having a clear and encompassing strategy for the whole corporation. Then he asked the audience, "Now that you have heard each of the divisions' strategies, how do they fit together and how do they contribute to the strategy of the whole corporation?"

That sparked an impressive eighty-person silence. Espen started counting the seconds to himself. The tension in the room palpably increased. When he had reached thirty-two, one of the division vice presidents *had* to break the ice, and that was it. The discussion flowed back and forth and the list of speakers grew until the CEO quietly sent Espen a note saying he would cut his final talk from half an hour to five minutes, since it was much more important that this subject be extensively debated.

So silence works. Most of the time.

Using the Physical Space

In most schools, classrooms are designed to be faculty-centric and support lecture pedagogy. Sight lines converge on the podium in the front of the room. Access to the rest of the room from the front is often limited to narrow rows behind seated students. The more you can do to open up the space and physically signal that you will be sharing the space with the group, the better. The first thing we do when we enter a classroom is move much of the furniture at the front of the room out of the way. Often, students arriving early in subsequent classes will move the furniture. Take down anything in the way that you don't need, including a boom microphone on the podium, a projector sitting on a table, or even a computer monitor, if you're not going to use it. Making the room your own sends a powerful signal to the group and improves the quality of the experience.

If the students are seated at individual desks, arrange them in a U-shape, if that's feasible. If there are longer tables that are mobile, rearrange them into a U-shape. If the U-shape is not practical, given the limitations of the space or the size of the class, consider other arrangements that aren't the traditional lecture format.

You have to both involve and see the whole class. Even in the best classrooms, the degree to which students are visible will vary. In a U-shaped, tiered case classroom, the students who are hardest to spot are those off to either side, especially those on the first or second row (see figure 3-6). Strangely enough, the first row in front can also be overlooked, simply because it is below the instructor's sight line. To counter this, you must make a conscious effort to see these students,

FIGURE 3-6

Zones of visibility in case classroom

Dark gray is easy to see; light gray is easy to miss

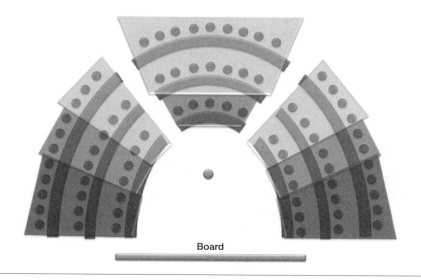

Board

and moving around, even up in the aisles if possible, will help you do that.

Seeing the students is not the only reason for moving about. You should try at all times to be *among* the students as much as possible, not in front of them. Don't stand still in one place. Good teachers signal energy and enthusiasm by movement. Many excellent case teachers almost run back and forth between the board and positions closer to the students, which one of our colleagues referred to as the physical instantiation of intellectual momentum. If the room has a U-shaped layout, spend much of your time in the "pit"—deep in the U-shape, toward the middle of the room. This may be uncomfortable for you in the beginning. Your back will be to some students, and you may feel that you are trespassing on their territory. You will find it easier over time, and students will grow accustomed to your presence.

But don't limit yourself to the pit. During each class, try to make your way deep into the room. It is not only a powerful signal but also a great opportunity to gain some perspective on what's happening in your classroom. Pay attention to what is on the students' computer screens, the extent to which they have marked up the readings, and what other materials they have.

Some teachers worry about losing dignity by moving around too much in the classroom, and some feel uncomfortable outside the place of authority, which is why many classrooms have physical barriers (in the form of a desk or a dais) between the teacher and the students. We don't believe this is a risk as long as the movement is tied to what is being said or happening in the room. Enthusiasm is contagious, and moving is a great way to raise the energy level.

Picking a Lecture Spot

One of our colleagues recounts a story of a professor who picks a specific location in the classroom. When he needs to present lecture material, he walks to that spot, lectures, and then, when he moves off the spot, the discussion resumes.

Students Moving You Around

Students can influence you—and your location—quite subtly by giving or withholding attention. One professor of organizational psychology told about a class of psychology students who colluded to influence his location in the classroom. Without his knowledge, the students changed their behavior based on where he stood in the room. If he moved to the right, the students would display signs of paying attention by looking at him, smiling, nodding when he spoke, and so on. The further left he moved, the more they would display signs of indifference and lack of concentration, such as averting their eyes, gazing out the window, or fiddling with their notes. Without being aware of it, he found himself drifting further and further right until he was teaching the last part of the class from the corner of the room.

Your students may not deliberately manipulate you, but be mindful of picking up on cues from the class. Watch for patterns in your behavior.

The TV Host: Asking Questions

Asking questions in class has much in common with asking interview questions, if you are a journalist, or panel questions, if you are a TV or radio presenter. You can learn a lot from studying good interviewers. The classic advice is to never ask questions that demand a very precise answer. There are exceptions; you can, for instance, ask a student what his or her answer to a numerical problem is, but this should be done as a starting point for a discussion of how the answer was derived. Similarly, never ask questions that can be answered with a simple yes or no, unless you follow it up with a "why?" question right away. When at all possible, refer the discussion back to the class: "That's an interesting choice. Anyone have a different analysis?"

Spiraling a Case Discussion In or Out

A useful way of thinking about how you explore is *spiraling in*, starting with a large overarching question and then gradually homing in on the details or *spiraling out*, starting with a very specific question and then using that as a launching point for the larger, less specific discussions. Discussions tend to follow one or the other pattern and should. One of the advantages of the case method is the ability to change the level of analysis and sometimes even to observe the almost fractal nature of organizations. The patterns that you see in the small may also be visible in the larger context.

Asking questions comes naturally with practice, but new case teachers should avoid certain errors. Chief among them is asking very general questions while looking for a specific answer, which happens if you have locked yourself into wanting the discussion to go in a particular direction. There is a tired old joke about the driving test with the question, "What should you always have over the car?" The not very intuitive answer is "control," but quite a few people will answer "a tarp?" Choosing questions for a case discussion is very similar to designing an interview guide for a field research project. You have to avoid questions in your own terminology and context and avoid imposing your vocabulary and theoretical ways of thinking directly on the interviewee. Don't make the underlying variables that you want to surface directly visible. If you do, you run the risk of turning the whole class into an interrogation about "what is the teacher thinking now?" rather than a debate.

Questions serve many purposes. You use them to start discussions, to guide the discussions deeper or higher, to follow up on student contributions, and to make transitions between students and topics. The C. Roland Christensen Center for Teaching and Learning has a list of case question examples (see http://bit.ly/Y5yoHb), which is also useful as a refresher. It is easy to fall into habits, relying on some types of questions while not using others. The greater variety

Asking an Open Question

If you ask an open question and are not met by a sea of raised hands, here are two simple techniques that can help. First scan the entire room. This shows students you are genuinely interested in hearing from them, increases the pressure on them a bit because each will think you are looking at him or her, and gives you something to do while you wait for a raised hand. If that fails, try making brief but sustained eye contact with a few students who are not avoiding your glance.

of questions at your disposal, the richer you can make the discussion. We discuss metrics for evaluating questioning style in chapter 8.

Try to make your questions inviting and turn the discussion back toward the students as much as possible. And remember that you are not the only one in the case classroom who is nervous. Quite a few of the students will be trembling as well.

Sometimes students, particularly younger ones, will start asking you questions rather than offering comments. It often starts out as an innocent question about something they didn't quite understand in the case, and before you know it, the tables are turned and you are being interrogated. Questioning can also happen if you *are* the undoubted expert in the room or have a lot of passion for a topic. As always, patience is the key. Let the students figure things out themselves by turning the question back on them: "Would anyone like to explain how this works?" If the pattern becomes too obvious or the student (this sometimes happens with executives) takes an aggressive and interrogatory stance, you can always say (with a smile), "Hey, this is a case class. I'm supposed to ask the questions here!"

Giving Up Control

It is statistically obvious that a room full of people, given some variance in their backgrounds, should collectively know more and be better able to analyze a complex case than one person. As a case teacher, you need to know and believe in this. In industry-specific subjects and in executive classes, you can count on at least one student in the room knowing much more about the case than you do. Even motivated undergraduates might have done enough outside research on the Internet to exceed your knowledge of the company and industry details. Rather than seeing this as a threat, you can turn this to your advantage by treating these people as resources. Sometimes, you might have to give up your teaching plan altogether.

Some years ago, Espen arranged a seminar for the Norwegian Polytechnic Society, a technology discussion club. He and his colleagues Øystein Fjeldstad and Knut Haanæs planned to discuss why Norway is not a hotbed of software development, despite the fact that object-oriented programming (the dominant technique for almost all software development) was developed in Norway with the programming language SIMULA in the 1960s. When the meeting started, the presenters found that the audience was not the usual random collection of more or less interested people, but that the entire Norwegian SIMULA community had shown up: researchers, technologists, and some entrepreneurs who had tried to capitalize on the invention and failed.

The presenters immediately discarded all their slides and asked the audience their opinions on what had happened. It became a lively discussion on technology history, policy, and the relationship between academia and the business world. The collective insight was much deeper and better expressed than anything the three professors would have provided.

Giving up control like this is not something you should do every time and requires self-confidence. Many teachers are afraid of losing authority by letting on that they are not the biggest experts in the room. We have found that in situations where it is obvious that you are not the sole source of knowledge (or even the most important one), you maintain your authority better if you don't try to hide that fact and instead facilitate knowledge exchange.

Time Management

Time management can be a tricky detail when lecturing, but in case teaching, it is crucial. Almost all new teachers initially think they don't have enough material to fill the allotted time, only to find that

Parkinson's Law has jurisdiction in the case classroom: discussion tends to expand until it fills the time set aside for it. Time is a precious resource, and to preserve it, you must start the class on time and make the most of every minute. There are many ways to do this that we relate here, but it is important to note that this is one area, like board writing and body language, where practice really helps.

How Long to Let a Discussion Go

Most classes, particularly if students are relatively new to case discussion, will stay on a topic far longer than is optimal. Many new case teachers fall victim to the idea that trusting the class means letting the discussion go unmanaged. You need to decide when to move off a topic, although, as the students get more accustomed, they will be of more help and hindrance as they move off topics on their own, sometimes prematurely. We apply a few criteria when deciding whether or not to move on:

- Have the major points been covered?

- How is the energy in the room?

- What else do I need to cover in the session?

If You Are Running Out of Time

If you have a break during the case discussion, you should have time to triage your teaching plan, adjusting for topics not covered and time left. If you are pressed for time, be prepared to jettison material that isn't crucial to your primary intended takeaways for the case as well as material that addresses issues you can cover in later sessions. If you don't have a break, then you need to do this assessment on the fly, preferably without looking at your notes and certainly without obsessing over them.

First, try not to wait until there are only a few minutes left to make an adjustment. When you first start deviating from your schedule, think about what you will drop from your plan. Don't try to rush through everything; prioritize. If you can't remember the major topics left to cover, glance at your notes and decide which one you can skip or truncate. If you don't get to a crucial topic and you won't have time to return to it, perhaps skip your summary and leave the students with the topic as a question: "So how will this merger turn out?" And then let them leave—on time. We try never to run even a minute over in order to reinforce our position that everyone's time is precious. If we do choose to run over, we will always acknowledge we are going to do so, estimate how long it will take (never more than five minutes), and promise to return those minutes to them in the next session.

Breaks and Other Interruptions

The timing of breaks is normally not too hard to change, as long as you stay within the limits of the total meeting time. We recommend being flexible about breaks. Some schools have set times for breaks, often fifteen minutes every hour. This works OK for lectures, but a case discussion normally requires more time, typically sixty to eighty minutes. Take charge of setting breaks, but let the students know in advance, so that they don't have to skip out of the classroom because they have another commitment (this is especially important for intra-company and executive classes). Never keep the students more than ninety minutes without a break, unless you punctuate things (for instance, with some group work). Concentrating for more than ninety minutes, in our experience, just isn't doable.

Managing Breaks

Getting students to be punctual about breaks can be hard. Both Bill and Espen seldom take round-number breaks, preferring instead to say, "We will now have a break for 13 minutes, and start again at 11:07 according to the clock on the wall." We will then start precisely at 11:07, whether or not students are all seated and ready. It only takes two or three times and then the students are precise and like it.

Interruptions, unfortunately, are part of a teacher's life, most commonly in the form of requests from student organizations and administrators to make announcements or give brief presentations in your class, particularly if you teach undergraduate or graduate compulsory courses. We tend to accommodate these if the topic is relevant (student government announcements, for instance), but we insist that they be brief, come right after a break (before we have started teaching), and try to dissuade presenters from booting PowerPoint slide decks if at all possible.

Teaching Long Class Days

The longer the session in a given day, the more the quality of students' attention and preparation erodes. It is much harder for module-program students, who frequently have full-time jobs, to prepare for a class session than it is for a full-time student in a weekly course. More than three cases in a day (especially if they are on the same subject) can make the students very tired and confused. The content begins to blur across the material, and even very diligent students run out of energy, both for discussion and preparation.

You simply cannot make a calculation based on hours and cases— "one case per 1.5 teaching hours" for full-day programs. You need to break the day up with pedagogical alternatives such as individual and group exercises, presentations, audiovisual material, and discussions beyond the case studies.

When sharing a room with the same group of students for more than a few hours a day, we tend to lower the formality a bit, relative to a class that meets for only a little more than an hour a day. This acknowledges a "we are all in this together" mentality that builds empathy for the physical and mental toll the long class days can take on everyone.

We also try to foster more cohesion across the material we are covering that day than we would if we were teaching the same four cases in four separate class sessions. For instance, if two of the cases include vendor management issues, we might discuss them at the same time, even though that breaks the flow of our "regular" teaching plan for each of the cases. This makes the day feel more cohesive and, given that the cases are likely to meld together in students' minds anyway, such combination of the discussions can be helpful. If you have the board space or flipcharts, consider keeping some material from early in the day visible in the classroom and refer back to it later on. You may even return to what you wrote earlier and simply add to it in the subsequent discussion to flesh out the implementation of a framework, for instance.

If you are teaching the same case to different groups of students on the same day, do not assume that the discussions will be similar and be sure to let the comments in the later groups guide the discussion, rather than be driven by what you saw in the first discussion. This is not to say that you can't learn from what happened in the first class session. In chapter 8, we discuss what to do after you've taught a class and how you can use the experience to improve the next time.

Beyond Discussion

So far we have focused on the mechanics of running the discussion, but case teaching is about much more than the core method of a single teacher guiding individuals in a discussion of a case in a plenary setting. In this section, we start to look at some of the more common deviations from that model and how to make the most of them.

Using Theory and Other Noncase Material

We love case teaching because it allows us to deal with one of the most common shortcomings of student learning—and our most common comments on student papers—that the students "mention theory but don't apply it." Plenty of students can recite theories and framework; a much smaller proportion can examine a real-world situation (the situation itself or as represented by a case, a newspaper article, or anecdotes), apply a theoretical perspective to it, and from that, draw conclusions about how to proceed. Cases and other examples give the students mental hooks for hanging the theory on, often in the shape of stories. For years after, they will remember the stories and therefore also the theory.

Inductive versus Deductive Case Use

We distinguish between inductive versus deductive case teaching:

- The *inductive method* is to teach students one or several cases and then use the cases to have the students draw out useful frameworks of theories from them. This is the "classic" way of using cases when the method started at the Harvard Business School, and many professors consider it the gold standard for case teaching. It has the benefit of drilling concepts into the students—for one thing, many will think they came up with the concepts by themselves—but can be time and energy consuming. It works best with very good, very competitive students interested in the topic.

- The *deductive method* is to give the students theoretical material (frameworks, overview articles, and so on) before the case is taught and then use the case as a vehicle to apply the theory or framework. This method is perhaps simpler to use in schools where case teaching is not the norm, but runs the risk of not diving deep enough into the richness of the cases. A bonus is that the students will learn the required methods, theories, and frameworks in the "correct" way—that is, one that causes them to repeat the theories back using the correct terms—but runs the risk of losing the tacit knowledge aspect that case teaching can confer.

In both situations, the goal is to have the students internalize the theory so that it becomes second nature to apply it appropriately—in the first, by evolving it themselves, in the second, by repeated and varied application. We think both methods have merit and detriments; which one you choose will be a matter of what kind of course you are teaching (it is perhaps a bit of a stretch to ask students to discuss their way to the capital asset pricing model or queuing theory), your own preference, and the quality and stamina of the students. We do, however, think that case courses should contain both, and that however hard to teach, it is always worthwhile to have a significant aspect of induction in the course, since that is what managers have to do once they are out of the classroom and back in their organizations.

If the cases in a course don't sufficiently relate to all of the theory you want to teach, you need to generate your own examples or cases. While this work can be time consuming, it has the benefit of forcing you to be relevant to practice and to help you and the students think critically about the limitations of the theory when applied. If you don't generate such examples, the relationship of the theory to the rest of the course may not be clear to the students. Finding examples is not hard, given your knowledge of your field, and putting them into a theoretical context is not difficult. But examples need to be well documented and with enough scope for alternative interpretations.

We sometimes see cases used very sparingly, almost like capstone activities in regular lecture courses. These are fine as example-giving exercises, but if you really want to hammer in a theoretical concept, whether by induction or deduction, you need to use more than one case. Preferably, some cases should be clear-cut examples of the theory along with some that are not so clear-cut in order to show limitations and stretch the students' inductive and deductive capabilities.

The world is not a clear-cut place, even though theory might want us to see it that way.

Communicating Theory

In nearly all courses, you will want to teach material beyond what is contained in the case study. The temptation is often to return to the comfortable default of lecturing. You can use lectures in case classes, but keep them very short and let them come at natural points in the discussion. But it is rarely if ever necessary to resort to lecturing. The more you lecture, the harder it is to return to a discussion centered on the students.

If you believe that lecturing is the only realistic or best way to deliver the material, one solution is to prerecord the lecture on video and assign it for students to view before the class discussion. This approach, sometimes called the "flipped classroom" (Tucker, 2012), is precisely what an increasing number of teachers, both in high school and colleges, do. They use YouTube and other channels to disseminate short videos on key concepts and have the students work on assignments in the classroom, where the teacher can give them individual help.

If you have to introduce the model or framework in class, try to do it briefly and with little transition time. In general, try to avoid PowerPoint presentations. The transition between using the board and using a computer breaks the rhythm of the class, a situation not helped by the clumsy systems in many classrooms for moving between different kinds of electronic media or using boards and electronic presentations at the same time. Instead, use the computer only where it is absolutely necessary—to show spreadsheets or web pages or other things that cannot be done on just a board. Show frameworks and graphs by drawing them as you explain them. Drawing a framework on the board has the advantage of pacing you so the students can take notes, offers interaction opportunities at any point, and does not force you to follow a particular sequence of points the way a PowerPoint presentation can.

If you need to show a video—quite common in case discussions, often featuring the case protagonists reflecting on the case at the end of a discussion—try to keep the running time short. Use software to edit out all but the part you need or at a minimum to start the video precisely at the point you want to get across. Any transition time spent watching titles or watching the teacher fiddle with the computer setup or any extraneous material on the screen are distractions that impede your ability to get back to discussion after. Have a clean computer (your own rather than whatever's available) and download videos to the local drive instead of relying on the Internet connection. If the classroom has a cumbersome projector screen, consider running the video on the wall or board if applicable; you can sacrifice some picture quality for shorter transition time. You can also shorten transition time by freezing the video at an opportune moment, leaving it on the screen as a discussion starter.

If a video is the main discussion topic (rather than the wrap-up after a discussion or an illustration midway through), we recommend you start the class with it. Students generally begin a class with a reserve of energy. If you have dimmed the lights and lowered the projection screen when they arrive, you can start the class by announcing the video, run it, and bring up the lights and the screen immediately after it ends. This means you have just halved the transition time and can crank up the discussion with little loss of energy.

Role-Playing

Role-playing creates an immersive environment, bringing the case and related analysis to life and fostering empathy for the players involved in the case. It can build insight and increase commitment to the case. It can also be a source of entertainment and greater engagement.

If there is dialogue in the case, pick an instructive subset and assign students to read each part. Use your knowledge of the students' backgrounds and personalities to cast the role-plays. Pause after some exchanges and ask members of the class what they notice. You can also call for different interpretations of how the dialogue may have sounded.

You can assign students roles from the case and then ask them questions or, better yet, have the class ask them questions. The role-playing can be between two students in the class or one student playing a role and the rest of the class taking turns playing other roles. You can also extend beyond two roles, giving several students specific roles and facilitating discussion among them.

Impromptu role-plays can also be extremely effective at engaging students and exploring alternative perspectives on a situation. When students are presenting plans of action, press them on how they would actually do it. Nearly all plans of action will require nontrivial interactions with others in the company. Seek volunteers to play the counterparts and have the student presenting the action plan play out the conversation. These interactions ground the discussion in reality.

Manage the time taken up by role-plays aggressively. You want to maintain a high level of intensity and keep the students on point and grounded in the case, rather than trying to squeeze every last insight out of them.

The Job Interview Role-Play

One of the easiest role-plays to implement is also one that business students receive best. Place students in the role of interviewer and/ or interviewee at the company in the case. If you prefer, you can also frame a consultant role and have the students either interview the consultant or interview as the consultant.

The most obvious way to set up the role-play is to use the role of the protagonist in the case. But it is often more effective to present the role as someone senior to the protagonist who is considering replacing the protagonist. This need not be presented negatively; you could pose hypothetically that the protagonist is leaving for a more attractive position elsewhere.

If you are teaching students who have no work experience, you might find that the subtleties of inquiring about the challenges at a company while interviewing for the job may require too much nuance. But even inexperienced undergraduate students can sink their teeth into the role of an executive or board member asking an applicant how he or she would address a situation. You can then have another student play the applicant or choose to take that role yourself if you want to press a particular student.

A great way to seek volunteers for such a role-play is to poll the group asking, "Which of you would want this job?" You can vary the job or ask them what they would do on the first day on the job.

Multipart Cases

Multipart cases—those with B and C cases—come in many variations and can be useful tools. The B and C cases are normally rather short—one to two pages—and designed to be handed out in the classroom or electronically revealed after the discussion of the A case. Some cases also come in series (or can be used in series), usually tracking a single company or industry over time.

B and C cases are often written with an element of surprise and can be great tools for the inexperienced case teacher because they tend to engage the students and make it easy to structure the discussion. Your main concern will be to keep the discussion from revealing the B case's contents before the B case is handed out, but that should be rather easy. Limit the discussion to "What should the company do?" and then use the B or C case to reveal what it did. Alternatively, limit the discussion to one particular time period of the company's development.

If you are going to incorporate information that is not in the case, whether from a B case or outside sources, introduce it separately. You can do this during the discussion of the case (or A case, if there is a B) or at the end. For instance, we often teach cases that are a few years old. During the discussion, we tend to stick with things as they were when the case was written, but at some point, we might ask how new technologies or other changes would alter the situation.

Time management becomes important when you use multipart cases. Set aside time for students to read the B case during class. Estimate the reading time yourself or simply ask the students to look up when they have finished. Reading time varies, and there are usually one or two very slow readers in a class, so you will almost always have to start the discussion before everyone is finished. We find it very hard to get more than a B and a C case into a session, and the students also tend to lose interest after a while. If you are running out of time, you can leave the C case for students to read after class, in lieu of a conclusion, or you can very briefly recount what it says and start the discussion from there.

Group Work

Group work is often seen as something that is good in itself, to the point where some teachers' evaluations will include group work as something unequivocally positive.

We do not see it that way. We do use group work in case classes, but we think it must be done with an explicit purpose and managed tightly. Do not use it because it is trendy or you want to reduce your workload. While group work can be great for learning, it presents challenges for grading and managing group dynamics. (We address these issues in chapters 4 and 5, respectively.)

We enthusiastically advocate that students form study groups to help each other prepare and discuss the cases before class. Study groups can be assigned or self-formed, depending on whether the students know each other and have other case classes in addition to yours. If they do know each other and have other case classes, let the students form groups by themselves; if not, assign them. Other variables are the students' ages (the younger, the more you will use assigned groups) and their backgrounds (if homogenous, let them self-form; if not, assign them and make sure you have eclectic backgrounds in each group). Bill, incidentally, uses a random number generator to assign groups, scoring nerd points in his technology classes.

Group Presentations

If you have problems with lack of preparation, or students with varying levels of English or new to the format and unsure what to do, you can have the groups prepare the cases and answer or present their solutions in class. We sometimes use this for evaluation purposes. Some teachers assign responsibilities ahead of time: "Tomorrow, groups two and four will present their suggested strategies for case X." Ordinarily, we don't like to do that because it generally leads to less preparation in the groups that are not scheduled to present. It's better to have them all prepare, which leads to a much better discussion. When you open the discussion to the entire class, those groups that have not been picked to present will want to have their perspectives heard and can be much tougher critics than you would be yourself. Collecting the supporting materials for the presentations ahead of class time affords you the opportunity to screen which groups will present according to your preferred criteria (quality, approach, frameworks employed, and so on). One colleague likes to pick two groups that offer conflicting analyses and then let them debate. Incidentally, always start the day with the group presentations. Otherwise, the students will think about their presentations, rather than the case at hand.

When groups are presenting their analysis, we like to set a scene. Rather than having the students present the case analysis as students, we have them role-play as a consulting company competitively presenting a bid for a consulting gig, a middle management group suggesting a project to top management, or a start-up firm presenting to a venture capitalist. Not only does this inject some realism, but it can also sharpen the presentation; very often the students put more effort into framing their presentations and analysis. We insist on details such as including the names of all the participants on the first slide. Students can show remarkable creativity in coming up with names for consulting firms and other details that lighten everyone's mood. This also primes the audience to ask good questions and, depending on the maturity of the presenters, can raise the intensity by encouraging the audience to be skeptical and vocal.

Make sure the presenting group addresses the class, not you. A case presentation and subsequent discussion should be between students, not an examination with you as the Lord High Inquisitor. Think about where you sit in the classroom. We prefer sitting far to one side, which allows us to see the presenter and the whole class. If the students persist in looking at you rather than the class, move to the middle back of the room.

For presentations, set a precise limit on time and presentation material. For example:

> Espen regularly teaches a four-day MBA module with fifty to
> sixty-five students. Each day (except the first) starts with four
> student groups presenting the case they have analyzed the day
> before. Each group can use no more than three PowerPoint
> slides (fewer slides means that the students must prepare
> better, since they cannot use the slide pack as speaker's notes)
> and gets ten minutes to present, followed by five minutes
> for questions from the other students. When a group starts,
> the next group is told to stand ready to minimize transition
> time. The eight to ten groups are randomly picked; at least the
> students think so, but Espen does take student backgrounds
> into account. Because there are more presentations than

groups, all groups must prepare every day since they risk being called at any time.

Group Discussions

Group work is, of course, not limited to formally organized groups preparing together. You can break off the plenary discussion at any point and have the students discuss in ad hoc groups in the classroom. This is a great exercise to use if there are several distinct categories of students—say, some from finance, some from strategy—and you want them to explain things to each other. You also may want to generate detailed discussion among the students on some smaller points along a well-defined scale, such as price setting, capacity planning, or timing of a market introduction.

You can have students work with people seated near them to save time, but if you are assigning a lot of group exercises, working with the same partner(s) can get tiresome over the span of a course. To foster discussion and alter the flow, you can also assign a group identity, such as a position or perspective on an issue, to subsets of the class, such as the left side versus the right, different rows, or wedges of the classroom.

Ideally, groups should be set up so that each group reflects the variety of the whole class. You can do this by carefully assigning groups based on student backgrounds, gender, age, and so on. If you don't have the information or time to do that, shoot for some element of randomness. If the students have chosen their seats themselves, you can count off groups by having each student count out loud from one up to the number of groups you want and remember his or her number. This quick method has a disadvantage: when the students return to the classroom after their group discussions, each group will be scattered. If the students are seated alphabetically or in some other order you have chosen, you can simply divide the students into groups based on where they sit in the classroom. In plenary sessions after the group exercise, the discussion tends to be livelier, since each group sits together and members assist each other.

The Everyone-Asks-Everyone-Else Method

A colleague introduced us to a wonderfully elegant, easy-to-implement exercise that can dramatically increase the energy in the room quickly. Have each student prepare a single question related to the course content about which he or she would like some advice. Then have each student pair off with someone nearby and have both ask the question of the other person. Allow only a brief one- or two-minute answer.

Once each dyad has answered both questions, have those students raise their hands and look around the room for a different student to pair off with. Repeat the question and answer. The entire room will be filled with voices and people walking around the room looking for others. This exercise provides a powerful break from sitting still in the classroom. It is particularly useful if you are teaching an all-day class, but can be used with modifications as you see fit in any course. If you are teaching less experienced or inexperienced students, you should make sure that the topic of the questions is something that fellow students can answer credibly.

We tend to use in-class group work when students need to move around the room more in class sessions longer than seventy-five minutes devoted to one case. And given the high proportion of the grade dedicated to class participation, we tend to keep group time in class under 20 percent.

Team Teaching in the Classroom

Sometimes you have the luxury of fellow teachers in the classroom with you. If managed well, this can be a great experience for the faculty and the students; the varying styles and perspectives of the faculty can greatly enrich the discussion. But you need to resist the temptation to spend most of the time discussing issues between yourselves. And you need to coordinate up front, primarily by assigning roles and responsibilities. Whatever you do, don't deliberately put your

Group Logistics

Try to keep the time devoted to the logistics of group work in class to a minimum. If you are preassigning groups, display the full list on the board. If the students don't know each other yet, preassign meeting locations as well. If they are staying in the room, post a seating chart with locations for each group clearly marked. If you have the students count off, tell them where to meet their groups. If they are leaving the room, know where they are going so that you can visit them during the exercise if appropriate. Bill once lost a group that had decided to convene in another building entirely and then never returned.

For classes we meet regularly, we do not seek out tardy groups when it is time to resume; we start again on schedule without them. But when teaching classes where norms haven't been established, we have found that explaining the importance of returning to the classroom from a group exercise on time may be insufficient, depending on the country and school culture. In those situations, we give reminders about time, including a five-minute warning to the groups, and when time is almost up, we collect them ourselves or ask a student to do so.

---

coteacher in a situation he or she would find uncomfortable, at least not until you have taught a few courses together, at which point some horseplay may be permitted.

If you don't have experience working with fellow teachers, it is easier if someone takes the lead in the classroom and is in charge of orchestrating the discussion. Confer ahead of time on the norms regarding when the other faculty member can chime in, call on students, and so on. If instructors who aren't currently leading the discussion are going to sit down, they should sit out of the way and not in the front of the room so that students do not watch them rather than the discussion. Having two or more faculty moving around in the room at the same time can be distracting, but if done with purpose, it can actually lead to more focus on the discussion; the message is sent that the faculty are not the focal point. Everyone should be paying attention to the person speaking.

We have taught together in person and online for more than twenty years. We develop the syllabus jointly either by passing a draft back and forth or by editing the document in a shared workspace and coordinate individual class sessions by sharing and discussing teaching plans and anything idiosyncratic for that day, such as which students to call on or props to use. Over time, we have learned to read each other in the classroom and work together smoothly.

Are You Getting the Most from Each Student?

We don't want students to be bored in class or anxious from being hopelessly lost. Psychologists refer to the fertile middle ground between these extremes as an optimal level of arousal. Csikszentmihalyi (1997) extended this concept, describing the relationships among skill, challenge level, and emotion. He advocates for achieving flow, the state where you are fully absorbed and at your most productive, which requires applying a sufficiently high level of skill to a challenging task. The difficulty you face is that your class is likely to include a wide range of students with varying levels of prior knowledge, skill, interest in the material, and intellectual capacity. How do you keep the brightest ones engaged without losing the others?

Part of the answer is to move the discussion at a pace calibrated to keep average, well-prepared students at or near their optimum. Obviously, if students are not preparing well, you face more challenges. We address techniques for improving student preparedness in chapter 5. But when students are speaking, you want to keep them at their peak or above it to help them grow and to assess their knowledge and ability.

Save the hardest and most surprising questions for the most advanced students. Use follow-up questions to probe students' knowledge, and don't be afraid to push hard if they have the skills and emotional makeup for it. Bill likes to put at least a couple of students on the hot seat in each class, not by cold-calling but through persistent and sometimes quite aggressive follow-up questions. If you can remember a comment the student made earlier or in a previous class, reference that and have him or her tie the two together.

Following up with an individual student in this way sends several important messages:

- Everyone needs to be prepared, and just chipping in with a good comment now and again isn't sufficient.

- Even the best students in the class are challenged, so those struggling should not feel alone.

- Perhaps most importantly, the instructor is not just going through the motions and cares deeply about every student in the room.

When you have pushed students past their comfort zones, one way to move ahead is to ask if they would like some help from a classmate. This can be preceded by a compliment if one is warranted.

Humor in the Classroom

We both like to think we can be funny. If you enjoy making jokes, by all means do so as long as you are not deemphasizing the learning. The "we're all just talking here" feeling that case discussions can

---

Practical Tip on Students' In-Class Writing

Having students write during class time can be a powerful device for changing the pace of discussion, for encouraging students to focus and think through an issue carefully and work on their communications skills, and for drawing out reticent students. You can stop at any point, pose a question, and have them write down an answer. You can then call on students to read their written answers.

This can also be helpful if you need a short break to collect your thoughts and regroup. We typically allow them five minutes for the exercise, although sometimes much longer for more complex questions, such as redrafting a mission statement, particularly in daylong classes.

---

often acquire lends itself to drifting off-topic. Occasionally telling a particular story because you think it will be entertaining is a perquisite of the job; go ahead, but don't abuse it.

If your humor relates to the topics or cases in the course or program, so much the better. If your jokes are parochial, it's OK to use them, but you need to explain references that are not reasonable to expect people to understand. Apply the same standards to your stories that you would to students' stories to ensure those of other backgrounds don't feel left out.

There are many opportunities for humor when writing students' comments on the board. For instance, if a student makes a suggestion intended to spin a message for an audience, you could simply write "lie" on the board to summarize the comment. If you are going to use this technique, be sure you have the right rapport with the class and that you give the student an opportunity to defend the original comment.

Be extremely careful with any jokes that are at the expense of students. Some students can be deeply hurt by what they interpret as ridicule, even if you meant it good-naturedly. Even in a case discussion class, some students put tremendous weight on what the professor says. Some groups may also get defensive if they feel that one of the students is being attacked, even if that student has sufficiently thick skin and takes no offense at the joke.

Energy

The amount of energy in a class session is not finite. There are many things we can do to increase engagement and energy in the room. But it is unrealistic to think that we can we can operate at maximum engagement for an entire session, particularly a long one. Ebbs and flows are a normal part of even the greatest case discussions.

You should consider the flow of energy you want in a class. We advocate using high-energy openings and closings. The opening sets the tone for the session and helps students be fully present for the discussion. The high-engagement closing increases the chance that you can keep students thinking about the discussion after the end of class.

Your teaching plan is an initial effort at managing the energy level of your discussion. The various topic areas represent shifts in focus that are likely to make students more alert and engaged and potentially engage different students who may have more to say on some topics than others.

But sometimes even the best cases and teaching plans fall flat. This may have nothing to do with you, the material, or even the students' preparation, although poor preparation can often lead to low energy in the classroom. If your students are together in other settings than your course, what has happened there, the workload in the program (an exam or paper may have been due that day, for instance), or a social event the night before can have a dramatic impact on the energy level in the room.

Groups that don't know each other well are not immune to low energy. Issues on campus, the weather, traffic, or news can all have an effect on the entire class. Arrive at class a few minutes early and speak informally with a few students to quickly take the pulse of the group.

Raising the Energy Level

Once or twice during a semester, Bill jokingly acknowledges how little energy is in the room. Sometimes mere acknowledgment is enough to elicit a knowing laugh and renewed vigor among the students. But they may take something said too often as criticism and become alienated.

If you don't have a B case, create an energizing change of pace by sharing data from after the time of the case or just pose a hypothetical solution to change the focus.

Physical activity is a great way to punctuate a class and increase the energy. Having students stand up or temporarily change their location in the room will increase their energy level. If you are planning to ask a polling question, you can have students vote by walking to a location in the room to represent the answer they choose, have them confer briefly with students who chose the same answer, and finally return to their seats. You can also use group work to change the dynamics and boost energy.

If you lack the mobility or energy to run around the classroom, consider adopting facial expressions or hand gestures to serve the same purpose. And use the full range of your voice for dramatic effect. You could sit at the front of the room. But sitting with the group can actually raise the energy in the room because it shows you engaging in a different way, and many students will focus more intensely. If possible, do this when you want to shift to a particular topic that may require more careful thought or generate more emotion.

Using Props

The use of props is a divisive issue among case teachers. Many faculty fear students will see them as clowns or perhaps simply as someone not sufficiently serious about learning. We believe that judicious use of props can have a tremendously positive effect. We don't use them in the vast majority of our class sessions, but once or twice in a course, we might employ a visual aid.

Props might be samples of the company's product or a technology described in the case. The samples can illustrate the case, but you can also use them to reward students for hard work. For example, if you have had a string of very complex cases in "hard" industries, have a case on a cookies or ice cream company and bring some samples to class.

Less frequently, we do something more dramatic. During a class session on managing web site development tensions between graphic artists and programmers, Bill ducked out during a break, changed from his suit to an all-black outfit, temporarily colored his hair bright red, inserted a magnetic nose ring and piercings, and taught the rest of the case from the perspective of a graphic designer. On a similar note, Espen once came to a case on Cisco, an Internet technology company, in a black Cisco T-shirt, cargo shorts, and sandals. These grand gestures are fun, and they also serve as valuable reminders to us to not take ourselves too seriously.

Relationships among and with Students

Case discussion classes tend to increase bonding among students. In lecture classes, it is not uncommon for students to complete a semester and not know the names of their classmates. In a case class, the community that develops within the classroom typically extends outside of it as well. There are often myriad opportunities for faculty to be involved in the group's social life. You don't need to have social contact with students outside of class (though expectations may differ around the world), but we do encourage you to keep abreast of the class's social life through informal conversations before and after class. Knowing when there are classwide events and which group of students might be partying hard during the week will help you understand the dynamics within the class.

If you do choose to engage with the class socially, make sure it is never exclusionary. This is not the time to build relationships with those you like and avoid those that you may not. As an undergraduate at Williams College, Bill had several class meetings in the homes of professors, greatly enhancing the learning experience. We have had many lively discussions with students at organized or informal pub nights and other gatherings. We also attend parties organized through the school; we avoid the informal student parties, even when enthusiastically invited, to maintain some professional distance. If students don't invite you to organized social events and you would be interested in attending them, be sure to indicate casually that you are open to such invitations. In many cases, students are only excluding you because they don't realize you are interested or willing to attend.

Participating in social events is a balancing act and requires some thinking, especially in company settings. If you are leading discussions at a company, for instance, there is normally a dinner afterward. Think carefully about whether you should participate. Do you know the company well (which means knowing more than one person)? Has the discussion highlighted some unresolved issues within the company? Were people energized by it? Be careful; you can quickly become a fifth wheel in this setting (especially if you are the only outsider) and ask yourself whether your participation will increase or decrease the quality of the company's experience of you.

You don't want to find yourself answering questions about what the "right" solutions to a company's challenges are. It's better perhaps to leave them wanting more of you at a later point in time.

Online social networks give new dimensions to communicating with students. How you want to use them is up to you. We have used Twitter for course communication, are happy to connect to students via LinkedIn, but reserve Facebook for more social communications and don't connect to students there, at least not until they no longer are our students. However, at least one well-known case teacher has a policy of not connecting to students on networks until after the course is finished. You have to decide what works for you.

You also need to think about how much to share of yourself. Case discussion classes can become intensely personal for participants. We encourage students to speak openly about difficult experiences and engage in discussions that relate to deeply held beliefs. As instructors, in each class we have opportunities to share ourselves. Sharing some personal details helps humanize you and deepens your bond with the group. But oversharing can erode your authority and even reduce the legitimacy of the material. There is a wide spectrum of viable choices, and you need to assess both your comfort and your ability to manage self-disclosure.

Concluding a Discussion

The end of a case discussion should be at least thought about, if not prepared in detail. Include a conclusion in your teaching plan but be prepared to abandon it if the discussion moves in a different direction or if the points you want to end on have been addressed during the discussion. The goal of the conclusion of a case class is not only to summarize and focus on the key learnings, but also to finish with a flourish—to have the students continue the discussion among themselves after class and to provide a transition to the next class.

The instructor usually summarizes the discussion a few minutes before the end of class, perhaps by relating it to a theoretical framework. While this is important, we would encourage you to *not finish with a conclusion, but with a question,* to aim not at wrapping things up, but at leaving the students discussing after the class is over. In case teaching, the discussion, not the answer, is important.

It is also important *not to conclude a case based on hindsight*—to see what happened to the company or the case protagonists after the case ends. There is nothing wrong in telling students (it is good practice to look up what happened in the company anyway) but be clear that what the company actually did is only one alternative of many. The fact that the company chose a path does not mean it is the right one. We often answer the question, "What happened afterwards?" with "I don't know—and I don't care." This can be rather unsatisfactory for students seeking some kind of closure, but it sends a strong message about the goals of the class.

Be clear and consistent that there is no unique, correct answer to a case. If you do not, the students will forever hunt for the "right" solution. But as one of our professors liked to say, "There is rarely only one correct answer, but there are wrong ones." Analysis and discussions count, conclusion is an afterthought, and most cases are written so that many proposed solutions can be right anyway.

You can transition to the next class with a few remarks. Refer back to the syllabus, position the case and the discussion in relation to that, and have the students understand your reasoning for choosing the particular case as well as the next one. You do not need to do this in every class but should certainly do it when you are going from one topic to another, say, every third case or so. You should also encourage students to make links between cases they have discussed.

As with everything in case teaching, you can choose to do neither of these things. If the case discussions have been highly spirited and contagious, you might choose to end the class almost midstream, to preserve the energy. Assuming the next class will be soon, you can start with a few remarks about the previous discussion. In any case, don't make conclusions and transitions long-winded affairs. As with the teaching goals of the class, it is much more important that the students understand one point well than many things cursorily.

You may also choose to have students provide the takeaways for the discussion. You might warm-call a student or two at the beginning of the discussion and let them know that you will call on them to tell the class what they've learned from the discussion. You can also have the entire class provide takeaways.

This chapter has been about the conduct of a single class—how you prepare for it, how you behave in the classroom, how you guide the discussion. But as a teacher, you do not just have to teach. You are also responsible for evaluating the students' performance and giving them feedback. The next chapter explores that dimension of case teaching.

References

Caro, M. *Caro's Book of Poker Tells*. New York: Cardoza Publishing, 2004.

Csikszentmihalyi, M. *Finding Flow*. New York: Basic Books, 1997.

Porter, M. E. "How Competitive Forces Shape Strategy." *Harvard Business Review*, March–April 1979, 86–93.

Tucker, B. "The Flipped Classroom: Online Instruction at Home Frees Class Time for Learning." *Education Next* 12, no. 1 (2012). www.educationnext .org/the-flipped-classroom/.

4

FEEDBACK

Assignments, Grading, and Guidance

Feedback is a valuable tool that gives an opportunity for students to improve and teachers to share expectations about what constitutes good work in a course. Evaluation has three main purposes:

- To *measure* to what degree students have achieved the learning objectives of the course.

- To serve as a mechanism for *feedback* to the students.

- To *motivate* students' efforts.

Measuring learning from case classes is different from lecture-based classes. Since a case class is about applying knowledge to problems, the evaluation should reflect that. Exams and assignments should be about solving problems similar to those students might meet in their future workplaces. Given that cases seldom have a single correct solution, simple fact-checking exercises, such as ordinary multiple-choice exams, are out of the question. Students should not be judged solely by whether they hit a specific answer, but by the way they have used judgment based on the theory and concepts of the course to arrive at their conclusions.

In many case courses, the only feedback students get is their course grades, a very narrow flow of information. When we were students, we found it hard to predict the grade of our own exams, and sometimes received grades we did not understand, better or worse than expected. The result is either that the students just accept their grades—with no understanding of how they can be better—or that they flood instructors with requests for grade justification, sometimes backed by institutional or governmental rules about how and when this should be done. We strongly recommend that you give the students good feedback—even in large classes—and will outline a few strategies for doing so in this chapter. Not only is this beneficial from the students' point of view, but constant and good feedback will shine on your teaching record.

Grades as motivation for effort are seen as gauche in some pedagogical circles. Students are supposed to seek knowledge because they want it, not because they want a grade or a degree. We are a bit cynical in this matter (especially Bill) and consciously use grading, particularly participation grading, as a motivator to have students come to class prepared. Unless all students come prepared, all of them suffer. You can appeal to the students' consciences and underscore the importance of your course for their future careers, but unless you back it with something concrete, the demands of work, life, and the Internet may crowd out your course, unless it is a highly sought-after elective.

The Evaluative Mind-Set

Grading is hard work; for us, it is our second-least favorite activity, after administrative meetings. By the time we have read a few dozen exams, we are sometimes tempted to live out the apocryphal stories of professors grading papers by throwing them down a flight of stairs labeled with grades or assigning grades by weighing papers.

It has become somewhat fashionable to refer to students as customers, which sounds obvious until accompanied by the notion that the customer is always right, even when it comes to evaluation. We do not see students as customers. Bill prefers the term used by a onetime dean of the MBA program at Harvard Business School, who liked to call students *partners*—someone you work with to achieve a common goal, the difference being that in the end, you can fire a partner. Espen, in his more cynical moments, will curtly inform students that to him they are not customers, but product, and that his responsibility is to society in general and their future employers in particular.

All of these viewpoints are to some extent correct, of course. Students are customers; they hire the university to change them, as advertised. They are partners in the case classroom in that they have a co-responsibility in the production of learning. And they are product when done, facing a market for their services. The evaluation and feedback during and after a course need to measure all of these relationships: the degree to which the student changed, the degree to which each helped others, and the level of the finished graduate in relation to others, not just at your own school, but in general.

For this to work, the teacher must thoughtfully design and judiciously apply the tools of student evaluation. There must be a direct link between what the students do during and after the course and the grades they end up with. The grades need to differentiate among students, which puts the teacher at risk because he or she has to use judgment. Grading should be fair, consistent, and well anchored, and if it is, it is also defensible when the students complain, as some will, not realizing that they are paying for an education, not a degree.

Designing Evaluation

Case class evaluation tends to boil down to two questions:

- How much of the total grade should be based on participation in class and in other forums, such as online discussion groups?

- How much of the grade should be based on individual effort and knowledge and how much should be group-based?

We strongly advocate that at least some of the grade—up to 50 percent—should be based on participation. The percentage does not need to be very high—for undergraduate classes with eager students, you can sometimes get away with just 10 percent—but it should be there as a motivator, if nothing else. We generally use 30 percent to 50 percent.

Smaller classes, more-senior students, and elective courses all pull in the direction of a higher percentage for participation. With a small class, you get to know the students well and hear their contributions often, so you can more easily set participation grades accurately. More-senior students (including executives) have a broader knowledge base and more outside school experience, and thus a solid background for forming opinions based on more than the basic textbooks. And in elective classes, students are there because they want to be and are interested in the topic. Consequently, they are more willing to do the preparation necessary to talk intelligently in class.

If you don't have the option to grade participation, you need to create an incentive for students to show up and participate. Tell them that while the literature (that is, the cases) can be read outside class, the understanding of how to analyze a case and communicate the result requires classroom presence. Reading about case analysis without practicing it with others is like serving a dinner you have never made before—it might work out, but the odds are significantly improved if you practice first. Then set up the final exam to be an individual case analysis done the way practiced in class. Once you have the students in class, you will need to rely on your personality, the material itself, and some of the techniques of chapter 3 to get them to speak.

Individual versus group grading is a question of your workload (the more group evaluations, the less reading for you), the desired quality of the finished work, and the extent to which you need to differentiate the performance of individual students. In general, the more time and work associated with something, the more it will benefit from group work. Term papers, for instance, are almost always better if done in groups of two or three, where the students can shave away each other's idiosyncrasies and stop each other from heading down interesting but ultimately very blind alleys. On the other hand, you need some individual evaluation to take care of those students who do not speak very much in class and to handle the ever-present free-rider problem.

Another option, used by some schools that offer only module-based courses, is to evaluate precourse work, that is, the students do assignments for grading before showing up for the course. This is great for preparation, but does require institutional support to work.

Designing Assignments

Table 4-1 outlines the wealth of options for assignments. Depending on your goals and resources available, you may choose to require some or none of these. Keep in mind that not all assignments need to be graded. Next we discuss each of these options and how to grade them.

Individual Oral Assignments

An individual oral assignment during class is a special type of a warm call: you notify students ahead of time that you will ask them to address a question or topic during class time. But the assignments typically have a higher degree of formality when the students deliver them. You can grade the assignments separately from class participation, or, for classes where participation is a particular struggle (more on this in chapter 5), you can include the assignments in the participation grade.

TABLE 4-1

Options for assignments

	Before class	During class	After class
Individual oral	Preparation for class, warm call	Discussion in class, warm or cold calls	Reflection, oral exam
Individual written	Pretest, short assignments	Short writing assignments, online collection (Google Docs)	Exam, individual term paper
Group oral	Prepared presentations	In-class group work with presentation	Case analysis with group presentation
Group written	Prepared group pretest	Group work	Group term paper, take-home exam

These assignments can be especially useful in extending content coverage beyond the cases themselves. We sometimes use this technique when teaching courses about technology. We assign students specific technologies to explain to the class, perhaps a technology referred to in the case or competing technologies. In many instances, there are several technologies per case, and over the course of the semester, we can find an individual assignment for each student. The same structure works well in other disciplines, where students can make presentations on processes, techniques, laws, frameworks, and so on. Technology has created wonderful opportunities for students to complete oral assignments before or after class. We will discuss the use of these technologies in chapter 10.

Individual Written Assignments

You can assign a variety of written work. Assignments can range from a problem set to an essay answer to a question or the creation of an artifact for the case, such as a model, mission statement, or marketing plan. You could collect them to grade formally or have students exchange papers and evaluate one another's work, or both. The individual writing assignments can also be done in shared electronic forums (see chapter 10 for a discussion of such tools).

Many instructors have students turn in written answers to the case preparation questions. This serves as an incentive for student preparation and helps students develop writing skills, assuming they are getting feedback about their writing. This has the potential to generate an unmanageable amount of grading for you, even if the answers are relatively brief. You have several options to reduce the burden of grading:

- Have students write about only two or three cases over the course of the semester. This means you only need grading rubrics for those cases and you achieve some economies of scale in the grading. The downside is that if you are using this as a mechanism to improve the level of preparation, it is not likely to have much of an impact on the cases you have not assigned for write-up.

- Have a few students write about each case. This gives you a base of students who are much more likely to be well prepared, which can improve the discussion.

- Require a write-up from all students for each case, but don't grade all of them. You can mark down students who do not submit them, but choose to grade them randomly or only grade papers on days when you feel the class was not well prepared.

- Ask the students to email a short presentation (a maximum of three slides) before class. You can scan through quickly and use the slides to start discussion in class.

- Choose questions that require relatively deep case analysis, but are simple to grade ("How many widgets will company X sell next year, and why?" "What salary would you offer the new head of sales, and why?").

We recommend case write-ups only as a last resort, if other means of motivating preparation are unsuccessful. If you would like students to do written work, there are other types of assignments that do not duplicate topics for class discussion. This reinforces the message that the class discussion is central to their learning.

Group Oral Assignments

You can have students do a presentation as part of the evaluation, whether or not you choose to have it as part of the participation grade or as a separate evaluation on its own. This can, for instance, be a very effective way to grade MBA students toward the end of a course—divide them into groups, give them a case to analyze, and let the groups present their solutions. We tend to use groups for presentations; individual presentations eat up classroom time, and the individual pressure of what would in essence be a public oral examination would be too much. For all group evaluations, there is a danger of free-riders. See the discussion of group presentations in chapter 3 for ways to deal with it.

During both group and individual presentations, you can choose to give feedback or not, and you can give feedback on both the content and the presentation itself. Students do not get enough feedback on their presentation style and performance, and most think it very useful, as long as it is presented in an acceptable format. You have to be rather sensitive when giving criticism, using phrases like "I see this quite often ..." or "You are doing something that many people do ...," and also limiting yourself to one piece of feedback per person or group. Most people can only take one piece of advice after having done a presentation, so stick with the most important and keep it very constructive. Another approach is to give one piece of feedback on what a student does well and one on what he or she needs to improve. Alternatively, you can develop a checklist of critical presentation skills, note brief feedback during class, and provide it to the students with more detail on the presenter's single greatest strength and weakness.

Group Written Assignments

The design of group writing assignments is similar to that for individuals, but you should expect more. Group assignments do not have to be longer than individual ones; the difference could be in the quality of the work or the depth of analysis or research. If forming study groups is not common at your institution, assigning a group writing exercise early in a course can be a way to make the students form them. In-class writing could include brainstorming exercises prior to generating documents such as branding messages, strategic positions, or human resource policies.

Designing Exams

If you have based your course on cases, the fairest and most accurate way to test students is with a case-based exam. You'll need to decide on a case or cases on which to base your questions, craft the questions, and grade the results.

Selecting Cases for Exams

If you have sufficiently long blocks of time for exams, you can distribute the case to students at the time of the exam and have them read it and then answer the questions during the exam period. How long you need to allow for students to read the case depends on the length and complexity of the case and the students' facility with the language in which the case was written.

For typical Harvard Business School cases, you need to allow three to four hours. If you don't have that long, you might be able to find a published case, news article, or blog posting brief enough (one to two pages) for students to read during a shorter exam period. Or you could write a case yourself. Some instructors prefer that the case present an issue that was not covered in the course, testing students' ability to learn new material as well as perform analysis. We tend to avoid this if we are teaching the only case course for some of the students.

If you cannot find or develop a case to be read during the exam, then you need to test students on a case they have already read. You can assign a case specifically for this purpose, or you can revisit one or more cases you have already covered during the course.

If you choose a case just for the exam, you can release it to students shortly before the exam. Depending on their schedule, you could do one or two hours before your exam or a day or two before. Bill likes to choose long, complicated cases for the last class of the semester and cover only a few aspects during class time; he then asks exam questions about unaddressed aspects. These cases are usually sufficiently comprehensive that he can craft questions about most if not all of the major topics of the course.

Writing Exam Questions

On exams, we are careful not to limit ourselves to the obvious questions about the case, particularly if students have access to it before the exam. This reduces the risk of collusion and other forms of academic dishonesty.

Here are some useful types of topics you can ask students to address:

- *Analysis of what happened.* Asking students what happened, as the first question worth relatively few points, helps ground them in the facts and prepare them for more challenging subsequent questions.

- *Analysis of the current situation.* Similar to the purely retrospective question, this analysis can help students develop their thinking about the case in order to make recommendations. This question stops short of asking for an action plan, but offers students the opportunity to show their insights about the issues and options.

- *A right answer.* These are certainly the easiest to grade and more common in quantitative courses. ("What is the maximum throughput?")

- *A numerical answer.* There need not be a single correct answer, but you might ask for an estimate of how much a company is worth or what unit sales will be next year—and also ask the students to support their estimates with arguments.

- *Apply a specific framework.* We tend to use this type of question more in undergraduate courses, preferring that graduate students choose frameworks themselves to answer broader questions.

- *Action planning.* Have students outline the steps that the case protagonist (or a consultant to the company, or someone else) would need to take to address the issue(s) in the case. Depending on the maturity of the students and their experience with cases, you can adjust how explicit your guidance is on what to consider.

- *Predictions and estimation.* Such questions force students to move beyond the case facts and use their analysis skills.

- *Production of artifacts.* You can have students create financial statements, marketing plans, strategic plans, mission statements, HR policies, technology architecture diagrams, or any other product appropriate to the domain you are teaching. These are particularly useful to test domain-specific professional knowledge.

Asking broad, open questions affords students an opportunity to show what they have learned and for you to evaluate their ability to abstract issues and apply theory. For undergraduate students, particularly in their first case course, we tend to offer more guidance.

We might suggest frameworks that could be of use or even explicitly ask them to apply a framework. Whenever possible, give the students a role, whether as one of the people in the case—a consultant, auditor, government official, or competitor. This helps them focus and often improves the quality of the answers.

Many students avoid creating spreadsheets and doing numerical analysis when analyzing cases. If you expect them to do numbers, it is a good idea to specifically ask for this in the exam question, either by saying that you expect them to evaluate options both quantitatively or qualitatively, or by asking questions about specific numerical exhibits ("What is the significance of exhibit X?" "How would the numbers change if the company chooses strategy B rather than the current strategy?").

We typically ask two or three questions on an exam because this helps students allocate their time better and reduces test anxiety, compared to a single all-or-nothing question. We also like to offer students some choice of questions (pick two of three or three of four questions, for instance), although we may require all students to answer one of the questions. The points or percentages allocated to each question give students an indication of each question's complexity and importance. You can also describe a question as difficult, intended to give the best students a challenge; this can bring some spirited writing for you to enjoy. We like to give challenging exams to ensure a sufficiently wide distribution of grades, but we do not want the exam to be demoralizing; students who have worked hard in the course want and deserve to feel they have learned something after taking the exam. If students will be told the number of points they scored in addition to the resulting grade, when appropriate we emphasize that relatively low numerical scores still might represent respectable or good grades.

Take-Home Exams

You can avoid many of the challenges of timing by allowing students to take your exams home. If you trust the students, you can also limit the time they can spend on the exam by simply telling them they can only spend a certain number of hours on it. We like to set word limits for the exams to manage grading and help students focus. With undergraduates, we may set word limits for each question, while with graduate classes, we will typically set the limit for the entire exam.

Cheating can be a major problem with take-home exams, particularly if the students submit them individually. We recommend using an electronic submissions system with automatic plagiarism detection to counter this and making the students aware you will be using it. See more about this under handling academic dishonesty later.

Designing Term Papers

Many of the considerations that go into designing term papers are the same for exams. The differences are largely that you will have fewer and more open questions and a support process starting fairly early in the course to help students gradually develop their ideas and learn how to write the paper.

A term paper should not just be a take-home exam involving more time and pages. There are differences in the types of term papers in Europe and the United States. In Europe, a MSc education in business is more research based, and students' term papers and master's theses are supposed to be more academically oriented than those typical of the more vocational, hands-on business educations in the United States. A case course lends itself to term papers with a practical bent, with students applying theory and frameworks they have learned in class to real-world problems. Moreover, you can use the term-paper writing process as part of your own research or to develop teaching material for future years (see the following section "Term Papers as Research Method"). We highly recommend term papers be written in groups of up to three students.

With this in mind, we suggest that questions for term papers be open-ended to let the students formulate the details themselves. You can give them a data set to analyze, a trend to explore, or a set of examples from newspapers or books to analyze. The question or questions asked should let the students demonstrate that they know the course content and how to think like a person in the role for which the course is supposed to educate them.

We also recommend that the students receive support during the term paper process. For this to be effective and equitable, you need to structure it. Espen uses an electronic shared document in which the students can present their term paper ideas to each other and recruit groups. He likes to end his courses with a session or two, depending on the size of the class, in which student groups present their term paper ideas and the class and instructor give feedback. These presentations should not be part of the participation grade. Because they are exploring ideas, the students should not feel that they are under pressure to perform to a standard. This process reveals many good ideas from the students, and everyone generally sees it as helpful and a positive experience.

We like to use an open approach to term papers—let students choose the subject of their own term papers—and focus on relevance, as long as the topics are within the course topic. Students like to explore things that are relevant, such as new technology and real companies. Therefore, we try to get them to write theses that are interesting to them and to us.

A former colleague encouraged his students to write their theses or term papers in areas where the collected data would be interesting for its own sake. When students set out to write a term paper or thesis, it is expected to be solidly based on research, but the result will often not be particularly spectacular; at most, students will confirm something someone else has done. A term paper is not just a means of evaluation; it is first and foremost a learning opportunity, so encourage your students to choose topics they want to learn something about (and if you want to learn this as well, so much the better). It doesn't hurt that the term paper is also useful to the student—that it can contribute toward a thesis project, if the program has such a requirement, or that it can help the student get a good job afterward. By writing the thesis or term paper, the students can demonstrate their knowledge of a particularly hot area. Solid research gets them a good grade, but relevant domain knowledge can secure them a plum job.

A strong connection to practical business motivates students, helps them establish a network, and increases their job prospects. In the long run, giving students this opportunity also establishes the professor as a dependable source of qualified labor to employers and someone whom it may be useful to assist with research money, prestigious speaking opportunities, and lucrative consulting gigs.

Term Papers as Research Method

If you are doing research in an area pertinent to the course, consider using the students as research assistants, for instance, by writing term papers that may end up as teaching or research cases. But be prepared for significant work on your part to convert what the students submit into something useful. You must, of course, explicitly recognize their contribution in your own work.

Whenever we have term papers as a component of the evaluation, especially group term papers, we like to offer students the opportunity to write a case on a company, whether the students choose the company themselves or pick from a list of companies we suggest because we think the companies pertinent and might use the student paper or a case based on it in the course. When doing this, we explicitly warn the students that this is likely to be fun; most students are quite enthusiastic about a particular company, frequently the one they work for, and think writing a case more interesting than yet another theory-based essay. However, we also tell them that it is significantly more work than they anticipate. We give the students information about case-writing style, content, and structure (see online resource 10 for a sample) as well as how to approach companies.* If you have international students, you can use this opportunity to develop a more diverse set of cases for your courses. If the course has a big theory component, we ask the students to complement the case with a reflection note in which the link to the theories and concepts of the course is explained—why they chose this case, how it fits with the content of the course, and what they learned during the case production process—in short, anything relevant that doesn't explicitly fit into the case story itself. This reflection note should also contain contact information for

---

* To see this and other online resources for the book,
visit the web site: teachingwithcases.hbsp.harvard.edu.

the company they have talked to, as well as a list of interview subjects and other information you might need to develop the case further.

Do not expect the cases to match the standards of commercially available teaching cases, unless you happen to have a class full of business journalists. A full-fledged case requires very careful writing and access to company executives beyond what students can achieve. But you can expect to get much of the digging from company reports and newspapers, and if some of the students work for or do business with the case companies, the results can get very interesting, with proprietary data and colorful stories.

Using teaching as a research method is, of course, not limited to evaluation. Your classroom can attract executives from interesting companies, and you can employ their input in your research. And there is always the time-honored tradition of having students be research subjects for experiments, simulations, or simple polling on matters economical, ethical, or political—always good fodder for a discussion.

Grading

Once you have designed the evaluation, you need to set up a system to do the grading as easily and fairly as possible. This involves deciding on a grade scale (for your own use; the official scale for reporting grades is normally predetermined), a grading process, and a way to communicate the grades and other feedback to the students. Of special interest to case teachers is the grading of participation, which can be a source of conflict unless it is done right.

A Matter of Scaling

Grade scales, in the United States and in most of Europe after the Bologna Agreement (an EU-wide standardization of grades and program structures), consist of letter grades: *A–D* with *F* for fail in the United States, and *A–E* with *F* for fail in Europe. Generally, grades should follow a normal distribution (or something close to it). They seldom do; the distribution tends to be skewed toward the higher grades, at least in business schools. The relative coarseness of the scale—in Europe, plusses and minuses don't make it onto official transcripts—is one reason that students have a great incentive to complain about their grades, with little downside risk.

Case classes can be complicated to grade. A significant factor is participation, which many students are uncomfortable about, especially outside the United States. A second reason is that you are not just evaluating the students' ability to understand a certain topic, but also their ability to analyze complicated issues and communicate findings; in short, you make yourself a judge of their analytical, management, and leadership abilities.

Some schools use a forced curve in their MBA programs, and in our opinion, more should. At Harvard Business School, the grade scale is very simple: there are three grades, *I*, *II*, and *III*, with *I* considered the best. (There is also a category *IV*, rarely used, for particularly egregious cases.) A fixed portion of the class, normally 15 percent to 20 percent, gets a *I*, about 10 percent get a *III*, and the rest a *II*. A typical course has 50 percent of the grade based on participation in class, the rest from a written exam (three to four hours in which the student analyzes a case).

This grading has the advantage of simplicity, particularly when grading participation, and the fixed distribution protects against grade inflation. The individual grading, however, is just as difficult. It may be easy to find the best and worst students in the class, but the borderline cases can take a lot of agonizing. You end up hoping for a break in the distribution to avoid someone getting a bad grade, even though only slightly different from another student. This grading system also requires fairly large classes and an assumption (borne out in admission statistics) that, from year to year, classes do not significantly differ in talent and effort.

Forced-Curve Grading

Bill believes the forced curve is the best grading system, but in his courses he implements the standard grading scale for the school at which he is teaching. Espen implements a forced curve in his courses as long as doing so is within the letter of the law of the school and country, even if his is the only such course in the university.

Our recommended format is to use a point scale (say, one to ten) for each graded component of the course, sum up the points, sort the students from top to bottom, and set the letter grades how you think fit. We tend to grade "on a curve," in the sense that we have a fairly fixed (and preannounced) distribution of the various grades, but not set points. The distribution is not absolute, however: when deciding cutoff points, we try to locate them where there are gaps in the point list, so that a student is not moved from B to C because of a difference in the second decimal. This gives us a solid and defensible basis, should any students complain about their grades. It also takes care of the problem of regression to the mean, which is why you cannot use the same scale and distribution on the component grades as on the final grade.

The chief problem with this approach, as perceived by students, lies in the need for each class to be somewhat similar to the previous year's, but that tends to hold true for large numbers. Changes in the admission criteria or changes in course participants—say, if it is so popular that you have to limit admission based on grades—are grounds for reevaluation, but only of the grade distribution at the course grade stage.

A second issue is that apportioning between evaluation components (say, 25 percent, participation; 25 percent, assignments; 50 percent, term paper) becomes somewhat imprecise since component grades with high variability will mean more for the final result than those on which everyone scores more or less the same. In other words, if all the students score a B on one assignment, that assignment really doesn't count in the summary. If all the students score particularly well or badly, you can shift the whole class a bit up or down, but you need to first take a look at the assignment and consider whether you have given the students something that is too hard or too easy.

How to Structure Feedback

Students deserve proper feedback that makes them understand your thinking about the grade and that has enough detail for them to learn from it. Feedback also keeps you honest about your evaluation standards. If students receive a single grade as the only feedback on their performance, many of them will ask for an explanation. Many instructors experience these requests as complaints, but that is not necessarily the case. To give educational value to a grade (and avoid student requests), you should provide personal, detailed feedback to all students.

That's noble, but how to do it without working yourself to death? The solution lies in being systematic and using technology, as well as carefully designing the feedback you are going to give before the course starts.

We use spreadsheets to keep track of students' performance throughout the course and to give feedback after the course ends. For each class, we give points to students based on their activity in the classroom (between one and ten, for instance). When we read exams or term papers, we set partial points either for each exam question or for content elements of the term paper (for example, theory use, problem description, data collection, analysis, language). Note that we use points, not letter grades. We do this to avoid the possibility that students will come back at the end of the course having carefully calculated their various grades and complaining that the final grade does not reflect the calculated one.

For each exam or term paper, we also write a short message, just a sentence or a few key words. We send this message, together with the final grade and point scores, to each student, together with a note in which we discuss elements of the exam that were common to the whole course ("In this course, we awarded x A's, y B's ...") and give some pointers about persuasive answers ("For question 1, a good exam answer will contain ...").

You should also automate the feedback as much as possible by producing emailed reports from your grade spreadsheets for each student. Figure 4-1 is an example of part of an email sent to a student in a graduate class on business innovation management. The grade is made up of individual participation and a term paper where the students create a new case.

Note that this quantitative way of giving feedback allows you to efficiently generate a lot of information, such as ranking in class (along with students' self-evaluations, which we describe later). In addition to this email, students receive one email for each group paper, as well as oral comments on their presentation style and content in a group presentation for the final class.

FIGURE 4-1

Sample automated feedback

Individual feedback GRA6834, Fall 2013

Student ID:	▮▮▮
Student name:	▮▮▮▮▮
Email:	▮▮▮▮▮▮▮
Grade:	A
Rank in class:	5 (of 49, 4 of which dropped out)
Total points:	8,883 (0-10)
Overall comment:	Congratulations - excellent work!

Breakdown term paper and participation:

Points term paper:	9,667
Case company:	▮▮▮▮
Content points:	10
Content comment:	Excellent choice of company and topic.
Writing points:	9
Writing comment:	Very good writing, the occasional error or lapse. The challenges section, particularly about the business culture paragraph, needs to be referenced or attributed. Some language perhaps needs to be toned down a bit, or set in quotes. But overall, an excellent effort.
Research points:	10
Research comment:	Solid research with interviews and quotes by the founders themselves. Well developed case and thought piece. The B case is a bit depressing - does perhaps need a little bit more fleshing out of why things went wrong, details about what the Green Phase Energy Award is, and so on, but that should be simple to fix. Confidentiality needs to be sorted out, but this is definitely a case I can use.
Pts participation:	8,10

The key lies in thinking through the feedback process in advance and making it appear as personal as possible while being very efficient. You normally save the most time by carefully writing the general feedback (the one that goes to all students and therefore only needs to be written once). Time spent on the feedback letter that applies to everyone with a thin coating of personalization is paid back, with interest, in sharply reduced numbers of requests for explanation and fewer complaints.

An added advantage of feedback like this is that the students catch errors in grading. Sometimes you write the wrong grade for a student, sometimes you mistake one person for another, or sometimes you misunderstand something the student has written. As with most things in life, a more open process is also a more just one.

Group Work

Grading group submissions has two clear advantages: the average quality is better and there are fewer submissions. You can use the same rubrics you would for individual assignments, calibrated appropriately, but differentiating the performance of individuals within the group is more difficult.

At a minimum, to keep the grades credible, you need to address any free-riders, as students often seek to minimize work. If you are not able to do this sufficiently through norms and group self-monitoring, then you should incorporate a mechanism to identify students who are not doing their fair share. For presentations, this can be mitigated if the instructor picks not only the groups to present their case analysis, but also the one or two students in each group to do the presentation. The division of work may still be uneven, but at least the students must all be familiar with the analysis before the presentation. Alternatively, you can deal with the free-rider problem by occasionally cold-calling the students in a group who are not presenting to answer questions about the case.

We also have students evaluate other group members. We have found that many students are hesitant to be frank about their peers in open evaluations. You may choose to make developing mature peer-evaluations skills part of the learning in your course; this will take time but can be a valuable exercise for the students. If you do not want to invest resources, you can mitigate their hesitance by allowing anonymous evaluations. Unfortunately, that is not always sufficient. If so, you can also force differentiation by having students rank-order their peers. Online resource 11 shows some sample evaluation forms. You can use this data for a portion of students' grades; we typically make it 10 percent to 30 percent.

Final Exams

Some schools forbid providing any comments on final exams to protect the integrity of exam questions that may be reused or to ease the burden on faculty. Given timing constraints on assigning final grades, Bill doesn't give final feedback in most courses. He has found that the vast majority of students, after performing self-evaluations and receiving feedback at midsemester, understand and accept their final grades. Fewer than one in fifty students seek more detailed feedback after the course is over. But even if they do not seek such feedback, nearly all students will read it if you provide it. If it is feasible, you should make every effort to provide the feedback and encourage students to use it.

Class Participation

Grading participation must be done with care and can require thick skin. Many students view class participation grades as unfairly subjective, favoring students with good looks, dominant personalities, and the ability to spout "chip shots" (comments with more style than substance). New case method instructors can fear the sheer volume of information to process, question their ability to accurately assess student knowledge, and dread the expected deluge of complaints after grades have been distributed.

Can you build a grading process that both you and students trust? You can, but you will have to capture participation systematically and in detail and spend some time setting student expectations.

When grading participation, consider both quantity and quality. Quantity is quite simple. Speaking more in class should be rewarded as long as the student is contributing to the discussion. As mentioned in chapter 3, be sure to scan the room so that you do not miss raised hands.

Quality is a more nebulous concept. What is the gold standard for a qualitatively good comment? The key word is *contribution*—does the student contribute to the other students' learning? Students can

---

"Hand Credit"

Bill awards credit to students for having their hands raised, even if he does not call on them. While this introduces a gaming element, he has found that students who bluff regularly are eventually caught. Espen does not award "hand credit," thinking that the sea of hands it produces makes the classroom environment stressful to the more timid and thoughtful students.

---

contribute with quality knowledge about the topic, but also by adding quality to the discussion through the way they conduct themselves.

One way to describe this to the students is to ask, "When you speak, are your classmates glad you did?" Did the student add something new by sharing knowledge, asking a critical question, explaining a tricky detail, raising a new possibility, synthesizing from examples, summarizing arguments, or pointing out a conundrum? Are students building on earlier points? Good insights or information delivered at the wrong time can impede a discussion. Are they challenging fellow students?

As you become more experienced as a case teacher, you will learn to recognize certain student personalities and how to play to their abilities. Typical personalities include:

- The shy but brilliant overpreparer, usually seated in one of the front lower rows, who excels at presenting case facts and answering set questions, but is quiet in the later stages of the discussion.

- The charismatic and experienced (sometimes in real life, sometimes just in his or her own opinion) "sky-decker" sitting in the front upper rows, who does not want to be called on to demonstrate detailed case preparation but is happy to summarize the discussion with more philosophical comments.

- The bookish theorist, generally located in the wing seats, who wants to apply models and frameworks.

- The contrarian—generally older than the others, quiet, sitting higher up on the side—who throws an often welcome wrench into the works by going against common opinion when everyone seems to agree.

They are all valued participants. Use them for their good contributions and challenge them outside of their comfort zones.

You also need to track whom you have called on to give everyone a chance to talk and gain participation points. In a small class, this is less critical, but should you teach a full room with ninety students, with each student only able to speak once or twice a week, you have to make sure everyone has a chance and record it.

Capturing Participation

Key to capturing participation is to have a very simple system for noting what the students do and taking those notes right after each class. So is this discipline: as soon as each class is over, make a note of how well each student did. We use spreadsheets to keep track of student performance but use lists with photographs for our after-class comments. The lists can be those the institution provides or, even better, printouts of the student photographs we took during one of the first classes. We print a complete set for each class; the photos are printed in weak grayscale so we can write directly on them.

We are agnostic about scoring notation. The important thing is that you are systematic and, if you use a spreadsheet, your scoring is numeric and therefore computable. One of our colleagues uses a point scale from one to five for each student as well as a set of symbols for specific, desirable behaviors, such as opening a class, answering another student's question, and wrapping up and presenting take-aways. A student with a symbol gets an extra point. Other teachers use plusses or minuses or just a point score and write comments when pertinent.

Whatever scoring system you use, you must be consistent and use it after every class. For one thing, you will need the documentation if the students complain about their grades. Done well, a point score system will also alert you early to students who do not speak in class so that you can make sure they get an opportunity.

Our experience is that it is fairly easy to identify the very good students as well as those who never say anything or, when questioned, are badly prepared. The middling, fairly anonymous students can be a problem. There are often quite a few of them, and the law of large numbers will work against you. Many students can have one or two really good classes but then be quiet in others. We have occasionally had teaching assistants or coteachers do the class monitoring for us. While this makes it easier to teach and gives you a second perspective, we have found that you cannot leave participation scoring entirely to a teaching assistant. You still need to score the students yourself to get to know them faster and better and to have a perspective on the quality of the observer's job.

Setting Expectations

Students often have inflated expectations for their participation grade. One reason is that they mistake quantity for quality, so make it clear that both quality and quantity count. Students also tend to overestimate quantity. They will remember every comment they have made, every comment they had formulated but never got to make, and every comment they wish they had made, and almost every time they have had their hands up. You will remember primarily the comments that were substantial, which is what matters and should count toward the participation grade. Clearly, some sort of calibration is required.

One way of letting the students know where they stand is to give them some feedback on their participation performance after one-third of the course, assuming, of course, that this is a course that meets regularly over a semester. As always, you need to minimize your own work while giving the students maximum feedback. A good way to do this is either to generate an email from your spreadsheet or to create a standard email. Here is an example of a template for an email feedback message:

> *Dear student,*
>
> *The following is some feedback on your performance so far. Don't take it too seriously. It is intended as a midterm guide rather than a firm indication of where your grade will end up.*
>
> *Your standard comment: X (see the scale below).*
>
> *Extra comments: You speak well in class and have in some instances driven the discussion forward. But try to provide answers and observations (from case or class) rather than questions.*
>
> *Explanation of standard comment:*
>
> *W. Good performance so far—well-prepared and frequent contributor. X: Satisfactory performance so far—good quantity, work a little on quality. Y. Satisfactory performance so far—good quality, work a little on quantity. Z. Could be better—either infrequent comments or apparent lack of preparation when called on.*
>
> *Please respond to this email if you want to discuss this further.*

Provided you can generate the email list automatically or clip the standard text into the feedback mechanism of a learning management system, you can quickly address each student with some calibrating feedback. The extra comments are optional.

Setting Expectations by Self-Evaluation

A useful exercise that we highly recommend is to have students suggest their own participation grades. We have used this technique in many courses, not to set the grade (for that we rely on our own notes), but to get an idea about each student's self-perception and expectations. This technique identifies which students are likely to be disappointed in their grades, gives us additional data about who they are and what they think, and provides excellent background information, should the students formally complain about their grades.

The method is simple: we hand out a form (see online resource 12 for a paper version or http://goo.gl/Cv8dzi for an electronic one) to each student and ask him or her to answer these questions:

1. Which participation grade (*A–F*) should I get, and why?

2. What can I do (could I have done) to improve my participation grade?

We sometimes include an additional comment field as well if we have specific questions about the course. You can do this in the middle of a course (which Bill prefers) or at the end (Espen's preference). The answers are always interesting, and we have found the students to be fairly accurate judges of their own participation. For most of them— up to 80 percent—we tend to broadly agree with their suggestions. They point out their strong and weak points, remember reasonably well what they have said in class, and also give other useful feedback.

The remaining 20 percent tend to divide neatly into two groups. The first group awards themselves *A*'s when they deserve much lower grades, sometimes as low as *F*'s. Their rationale typically ignores the grading guidelines entirely and relates to being well prepared, even though they don't speak in class. The other group gives themselves significantly lower grades than they have earned. This is almost always rooted in self-esteem and confidence issues; these students benefit greatly from constructive feedback and coaching. Checking these grades for patterns along cultural and gender lines can be useful. We discuss how to address such issues in chapter 5.

Amir Sasson, a colleague of Espen, has come up with an even more ingenious approach, which so far we have not tried ourselves. On the back of each student's name card, he prints a table, shown in figure 4-2.

Amir requires the students to turn in the name cards after each class. The beauty of this approach is that the students track their own performance systematically and are constantly reminded that they must contribute in class. As a bonus, they get their name card at the beginning of each class with written feedback. To make sorting and data input easy, Amir writes the student spreadsheet row on each card, next to the student name.

Exams

If you have a large number of exams, developing a formal rubric (formalized set of scoring criteria) can be helpful. For smaller sections, the rubric might just be a set of notes. The key is to know the main topics you are looking for in an answer and the number of points they are worth.

Many of the points you allocate on the exam will be driven by the content of the course you are teaching. Here we list factors that are often helpful to consider, independent of domain, when developing a rubric. Online resource 13 includes a sample rubric.

- *Analysis.* How deep is the analysis (first-, second-, third-order effects)?

- *Use of language.* Is the language understandable and appropriate to the setting? If you charge the students with writing a memo to the board, does it read like a memo to the board?

- *Time frame.* Did the student consider immediate, short-, and long-term issues as appropriate?

- *Use of theory.* Did the student draw on the right theories and apply them well?

FIGURE 4-2

A self-evaluation name card

My contribution was characterized by:	Session	1	2	3	4	5	6	7	8	9	10	11	
Careful analysis leading to appropriate and inventive conclusions supported by evidence, showing clear signs of independent thinking, and mastery of the subject.													INSERT YOUR PHOTO
A thorough familiarity with the subject, showing well developed capacity to analyze issues, some original insights, and capacity for creative and logical thinking.													HERE
Reasonable familiarity with the relevant literature, showing understanding of the ideas but not supported by well-reasoned arguments.													
Some familiarity with the subject, limited development of arguments, restatement of information/material, and lack of supporting evidence to provided conclusions.													
Irrelevance to the subject discussed.													
Absence (no contribution was provided).													

- *Finances.* Has the student considered the implications on revenues and costs? Are the estimates appropriate and based on solid analysis?

- *Political realities.* To what extent do students see the complexity in the situation and suggest viable solutions? Can students identify personalities and power dynamics?

- *Big picture.* This might include analysis of the industry or environment.

- *Domain-specific issues.*

We prefer to keep the number of elements on the rubric for a given question to single digits, preferably to a half-dozen or so. This means we can be aware of all the criteria at once as we read the answers. If more than one instructor will use the exam and you want uniformity of the grading across classes, then the rubric needs to be more detailed.

If you are using the rubric for the first time, it is helpful to grade a dozen or so exams with it, being careful not to place marks on the exams, and then review the rubric to make sure you are comfortable with the results. If you need to adjust it, you can change the grades on the exams you have already reviewed as appropriate.

Grading Exams on Paper or on Screen

Bill always prints out all exams and grades them using a pen, going through them question by question (that is, he grades all question one first, then question two, and so on). He writes comments on the papers themselves, enters the grades into a spreadsheet, and returns the hard copies to the students. Espen uses two big computer screens, reads each exam on one, and enters comments and grades into a spreadsheet on the other, before sending feedback to students electronically. The advantage of Bill's approach is that it is easier in the grading phase and you can work into a flow, particularly by concentrating on one question at a time. The advantage of Espen's is that he has both grades and comments electronically captured, easy to find when students ask for more feedback.

If you are grading many exams, particularly over more than one day, it is helpful to compare one or two you graded early to those you grade later, to ensure that you haven't drifted.

The Dreaded Extra-Credit Requests

Most teachers, especially in undergraduate classes and in the United States, will have requests from students to do some form of makeup work to compensate for doing poorly or missing class, especially in lieu of participating in class.

Our advice is simple: don't do it.

We mean that. Makeup work is more work for you, no extra learning for the student, and an injustice to those students who do not ask for something extra. Of course, no rule is without exceptions. If a student has had some sort of personal catastrophe or has a disability that prohibits normal participation, then allowing him or her to do something different is reasonable. These exceptions should be rare.

Some faculty like to include planned extra credit as part of the grading structure. We avoid this because we feel it reduces the focus on doing well on the core parts of the course for which the students are being graded. Rather than doing extra work, we would prefer students focused more on the core work assigned.

Missing Class and Grading

The class participation grade reflects engagement, which requires presence as well as contribution. Espen addresses this problem by giving students one point just for showing up in class and a zero if they do not. If they have a valid excuse for not showing up, such as illness or a class conflict, he grades them as if they had been present but not said anything, a reward system roughly similar to what would happen in a work relationship. Bill's policy is that just showing up does not earn any points, but missing class without a valid excuse results in a penalty. He requires students with valid excuses to participate more actively in the sessions they do attend to compensate for missing class.

What constitutes a valid reason is up to you, but it can be useful, in this as in many other things, to be quite strict in the beginning of a course. Sometimes it can be quite funny. Espen once had a student inform him that he would have to miss the last forty-five minutes of every Monday class because he had to go to handball practice and asked if that would affect his participation grade. Yes, Espen said, and suggested the student instead tell his coach he would be forty-five minutes late for practice on Mondays. The student protested that he was playing handball "at a national level." Espen replied that he was teaching at an international level. The student stayed to the end of the Monday classes and did very well.

Neither of us spends a lot of time on missed classes, and with executive classes, we seldom bother with this at all. Either the students are interested and show up, or they don't. It's their choice.

Handling Academic Dishonesty

Cheating is rampant and growing in many schools. Key concerns are how to foster academic honesty, the mechanics of detecting cheating, and the realities of addressing it, including in environments where tight enforcement is tacitly discouraged. Case classes are less vulnerable to cheating than lecture-based classes because a big chunk of the grade comes from class participation, but in exams and term papers, cheating can occur.

In most schools, students can access information about prior exams. In many situations, this is done openly and legitimately; in others, it is part of an underground system. We have seen examples of remarkably organized troves, including ones where students memorize exam questions and pass them on to future students. For exams that repeatedly use the same cases and questions, this form of cheating can be refined and effective: use these frameworks to illustrate these points, raise these key factors and these secondary ones, and create an action plan that addresses these factors. A boilerplate for an excellent answer can be distilled to a page or two. In fact, it's basically your grading rubric.

To ensure an effective exam, and to be fair to students who can't or won't use exam templates, you need to make the exam less predictable. The most effective way is to use a different case each time. This involves search costs, although those are mitigated by putting aside a case or two as potential exams when you are choosing the cases for the course. And creating a grading rubric takes time. Depending on your topic, you may also have limited access to cases.

At a minimum, we would suggest rotating the exam case (for instance, remove a different case from your syllabus each year and use it for the exam) or creating a pool of questions from which you can draw in any given exam. Write a new question every semester or two and make that question required of all students and worth more points.

If your school has an honor code you trust, then you can ignore this advice. If there are dishonesty issues despite the honor code, then you need to pursue the appropriate course of action, which may involve working with the honor system or implementing some of the controls we describe if they are permitted by the code at your school. Be sure there is a clear policy about academic honesty and plagiarism specifically, and share it with students. While this may not change the behavior of many students intending to cheat, it does eliminate ignorance as a defense.

Some students may claim a "cultural defense": where they were educated, the rules regarding academic dishonesty were different. This has not been our experience, though we know a number of teachers who have heard it. In one course we were teaching together, a student claimed this as a defense. With the student and us in the room, the dean contacted the educational attaché at that student's embassy. The attaché was unequivocal (and rather vociferous) in making clear to the student that the standards were the same as in the United States, to which the student eventually agreed.

Plagiarism is an increasing problem, facilitated by easily Googled information from the Internet and culturally accepted by students used to pirating software and music for their personal consumption. Increased use of projects and independently researched papers in grade school and high school without enough focus on intellectual honesty compounds the problem.

We are passionate about fighting plagiarism. Plagiarism demo-tivates the good students, devalues your work as a teacher and evaluator, and introduces the risk of graduating people without the qualifications their diplomas indicate. Fighting plagiarism is the duty of every faculty member, but unfortunately many are hesitant to deal with the problem because of exposure to uncomfortable situations, the amount of work required to document cases, and the wrist-slap punishments plagiarists often receive.

The control itself is easy, both conceptually and in terms of work. There are good tools available for doing automatic plagiarism control, and there is little reason not to use them. They also simplify your life when it comes to receiving papers. Allowing students to submit papers to the plagiarism checker and see the results before submitting can help avoid inadvertent problems. We use manual controls in addition to the automatic software. When we are reading a student's paper and find a sentence that seems familiar or at least above the student's usual level, we clip or type it into Google just to be sure. If you are teaching abroad, running some particularly convoluted paragraph through Google Translate into the local language often surfaces plagiarism.

If we find plagiarism, we *always* let it have consequences for the student. What kind of consequence depends on the situation, but the standard way is to report it to the disciplinary board. Plagiarists tend to do it a lot (Sorokina et al., 2006). We have had student groups that have plagiarized a term paper in one course, and when we checked previous term papers in other classes, we found that they were plagiarized, too. The students very often seem surprised to have been caught, we think because many faculty see the problem but don't have the energy or motivation to pursue it.

In some countries, plagiarism is a systemic problem. In some Asian countries, for instance, many students do not see plagiarism as necessarily wrong. Espen has had students clip material from the web and defend their actions by saying that they found something that was well written, and since they could not improve on it, well, they just used it. In the same countries, students face enormous pressure to perform, especially if they are executive students whose studies are paid for by their employer. We recommend using judgment when dealing with this; you should make it clear that you have zero tolerance for plagiarism, but measure your reaction somewhat depending on the consequences for the students. In some Asian countries, students being reported to a disciplinary committee risk much harsher consequences, including losing their jobs, than they would in the United States or Europe. When Espen finds students plagiarizing in Asia, he fails the students and gives them a chance at the next course, a punishment adequately harsh.

To reduce the problem, expect to spend quite a bit of time and energy explaining what plagiarism is and why students shouldn't do it, as well as giving information about proper citation technique. If you make your position clear and take consistent action, you will gain the respect of the students who don't cheat. It is well worth the time and effort.

Conclusion

Grading is hard because it requires making decisions that matter for someone based on what you will always feel is too little information. Our approach can seem time consuming, but it is defensible and open, and at least forces some accountability. If you find yourself longing for short-answer or multiple-choice exams, remember that good feedback is invaluable to students' learning and it can motivate them to improve far more than a solitary number. With forethought, you can reduce the burden of grading and feel more secure in your own judgment.

Do not fall into the trap of giving students good grades in an effort to make them like you (and recommend your course). Give a stellar course and be tough but fair in your grading, and the students will forget their disappointing grades over time and remember you as a brilliant teacher.

Reference

Sorokina, D., J. Gehrke, S. Warner, and P. Ginsparg. "Plagiarism Detection in arXiv." Sixth International Conference on Data Mining, Hong Kong. December 18–22, 2006.

5

MANAGING
CLASSROOM ISSUES

When we talk to teachers to try to promote the case method, they ask many questions about potential problems. We have dealt with many of the questions in the preceding chapters. This chapter answers the ones that keep popping up.

We emphasize that these problems rarely occur, but they can generate enough anxiety to keep instructors from using the case method. The method is robust and flexible and, with good preparation and an explicit contract with the students, serious, sustained problems seldom occur.

Issues with Individual Students

Students come in all kinds. Some are assets to any class, sharing their ideas and contributing to their peers' learning (and yours, for that matter). Some can be more of a challenge or even liabilities, detracting from the learning experience, but all of them can be dealt with. Here are a few typical scenarios and what to do about them.

How Do I Manage Students Who Hog Airtime?

Airtime hogs—students who grab the floor and do not relinquish it—can be a problem. They have numerous reasons for dominating discussions:

- An inflated self-image and a belief that they have the answer for everything (and, well, sometimes they do).

- A misunderstanding of the participation grading system: they think quantity is the only dimension rated.

- An axe to grind with the case or the topic that they feel free to grind at length.

- An unfamiliarity with speaking in public that causes them to drone on, frequently with very long explanations for concepts well understood by the class.

How to deal with them?

The question is twofold: what do you do in the classroom as it happens, and what do you do to manage the situation in the future—the next class, the rest of the course? In the classroom, you need to stop the person without damaging him or her, while maintaining your authority. Do not simply overlook the airtime hog, at least not when he or she starts to annoy the other students. Your passivity risks having the class take action on its own, which holds the potential for greater problems. Sometimes it is best to take direct action, but unless absolutely necessary, we recommend waiting for a break or acting before the next class. This has the advantage of giving you time to think through and formulate your approach.

There are many ways, with varying degrees of explicitness, to stop a student from continuing to speak. As mentioned before, striding forcefully toward him will get most talkers to take a break, which you can use to divert the discussion by calling on another student. If the talker is sensitive to your behavior, you can look away or, if really desperate, at your watch, stop writing on the board, or look a bit distracted to get the student to understand that it is time to stop. As you get practice, you can do this almost unconsciously, at no time alerting the other students to what you are doing.

If the student does not react to this, be more direct: hold up your hand and say something like, "So, you want to [do this]—any other views?" and turn it over to another student. You can be more direct, saying, "So, in conclusion …?" or "So, in summary … ?" forcing the student to conclude.

If students start talking without holding their hands up or interrupting other students, you are quite within your rights to explicitly stop them and tell them to hold their hand up and wait until given the floor to speak. In some cases, this can be an inopportune thing to do—for instance, if you are running a case discussion inside a company and the drone is the CEO—but normally this will be fine.

If a person is a recurring problem, you can talk to him or her discreetly—so that the class doesn't see it—about appropriate behavior in the classroom. Some students will complain that you never call on them, even if they speak a lot; the mind can be very selective in these matters. If you show good humor and make the students aware of their behavior, most will take the advice and at least try to abide by it. If they are unsure about what they are doing—lack of self-knowledge can be as common a cause as anything else—you can suggest a signal to them, such as pressing your hands together or touching the side of your nose when they are speaking too long. Underscore the role to help others learn and the fact that the quantity side of participation grading typically follows a curvilinear function. More at some point is worse, not better.

How Do I Manage Combative Students?

You may come across students who are overly argumentative and constantly challenge you and the other students. This may be because they have deeply felt opinions, consider themselves experts, and can't abide anyone else having opinions. In some cases, they seek to manipulate the classroom toward their will, whether it is to shut down one side of a debate or just show off.

Such students can be dealt with in many ways, depending on your personality, subject knowledge, and the mood in the class. You want to diffuse the situation, clarify what the student means (at least in terms of content), and then use the incident to continue the discussion with the whole class. It can be tempting, especially when you have gained some experience and cynicism, to employ some snappy repartee to cut the student down to size. While this looks great in a Robert B. Parker novel, it can backfire. Cutting someone down means playing it his or her way, demeaning yourself in the process.

We recommend a tactic we will call *catch, measure, release* (as you would with a fish that is too small):

- Pause to hear what the student is saying.

- Parse the statement, request more detail, and show that the issue has more depth or different angles than the student thinks.

- Reengage the class from that understanding.

Normally, students' combative statements will pop up when you are discussing subjects that are political or otherwise controversial, say, globalization, outsourcing, gender, regulation, and so on. The statements from the students will typically be rather broad—"You business school professors think globalization is good for its own sake!"—and lend themselves to analysis of what is good or bad about globalization: "Are we really dealing with globalization in this particular case?" "What are the effects of globalization (for rich and poor countries) and what do we gain or lose by it?"

What Can I Do about Students' Computer Use in Class?

The classroom is no longer a closed space. Students routinely surf the web, communicate with the outside and each other, and search Google and Wikipedia as soon as a teacher says something. Some teachers disallow computers in class, just as some executives insist on "topless" (as in "laptopless") meetings. The argument is that computers distract many students—and employees—and forbidding them will give you their full attention.

We disagree. Not only have we taken laptops to lectures and meetings for decades, taking all our notes on them, but it is our firm conviction that if the students want to surf the web rather than listen to you, you are not having a *technical* problem. Daydreaming and doodling long predate the web, as does sneakily reading the news-paper in the back row. But the vastly enhanced capability for search, calculation, and communication that computers provide introduces some issues in the classroom that you need to think about.

Aside from distractions, the computer allows students to instantly look up facts and figures. Some will use them to triumphantly correct anything you or another student says: "Professor, the population of the United States is not 300 million; it's 315 million!" Others will even search for content to contribute, some of which you will not know or will consider irrelevant. Your best bet is probably to treat the noisome students as you would any other unruly student and not worry that you do not know every fact out there. Instead, treat the class as Google—"... and you divide that number by the population of the United States, which is ... Can someone look that up on Wolfram Alpha?"

The most significant change, however, is not what the students bring into the classroom, but what they can communicate out of it. Blogs, YouTube, Facebook, Twitter, and other social media tools allow anything that happens in the classroom to be broadcast to the entire Internet via a smartphone and a few keystrokes. This is something you need to be explicit about early on to prevent dissemination.

You need to make clear to students that remarks in the classroom are meant for the classroom, not for public consumption, and that it is a violation of the contract between you and the students to publicize any of it outside the classroom unless given permission. Much of what is said in a classroom is spontaneous, designed to be provocative and to start discussion. If you risk being held accountable for things you really did not mean (at least not in another context), the whole classroom experience will be much worse for everyone, you included.

What Do I Do If a Student Does Not Pay Attention in Class?

Some faculty expect an unreasonably high level of continuous atten-tiveness from all students. A student zoning out once in a while is perfectly normal. If many of your students are not paying attention, you should look for ways to energize the class, as we discuss in chap-ter 3. And if an individual student is repeatedly not paying attention, then you should take action.

If your facial expressions and body language and movement toward the student don't work, then the most compassionate next step is to email the student about the issue. There may be a physical or psychological reason for what appears to be inattentiveness. And even if there is no such reason, the email usually suffices. If it doesn't, then call the student out on the behavior in class, using humor or a cold call (or both), depending on your style and the gravity of the situation.

What Do I Do If a Student Complains?

Students may choose to complain about a range of issues, from grades or facilities to pedagogy and classmates. Teaching the students' first case course or teaching cases when others teaching the same course are lecturing can provoke a disproportionate number of complaints, particularly in the first half of the course. Being clear in setting the contract for the course with students helps, but you are still likely to hear some complaints.

If the complaints arise during class, don't let them derail discussions and take them offline, if at all possible. Listen carefully to the complaints, but avoid validating them during the discussion. At the end of the conversation, calibrate your response, which generally will fall into one of four categories:

1. Help the student see that the complaint is petty, unreasonable, or unfounded. Reinforcing whining does not do you or the student any favors. As a teacher, you are responsible for helping your students develop, and, although difficult, these conversations can be some of the most valuable in their education.

2. Explain that the underlying issue will not change. This is very commonly a conversation with a student who is uncomfortable participating in class. Empathizing with his or her anxiety can be helpful. Explain, but never apologize for, the methodology or other issue.

3. Address the issue directly. If the complaint is valid and readily resolved with the individual student, then fix it.

4. Let the student know you will follow up. Perhaps the
    complaint requires more analysis or raises an issue
    that you need to address with the class. Do not try to do
    everything in the classroom if that is not realistic, but make
    sure to follow up and let the student know the result. One
    colleague had a student complain that he was never called
    on—that the teacher had a blind spot where he was sitting.
    The professor said he would check his data, did so, and
    discovered that this student was the second-most frequent
    contributor in class. When he relayed this fact to the
    student, the reply was, "Oh, it must be in marketing class I
    am never called on."

Not all complaints are worth listening to, and whatever you do,
don't turn your classroom into an introspective therapy session for
you and your teaching. Not only is this a waste of the students' time,
but it may validate a view that only a few students hold. If a few vocal
students think your class is bad, acknowledging that and discussing
it may cause the other students—so far quite satisfied—to think that
they are wrong and the class really must be very bad.

How Do I Accommodate Students with Disabilities in Case Classes?

Schools—and, by extension, faculty—are required to accommodate
students with documented learning disabilities. In lecture classes,
such accommodations may include note takers, specialized technology, reading assistance, and extra time and support on exams.
Students with learning disabilities are becoming more commonly
recognized, and classes in which at least one student needs to be
accommodated are the norm.

Case classes put extra pressure on these support systems. We have
taught classes with visually and hearing impaired students. The
pace and unpredictability of the discussions makes it much more
difficult for the interpreters, but with earnest effort from all participants and good communication about process, the discussions run
smoothly. The greater challenges are accommodating students with

learning disabilities and psychological issues that make processing information or speaking in class difficult.

Bill has had several students with severe social anxiety who would suffer panic attacks in class. The accommodation was to work with the students' therapists to treat speaking in class as an *in vivo* exposure where the students would apply techniques they learned in therapy (breathing, reframing thoughts, and so on) to manage their anxiety while participating in class. Early in the semester, the students were warm-called in advance of class with relatively easy questions. As the semester progressed, they got less advanced notice and the complexity of the questions increased.

For students with learning disabilities that affect them in class discussion, we also use warm calls to give them more time to process. When possible, we do this surreptitiously so that the student does not feel singled out. This can include an email before class, a quick word during a break, or subtle hand signals.

Issues with Groups of Students

Sometimes issues arise not with individual students, but with groups or even the whole class. Here we examine the most common questions about dealing with students as a group.

What Do I Do When Students Are Not Well Prepared?

When a class seems unprepared, be sure the problem really is poor preparation. If you are teaching the first case course for many students, their anxiety may be manifesting in ways that are easily confused with poor preparation. If preparation is the issue, try to find out why. Were your expectations about preparation clear? Do students know how to prepare? Are there competing demands for the students' time and they are not prioritizing your course? Don't immediately jump to the conclusion that the problem is sloth.

If you determine the issue is poor preparation, you need to do what you can to make sure it doesn't continue. We address that in the next question. Here are some ways to get the most out of a class session in which preparation is scant:

- Give students some time in groups to skim and discuss the case. If feasible, seed each group with one or two people who are prepared.

- Spend more time on issues that don't require having read the entire case.

- Leave some issues open and return to them in the next class meeting.

- As a last resort, you can always revert to a traditional, presentation-style approach. We have done this, especially when there was no case involved, but it makes returning to discussion in the subsequent class even harder, as you have signaled that if students do not prepare, you will rescue them.

How Do I Get Students to Prepare Better?

First, make sure the workload you demand is realistic. It can absolutely be higher than other classes, but if you are wildly out of line or the students have other demands and not enough time, then you may need to cut back on work outside the classroom.

If the workload issue doesn't seem to be salient, reinforce the messages around preparation we outline in chapter 3. If that doesn't work, then escalate your efforts in the following ways.

Reward Good Preparation

While this seems straightforward, if student norms are developing (or have developed) that frown on showing preparedness, then singling out students can backfire. While you should temper your effusiveness after a good contribution to avoid blowback, at the end of class thank those students who prepared well without naming them and email follow-ups to students who did well to reinforce the message. If you are teaching students who also take other classes together, speak to other instructors about how the students tend to prepare.

Help Them Along

Acknowledge the issue of preparedness and make your case preparation questions more comprehensive for a while. Make cheat sheets available, with a list of key names, events, and dates. Deliberately ask some easier questions. This will allow you to build momentum in the quality of the discussions.

Draw Out Prepared but Reticent Students

You probably have a few quiet students who are well prepared but are not speaking up. Warm- or cold-call them regularly to keep the discussion moving. Let them know by email or in person why you are doing it—that you are confident they have a great deal to contribute to elevate the quality of the discussions.

Require Case Write-ups or Give Pop Quizzes

See chapter 4 for advice about minimizing the grading involved if you try the case write-up option. You can try pop quizzes that require knowledge of case facts. You can give these at the beginning of class or online the night before. Executives and experienced MBAs find this technique infantilizing, but for undergraduates and inexperienced MBAs, it is fair game.

Give a Stern Lecture

Diatribes are tempting but rarely work. If you want to address students about preparedness, make sure your approach is balanced. To offset your expression of disappointment in them, be positive about the value of the course and clear that your desire is for everyone to succeed as best they can.

Make An Example of a Student or Two

If the lack of preparation is clear and in violation of your course contract, you are within your rights to make examples of certain students. Fear and shame can be powerful motivators, but be careful. You wield a great deal of power and aiming it all at one student is a drastic action. With students that know each other outside class, you may see the rest of the class defend the student and turn on you (this is less likely but not unheard of in other classes). Also, be confident that the student you are using as an example can handle the pressure.

We suggest choosing ways that work well for you in your context. Experiment with positive and negative reinforcement. Being positive is the better choice, when it works. We have found that it is often insufficient by itself, especially when teaching less-experienced students. By adding in some negative elements, we see better results, without getting draconian.

We have both responded to poorly prepared students in class by telling them that they are at risk of failing the class. But we don't do that unless we are confident of our perception of both the individuals (that they will be able to handle it and not react badly) and the class (it will not cause a revolt). We follow it with a reminder of why we want them to learn the material. It goes without saying that we wouldn't threaten to fail or mark down students in an executive class where they generally don't care about grades or in an undergraduate class when the students could simply drop the course without penalty.

How Do I Stop Side Conversations?

The fastest way to stop a side conversation is to cold-call one of the students. This does run the risk that the student is ill prepared for the question and could uncomfortably break the flow of the class. You may also prefer not to cold-call in your class in general.

Here are some alternatives:

- Ask them to stop.

- Pause the discussion and look toward the students. If they don't notice you doing this, their neighbors will and someone will tell them to stop.

- Use humor to remind them not to have side conversations.

- Walk toward them.

Allow Side Conversations?

Espen will only intervene in side conversations if they are disruptive to the class. Bill strictly enforces a norm that they should never occur, suggesting that students should pass notes if they need to communicate. We both try to understand why students are driven to such conversations: Did they have trouble hearing a comment? Was an unfamiliar technical term used? Is there a language issue? Are they talking about something important to the case that should be covered?

How Do I Manage Dysfunctional Class Behavior?

Dysfunctional behavior involving groups of students or sometimes the whole class can surface in a case classroom. This unusual behavior tends to arise when the students have known each other for a while, perhaps during several courses. The behavior takes the form of coordinated gestures or utterances designed to signal in-class social norms and sometimes to make students who don't agree with them toe the line.

You as a teacher might observe these behaviors, but miss their significance. Done with malice, they can be very effective social controls and need to be observed carefully. The following are some prime examples.

Hissing

Hissing can be triggered when a student says something that the rest of the class dislikes but no individual wants to argue against openly. Since the instructor cannot always see who is hissing, this is an effective way to signal dislike with a low risk of being challenged by the teacher or other students.

Genuflection

These types of gestures can happen when a student says something very smart, demonstrating knowledge beyond the rest of the class.

The other students hold their hands up and bow down until their foreheads touch the table, signaling sincere or sarcastic admiration for the student.

Sharking

Sharking happens when one student argues very forcefully against another student. Other students will then pick up their name cards, hold them above their heads in the direction of the attacking student, simulating shark fins sticking out of the water. It is intended to show support for the "attacked" student, and, if done often, can be very detrimental to students' willingness to challenge each other's viewpoints.

Sometimes these behaviors arise out of boredom toward the end of case courses, when the students have grown tired of each other's viewpoints and discussion habits. As the instructor, you need to monitor this behavior carefully and disallow it; the hissing can be especially destructive. In our view, the simplest way to deal with it is to tell the class that this behavior is unacceptable and should stop. If you want to deal with it more discreetly, take it up with the student representative.

What If the Class Turns against Me?

Another rare type of behavior is when a class, as a unit, disrespects or gets angry with the instructor. There is a difference between these two alternatives. In the former, the class thinks the professor irrelevant and not worth paying attention to; in the latter, the class might respect the professor but be angry with him or her.

For some reason, disrespect—the danger of not being taken seriously—scares more new teachers than the risk of antagonizing the class. The fear can be caused by anxiety about knowledge—Do I really know the subject I am supposed to teach?—or by the fact that you are significantly different from the audience in appearance or background. Sometimes anxiety itself can drive you to focus on some of your personal attributes—having a thin voice, for instance, or being over- or underweight—and drive fear that these attributes can lead the class to disrespect you.

These situations seldom occur for a reason. If nothing else, the students have signed up for your course, and you have been given the job to teach it. This in itself is an indication that they are interested and you are capable, and that's all that is needed.

You need to find some source of strength, something you are good at that is valuable to the audience, and make that clear as soon as possible. All the standard tricks we talked about in chapter 3—dressing carefully, being on time, making sure you project a confident image the first time you encounter the class—are helpful, but you also need to make your own, long-term value clear to yourself. Establishing academic stature can also be a way to do it. Include articles, cases, or some other material you have created in the syllabus, if only for legitimacy reasons.

But, most importantly, trust yourself.

Classes get angry with instructors occasionally, but seldom for reasons connected to the content, unless you are overloading the students, for instance, and being unreasonable about the workload compared with that of other courses. On the rare occasions when a class gets angry over content, it can be because you have taken a controversial position (being rational on an emotionally controversial topic, for instance, or being too provocative when playing devil's advocate), treated a student too harshly, or made a comment that was too flippant. Sometimes, the students' reaction has far less to do with anything you did and more to do with you as an easy target for transference of dynamics among the students in the room. Perhaps you were introduced as something you are not or the class was dissatisfied with previous instructors or other parts of the course and is taking it out on you. This occurs more commonly if you are teaching a group of students that developed norms while being taught by other faculty.

Elegantly handling this type of situation, while infrequent, demands a cool head and some experience. An inexperienced instructor should probably insist on maintaining his or her (well-developed) approach and rely on the class's internal system of justice to kick in at some point. Most students have a sense of fair play and most audiences want the class—and the instructor—to be good. If you can identify something you did wrong, then acknowledge it and apologize. Do not belabor analysis of the issue or your apology unless the issue is related to the course content. Move on quickly; overcompensating can be damaging to your credibility.

If there is nothing to apologize for, don't. But even if you did nothing wrong, you still have a problem to deal with. You have four basic options:

1. *Ignore the anger.* If you think it will blow over quickly, this is the best option. Reacting to every mood shift in the room will make the class interminable for everyone.

2. *Ingratiate yourself.* Go easier on the students for a while. Ask easier questions or cold-call students who are likely to enjoy speaking and will provide good responses. Make yourself a little vulnerable by sharing something personal. Get back in their good graces without an open acknowledgement of the issue.

3. *Acknowledge the tension in the room and suggest everyone accept and move past it.* You can also use humor ["Boy, today has been about as much fun as that (local sports team's recent losing) game. Let's shake this off and move on."] Students appreciate that you feel the discomfort, and the validation is often enough to get past it. You could then take a short break or have the students do a quick group exercise.

4. *Open a discussion, if appropriate, without apologizing.* To do this well in the classroom, you need good facilitation skills, as the conversation can escalate very quickly in counterproductive and unpleasant directions. If you are comfortable with your skills and the class, it can be an effective means of surfacing and dealing with the issues. If not, you might consider using a survey instrument or meet with smaller groups of students outside of class.

How Is Teaching Executives Different?

Many prospective case teachers are nervous about teaching executives; frequently case teaching and executive education programs are linked. Many who set out to learn case teaching do so because they have been tasked with teaching executive classes.

We love teaching executive classes—the more senior, the better—and think case teaching superior to other methods for this particular group. Executives—or, indeed, any class of people with work experience and eclectic backgrounds—are a more mature audience than college and graduate students; they are more confident in their own observations and opinions, less likely to demand a correct answer to everything, and more interested in seeing a problem from many perspectives.

Nevertheless, if you are young and inexperienced, being up on your hind legs in front of a flock of grizzled execs can be frightening. The trick is to remember that just as a first-year undergraduate student is nervous about a course—especially a case course—so are execs. Unless you are teaching courses toward the end of an MBA program, most of the students will feel rusty about studying and going to class. In fact, when we have MBA students (part-time, with work experience) and regular students (full-time, no relevant work experience) in the same classroom, the full-time students look forward to learning from the executives, while many of the executives are nervous about appearing in a classroom and being evaluated on their contribution against those fearsomely bright young things.

One issue with teaching executives is that it often takes place on *their* ground, not yours. The ground can be literal if you are teaching a class at a company. It can also mean that you are stepping into their territory in terms of knowledge, that is, when you are leading a discussion of people from one particular industry. We come into an organization or an executive class that is significantly different from our home institution or our backgrounds, and the students make assumptions about us based on where we come from.

Espen has faced this situation many times as a management speaker: as an Internet enthusiast speaking to paper journalists, for instance, or as the "invited enemy" panel member from a private business school in a discussion of school fees for publicly funded schools. Rather than attempt to ingratiate ourselves with the people in the audience through apologies, we advocate starting out by expressing some viewpoint or observation that surprises the audience and leads them to see you as a person, not a representative of something they do not like. Espen, who lives in Oslo, once taught a course about entrepreneurship in the north of Norway—the equivalent of flying in from New York to a small Alaskan town to tell people how to run their businesses. Northern Norwegians are known for their directness, so Espen countered the budding animosity in the room by saying that, yes, he lived in Oslo, but he lived on a small island where (a) no buses ran after 8 P.M., (b) he could only get one TV channel, and (c) one of his neighbors was a professional fisherman. So there! The atmosphere in the room visibly relaxed, and the course became a very good experience, both for Espen and for the students.

At other times, you can build your legitimacy precisely by being different from the audience and underscoring it. Showing up in front of an audience of programmers and other techies in a business suit to talk about business topics may give you legitimacy, especially if you are careful to use a few technical terms correctly early on. Similarly, you can ingratiate yourself with an audience of grade school teachers or publishing industry executives by showing some familiarity with their world, be it pedagogy or literature. The people in the audience will be fascinated that this apparition in weird clothes shows concern for their worries and addresses them on their terms. Demonstrated competence in your one field, even if unrelated, can give you legitimacy on other questions. Of course, you should not overdo this, lest you become one of the parade of sports and reality TV stars on talk shows everywhere, interviewed on topics for which their knowledge and analytical capabilities are thin to nonexistent.

How Should I Deal with Student Pranks?

As time passes, your students will feel more comfortable with you. At some point, especially if yours is only one of several courses with the same class members, they may seek to release the tension or break up the routine in the classroom with a few pranks.

The inventiveness of students in these matters is infinite, but over the years we have learned to recognize a few behaviors that we classify as pranks. Unless you are a really bad teacher, your first reaction to student pranks should be to see them as signs of affection. Pay attention, though; they can be subtle signals that you are taking your-self too seriously, that you are over- or underworking the students or boring them, or that you have missed something seriously wrong.

Some of the more common pranks played on the teacher are:

- *Turkey bingo* (the game may have other names) is prevalent in schools where case teaching is the norm. The students create "bingo sheets"—five-by-five tables with the names of students from the class randomly distributed on the grid—and give them to the whole class. As students comment in class, they are crossed off, until someone has "bingo," that is, five crosses in a row or another pattern. This student will now have to declare "bingo," but cannot, of course, shout it out. He or she has to make a comment that communicates "bingo" to the other students, by, for instance, including a predetermined phrase in the comment. The phrase is usually something ridiculous: "As Napoleon said at Waterloo ..." or "When I read the case for the fourth time last night ..."

- *Bullshit bingo* is a variation of turkey bingo that fills the bingo card grid with clichés instead of student names. For business schools, these could be jargon words such as "leverage," "empowerment," and "dynamic." Bullshit bingo, can, of course, happen in lectures as well.

- *Dressing up* involves students mimicking something the teacher often wears. Espen wears a bow tie to class and has gotten used to students all showing up in bow ties at some point. If you know about the copied attribute and are OK with it, take it as a compliment. If you don't—we heard of one teacher who always wore checkered lumberjack shirts and was quite hurt when all the students did the same—keep your mask. If they go to that much effort, it is because they like you.

- *Hidden board writing* is a final kind of prank in which students write something on a board before class and hide it from the teacher. We once saw a well-known case teacher completely flummoxed when he pushed a board aside and found an elaborate parody of his favorite two-by-two framework.

How you respond to these things is up to you. They can be quite irritating if you are in a bad mood and are pressed for time, but normally the best option is to try to keep your cool and play along, at least for a while. We heard of one case teacher who discovered that the students were playing turkey bingo and stopped it very effectively just by walking over to a student in the first row as another student was speaking and crossing off the speaker's name on the student's bingo sheet. Forewarned is forearmed.

How Do I Deal with Student Representatives?

In many schools, classes will formally elect a student representative (or several) to serve as liaison to the faculty and discuss problems and suggestions. They can be helpful, but you need to consider how accurate the representative's assessments are so you don't overreact. When the representative comes to you with an issue, treat the meeting as you would an individual student complaint, except you can feel free to discuss the dynamics of the entire class, which we typically avoid in individual student meetings.

Normally, student reps are good students with a sense of duty for the common good. Occasionally, a dynamic can develop where they feel under pressure to change things, more to prove that they are doing their job than for any substantial reason. A somewhat Machiavellian trick you can employ here is to steer the conversation to some aspect of the course that you are quite willing to change, put up a little bit of a fight about it, and then give in. This preserves both sides' position—you are seen as firm but willing to listen and the student representative is seen as an effective advocate of students' rights.

You can also use the representative as a source of information about what is happening in the class. It is entirely appropriate to discuss the dynamics of the group and how that plays out in your course as well as in others. You may learn about issues that have surfaced in other courses and manage them preemptively. You may also glean information that would be useful for scheduling assignment due dates and other work.

One thing you have to be careful about is accuracy in and documentation of student reps' grades. They should receive neither better nor worse grades because of their more frequent communications with you.

How Do I Deal with Dysfunctional Groups?

MBA programs frequently include group work, both for practical reasons and because the ability to work and function in a group is integral to management practice. Normally the groups are evaluated on a deliverable item such as a term paper, a consulting-like presentation of a case analysis, or a more long-term project for a company. In all these instances, you will encounter group issues. In our experience, if you have ten groups in a class, expect at least one to blow up if its grade depends on the common work and more if the work stretches over weeks rather than days.

In general, our preference is to provide guidance to groups when they start out and encourage them to be quite explicit about division of work, schedules, and sanctions against people that do not pull their weight. We might have some check-ins but try to stay out of their inner workings as much as possible.

The problems we see with groups fall into the following categories.

Free-Riders

Free-riders—students who don't do their share of group work—are a source of great frustration for many students. In chapter 4 we addressed peer evaluations, which will handle the majority of cases. When students complain of a free-rider, we ask what they have done to address it and send them on their way, with little additional guidance. Only if they return after failing to solve the problem do we get involved and only if necessary.

Personality Conflicts

Typically, problems arise between students who have quantitative or technical skills and those who don't, along cultural lines (particularly gender issues), and between students who want to do things by themselves and those who prefer to hash things out in plenary sessions. When this happens, we try to gently straighten out the students by talking to them individually and encouraging them to change their behavior. We point out that they are, in effect, in a work situation, evaluated as a group, and hence will have to adapt to each other. We advise against moving students between groups. You should only do this as an absolute last resort. Again, in a work situation, this would not normally be done.

Poor Project Management

Students can do good work, but manage a project badly, an issue that quickly can become a bone of contention, especially since it increases the danger that some of them will seem like free-riders. We try to teach some project management skills, help them set realistic goals, and, if necessary, restructure the assignment. We try to avoid falling into the trap of becoming the project manager ourselves. It should never be the responsibility of the faculty adviser to make sure a project is completed and of high quality.

Poor Performance

Some groups just don't do good work. This can be hard to foresee, though with experience, you will have your suspicions at the outset. We advise teaching poorly performing groups something about what you expect, both by explicit demands and by showing them prior projects to calibrate their work and their grade expectations.

In both our schools, we have psychologists who can deal with especially difficult student situations. In our experience, it is important to recognize your limitations and turn things over to them if simple measures cannot remedy the situation. Unless, of course, you teach group psychology and dynamics yourself and feel comfortable handling the situation.

Issues beyond Students

Placing blame outside yourself can be tempting, and whining about students is a favorite faculty pastime. But sometimes the problem is *you*. You may be short of material, you may lose track of the discussion, you may struggle with students, or you may just have a slow day. What do you do?

What If I Can't Find Enough Cases That Fit?

Although the number of cases available from various sources is large, you may not find enough cases specific to your topic to fill out your course. If your initial search comes up short, you can try some of these steps:

- *Cast a wide net.* Try multiple case clearinghouses, academic and practitioner journals, and textbooks for short cases often included at the ends of chapters. These shorter cases are excellent introductions to students less accustomed to case teaching. Online resource 14 has a listing of sources for cases.*

- *Look at cases outside your subject area.* You may be able to use cases that were not intended for your topic area. For instance, in technology courses, we often use cases intended for management, operations, or marketing courses.

- *Make good use of the cases you can find.* Spend more time discussing them and generate your own B and C cases from supplemental materials, whenever possible.

- *Use materials that aren't formal cases.* Newspapers, blogs, trade journals, journal articles, and videos can all serve the same purpose as dedicated teaching cases. Feature articles describing companies, technologies, and managers can serve as excellent cases. You can also cobble together material you find on the Internet, including videos, annual reports, short articles, marketing material, and opinion pieces. All these sources

---

* To see this and other online resources for the book, visit the web site: teachingwithcases.hbsp.harvard.edu.

together will give you all the information you might want about
a company or an issue; the difference is that you do not have
a narrative voice that comes with a well-written case. This
means you will have to provide some of the structure yourself,
for instance, by producing an introductory note to describe the
material in a certain sequence and be quite detailed about the
order in which the students should prepare it.

- *Have students find case material online themselves.*

What Do I Do If I Lose Track of the Discussion?

Even the best of case teachers can lose track of the discussion. You
might be trying to plan ahead to the next person you are going to call
on, calculate the time remaining in the class, and assess the material left to discuss, or your attention may simply drift momentarily at
precisely the wrong time.

The key here, as with many of the issues in this chapter and with
case teaching in general, is not to panic or overreact. The easiest
solution is to wait for the student who is speaking to finish, then look
around the room for the next hand, and call on that student to speak.
You can almost always pick up the thread of the discussion again.
Alternatively, you could ask the students to repeat the last part or, if
they were speaking for a long time, to summarize their point in one
sentence. To the students, these will seem like routine questions, not
an indication that you were not paying attention. If you are caught,
don't make a big deal about it. Apologize if appropriate, use humor
("Pardon me, I spaced out there for a second"), and move on.

Teaching can sometimes be excruciatingly boring, at least, if you
lecture. Espen once fell asleep while teaching or, more precisely, he
declared a break and then instantly could not remember what he had
talked about or how far into the subject he had gotten. He solved it by
sneaking a look at some student notes while the class was out of the
room and swore to adopt discussion-based teaching.

A colleague found himself giving the same ten-slide speech over
and over and resorted to randomizing the order of the slides to keep
himself alert, coming up with creative transitions between the slides.

Discussion teaching makes this less likely. The fact that you give up some control to the students means that no matter how many times you have run a case, there will be enough variety to keep you awake.

What If I Run Out of Questions?

This is perhaps one of the greatest fears of case teachers: you have covered your teaching plan but forty-five minutes remain in the class. We often experience this fear when teaching a case for the first time. Neatly planned blocks of time for discussion topics can sometimes collapse in seconds. But only rarely have we run into serious risk of having too much time to fill.

You can do several things to manage this fear. The first is to remind yourself that such a crisis is rare. Next, don't let things get to the point where you are without a closing question or two at the end of class. If you need to find ways to stretch out your teaching plan, do so as early as possible. But try hard not to overcompensate. Finding too little time on the clock is a far more common problem and is often caused by such overcompensation early on. You can always change some of the key facts of the case and ask students how that would affect their analysis.

Finally, keep some material in your proverbial hip pocket. If worse comes to worst, you can be rescued by PowerPoint. This could be a lecture on a relevant piece of theory, a couple of short cases that you can distribute to the class, or just some good stories that relate to the material. You may well go the entire semester without using any of this material, but having it at your disposal will make you less likely to overreact out of anxiety.

How Do I Deal with Problems in an Intensive-Format Course?

When a course meets for seventy-five minutes a few times a week for a quarter or a semester, it is relatively easy to make reasoned adjustments when issues arise. Intensive formats, however, present more challenges. In particular, having one bad class in a typical semester is rarely a problem; having a bad day in an intensive class might represent 20 percent or 40 percent of the entire course.

We have found the following practices helpful when teaching short, intensive courses.

Prepare Differently

Put extra effort into getting to know the students beforehand. This knowledge can speed up your bonding with the group and help you identify potential issues. Organize your notes so that you can make adjustments as quickly as necessary. Check in with your course plan at least daily during the course. With case discussion, you will likely have addressed some material planned for later in the course and missed some issues you hoped to cover in the previous session. If you stay and appear organized, you can head off many problems.

Manage Expectations

Calibrate everyone's expectations, especially yours. Daylong sessions cannot be the same as four classes distributed over a week or two in terms of time to prepare and intensity of discussion. But you can emphasize the benefits of the intensive format for learning, such as the immersive effect and the increased need to use different learning formats (group work, for instance) and play to those strengths, but you might also acknowledge the loss of time to absorb the content and the challenges of being in a room with the same people all day long. We often use humor to keep things light.

Manage Process Closely

Devote some class time to discussing the process. Acknowledge the challenges of the format and check in every day or two to see how everyone is doing. Email students (or write paper notes if they are not online during the day) to address issues. If urgent, you can write these during breaks or while groups are working; otherwise, do it after class ends so that the student can adjust for the next day. Have access to some private or semiprivate space. This is invaluable for discussing a behavioral or performance issue with a student during a break.

What Can I Do If I Am Low on Energy?

Case teaching requires more mental acuity and physical activity than lecturing. We find the process so invigorating that insufficient energy while in the classroom is typically not an issue, even if we are exhausted before and after. But sometimes that adrenaline rush is not enough, particularly when you are teaching all day or all week or if you are sick or distracted by other things. While it can be scary, teaching when you are not at your best is also a wonderful opportunity to practice some techniques you might not use as often when you are feeling well.

Whether or not you share with the class that your energy level is low is up to you. If you do let the class know, be sure to make clear that the discussion pace and intensity do not need to change. You can easily get wrapped up in the discussions and lose sight of proper nutrition. For shorter classes, Bill tends not to eat before class. But in day- or weeklong classes, that habit can be unhealthy.

If you need to conserve physical energy, sit down during class. But don't sit behind the podium at the front of the room; sit on a desk or take a seat with the students. Change seats to punctuate the discussion, emphasize a point, or retake control. Use a computer in lieu of the board or let a student write on the board for the class. If you would rather not sit, lean on student desks or against the back wall of the classroom. This practice is great for making better use of the space.

If you are mentally tired, adapt your teaching plan. Perhaps create a more thorough set of notes than you normally would, particularly about case facts and key analyses. Ask fewer broad, complex questions for which the answers might be harder to follow. Hold more tightly to your intended flow for the discussion to avoid keeping track of too many threads simultaneously.

During the discussion, make use of your best students in two ways: call on them for responses to the most complex questions so that the answers will be less likely to overwhelm you, and call on them immediately following a response that left you at a bit of a loss. Finally, be less ambitious in trying to recall prior comments or minor case details. Speak less and rely more on the class; let one student follow another without saying anything yourself. You can also put students into groups and have them report afterward. You might want to give group work (see chapter 4) and variations on it (such as group presentations) more prominence. It is a great way to reduce the burden on the instructor and keep up the energy level in the room.

What If the Administration Gets Involved?

Some students will not bring their complaints to you, but instead speak to student services, student advisers, your department chair, the dean, or even the president. The normal and correct response— which you have a right to expect—from these people is that they ask the student if he or she has raised the point with you and point the student in your direction if not. When this doesn't happen, it is either because someone *wants* to be involved or because the student has raised an issue she felt she could not raise with you. This can be about personality, feeling discriminated against, or overlooked, or a questioning of how you run your classes, perhaps even of the case-teaching approach itself.

The way to deal with such issues is to anticipate them and inform the administration and your faculty superiors about what you are doing in advance and make them aware that complaints of a certain kind may arise. This counters the "we have to do something" impulse many feel when students complain and increases your ability to keep the initiative.

Being as transparent as possible about your expectations in the course goes a long way toward preventing or managing such complaints. If your processes and criteria are clear, most administrators will be supportive, even in the face of vociferous students. In many cases, administrators will applaud you for increasing the level of student engagement by using case teaching. And once you are known to be reasonable, they will deem many complaints to be unfounded and quash them without ever coming back to you. While this may not be the way you want the administration to get to know you, being known as an organized, demanding teacher interested in student learning will serve you well, assuming the rest of your job performance meets your school's standards.

6

QUANTITATIVE AND
TECHNICAL MATERIAL

Case teaching is used quite commonly in subjects like strategy, marketing, and entrepreneurship but less frequently in subjects that are more quantitative or technical, such as finance or statistics. Tradition plays a big part here, but there are other reasons as well. Quantitative and technical subjects tend to have unique, correct, and presumably less debatable answers. Other factors are declining math skills among business school students that encourage lecturing to explain the basics, and—dare we say it—the disinclination of teachers of quantitative subjects, due to personality and training, to wait for students to inductively figure things out themselves.

We think case teaching of quantitative and technical subjects can help the students better understand the methods and concepts taught. Even more important, by anchoring problems in real-life situations and by having students discuss implications of methods used and answers found, it can move them from routine know-how to critical know-why. In fact, you can argue, as Bill Ellet, author of *The Case Study Handbook* (2007) does, that the recent movement toward the "flipped classroom" is essentially an application of case teaching methodology.

Students in a flipped classroom spend in-class time working on assignments and discussing them with the teacher and their classmates. Teachers of scientific and quantitative subjects—math, physics, biology, chemistry—are currently leading this movement, which is becoming more prevalent as the tools for video creation and sharing improve and become more widespread.

If you need students to do a particular calculation or statistical analysis and you are not sure if they know how to do it, rather than lecturing during class time, you can provide links to online resources explaining it. If you can't find a resource you like, consider creating a short video yourself and posting it online, publicly or privately. Done right, the case discussion in the classroom can be more in-depth earlier than otherwise possible.

Lectures at home, problem solving in the classroom. This is not too far from reading at home and discussing solutions in the classroom, is it?

Flipping the Qualitative and Quantitative

One of the most important aspects of business case teaching is to foster an intuitive understanding of a situation and to learn to think and make decisions like a manager—or a doctor or a lawyer, as case teaching is not limited to business management. It is easy to imagine a case in which a senior physician asks an intern, "Well, here is the patient. What do you do now?"

Cases create opportunities for learning by flipping the hard and the soft—by being qualitative on quantitative cases and quantitative on the qualitative ones. In practice, this means teaching students to question the basis for numbers as well as the results of analysis: Where do the numbers come from? Can we trust them? When we have done our calculations, what do they mean and how much should we trust them? It also means teaching how to do back-of-the-envelope numerical analysis, make assumptions, and use calculations to derive conclusions from descriptions that do not apparently lend themselves to numerical analysis.

The following are a few examples of quantitative-qualitative flips.

Being Qualitative about the Quantitative

You can talk through a quantitative case until most students have more or less the same calculation and then ask, "What do these numbers really mean?" The students will expect this exercise, and the better students will almost always have drawn conclusions based on the numbers. To further the discussion, question the basis for the numbers—where they come from. If you really want to push the students, question the rationality of using the calculations at all. It may be entirely appropriate just to follow the numbers, but challenging their use forces examinations of assumptions, which is always a good thing.

We have found that few students—including executives, though experience breeds skepticism—question numbers even when they should. Great teaching moments occur when presenting the students with numbers that are dodgy, luring them into spending a lot of time chasing quantitative conclusions based on data that, when subjected to common sense, turn out to be fabricated, false, misprinted, or simply nonsensical.

Espen uses such an exercise quite often. He gives the students a data set taken from a well-known trade journal—a listing of five hundred large companies that includes financials, number of employees, IT budgets, and so on. He assigns a spreadsheet containing the data, a copy of the article, and the question, "If you were the CEO of a large company, how would you use these numbers to determine how much you should spend on IT?" The students go to work using various strategies. Some of them (sometimes as many as a third) will not touch the data at all and lay out a verbal strategy for how they *would* have used the numbers. Most will do some perfunctory calculations, generally computing IT spending as a percentage of revenue or IT employees as a percentage of total employees and then observe that there are significant differences between industries. A few will go overboard on data analysis and do multifactor regression analysis without reaching very firm conclusions.

Espen then starts the class by asking a few students to give their analysis based on the assignments handed in the day before. This generates quite a bit of discussion back and forth about how to use the data set. At some point, Espen fires up Excel and asks the students how to do this (taking care to fumble a bit, as teachers are wont to do). The students quickly agree to calculate the IT-revenue ratio, and to look at it by industry. At this point, an interesting phenomenon occurs. For each industry, as many as half of the companies have exactly the same ratio (to the fourth decimal). This generates another discussion, with increasing frustration. Some of the students will even suggest that the companies have colluded to have the same IT spending. Eventually, a bright student will deduce that something is wrong: the magazine has estimated the data for most of the companies since it could not get a precise number for IT spending or even any number at all.

Espen likes to run this exercise toward the end of a course to underscore the importance of always looking at where numbers come from and understanding that they have an unfortunate ability to drown out other arguments. Espen has run this exercise for fifteen years and thousands of students. A total of three students has accurately spotted the data falsification and commented on it. A few more—mostly experienced CEO types—have said that they would never use the data anyway, that they would never base their budgeting decisions on superficial knowledge of what the competition is doing. Many more have told him after class that they were suspicious, but didn't dare say anything against the professor. And many of them were quite angry with themselves and occasionally with Espen for leading them down a track of intensive analysis when some quick eyeballing would have been enough to see the limits of the data.

There is learning in an experience like that.

Being Quantitative about the Qualitative

Being quantitative on qualitative cases means doing calculations in situations where there doesn't seem to be much data. This can make quite an impression on the students. We have seen excellent teachers ask students, "Did you run the numbers?" on cases that have no numbers and then go on to make some back-of-the-envelope calculations based on annual revenues (included in most cases), guesstimated size of market, and likely market share to make a point about, say, the size of a new warehouse.

Students may initially resist this exercise because it relies on extrapolation of case data and outright guessing at times, but it can be quite effective and reinforce the point that estimates help make sense of things, that errors in estimates tend to cancel each other out (and can be tested with sensitivity analysis), and that even quick-and-dirty models can allow for insightful analysis.

The following four techniques facilitate such impromptu analysis in class and help students build their skills. You can prompt such analysis at any point in almost any case, whether it is quantitative by design or not.

Explicitly Teach Estimation

Many students are not trained in how to do estimation. Encourage them to think about probability, perhaps with some sophistication if they have the mathematical background. Incorporate concepts from decision theory and help them understand the impact of cognitive biases on estimations. Domain-specific heuristics are also helpful; for instance, in information technology, the power of processors doubles about every two years. When appropriate, have students do quick-and-dirty calculations ("Can we get the right order of magnitude?") or even complete simulations to reach estimates.

Quantify Anything

For any topic, ask what metrics should be used to measure it. Once you have those metrics, give some hypotheticals and require students to calculate them. Sometimes, you may be able to use details from the case to drive this discussion. But if the case doesn't have any numbers, don't let that stop you.

Know the Industry Data

If you are teaching a reasonably sized, experienced MBA class, you will often have a student or two with experience in the industry and you can turn to him or her for rough estimates. If your students do not have such experience, then for each case you teach, spend a few minutes looking up some basic information about the industry, including financial ratios, basic organizational structures, nature and costs of technologies used, and labor statistics. This makes on-the-fly analysis remarkably more compelling. When you ask, "What would it cost to open a new store?" having a sense of the size of an average store, the number of workers, and other details that are grounded in reality

---

Back-of-the-Envelope Calculation Example

During the 1990s and 2000s, Dell Computer evolved a business model of selling computers made to order, first via telephone orders and then over the Internet. The company took payment by credit card and then sent the computer to the customer in two to four weeks, a business model with favorable cash flow. How much was this business worth?

You can set up a calculation by looking at its sales ($53 billion in 2010 with $9 billion gross margin) and making the following three assumptions:

- Half of what it spent was for components (probably too high, but the company is a combiner of components, not a producer).

- It paid its suppliers net sixty days (a bit low) and took ownership of a component when it was put into production.

- It had a 4 percent internal rate of return.

Here is the full calculation:

$$\left(\frac{\$53\,billion - \$9\,billion}{2}\right) \times .04 \times \left(\frac{60}{360}\right) \approx \$146\,million$$

This is a nice number, but it is just 0.28 percent of the $53 billion in revenues, which can lead to a discussion of how significant the financial aspects of build-to-order are. How does it compare to traditional manufacturing with work-in-process inventory? Perhaps the lack of technology obsolescence is more important? And is it worth the extra cost of flexible manufacturing, particularly as the technology matures and customers demand less customization?

changes the discussion. You don't need encyclopedic knowledge, just enough to pepper in some flavor, and you can often find quite good industry data with a quick search online, from industry associations and other organizations.

Change Assumptions or Problems on the Fly

Changing parameters is an excellent way to involve more students in the discussion of a specific technique. Changing the assumptions could include the sign of one of the variables ("Suppose sales were decreasing rather than increasing"), macroeconomic variables ("What would hyperinflation do to this analysis?"), or political ("What if the regulatory environment were more strict?"). You can also change the problem by asking about a different customer, industry, type of investment, or similar variables.

Teaching Quantitative Material

In principle, there is no difference between teaching quantitative and qualitative cases. You need to know the case in detail, have a plan for the topics you want covered and the order to cover them in, and have an open mind about how much you are in control of what happens. A key difference is that you will need a better understanding of the types of errors students make, something that gets much easier after you have taught the case a couple of times.

We often hear from faculty who teach quantitative courses that the "no right answer" standard for cases is well and good for management courses, but it doesn't apply in their courses. While we think there is generally a lot of room for qualitative analysis and for subjective analysis, sometimes there is a unique, correct answer. This requires adapting the teaching plan we discussed in chapter 3.

Making a Teaching Plan for a Quantitative Case

Naturally, your quantitative analysis will figure prominently in your teaching plan. When preparing the numbers, once you are sure your analysis is sound, consider what different assumptions or errors students are likely to make. If it is feasible, run the numbers several different ways to help you identify issues during the discussion. Teaching notes may provide some guidance, and speaking with faculty who have taught the case before can be invaluable. Be very structured, use good examples, and build up the content so that the students can create modules of learning that they can refer back to.

Many faculty used to lecturing worry that if every student in the room has the correct answer, then there is nothing left to discuss. As with qualitative cases, this need not be true. There are several options for dealing with this situation:

- Explore whether students took different approaches.

- Change the assumptions.

- Discuss the qualitative implications of the numbers.

- Integrate the analysis with concepts from other cases or class sessions.

Pacing the Discussion

The pace of coverage of topics in a case-based class will typically be slower than in a lecture, for two reasons. First, you become more aware of students who have not grasped the material, and, second, by asking students to apply the topics in practice, you are expecting a more sophisticated grasp of them. You will need to make a realistic assessment of how much material you can cover. While the amount of coverage may feel unambitious compared to what you could cover in a lecture, given the depth of coverage and exposure to student knowledge and thinking, you can be more confident in your assessment of your students' ability to apply the material in practice.

A primary driver of how much material you can cover will be how well students have prepared, as in all case discussion classes. All of the advice we have given elsewhere in the book about encouraging students to prepare applies for technical and quantitative material as well. If you do not have the luxury of a support system for students in addition to you (such as teaching assistants, tutors, or labs) and either you cannot require groups to work outside of class or they have not been effective, then you need to ensure that the discussion helps all of the students. You should not feel obligated to ensure that every student leaves the class with a complete grasp of all the material covered. Some students will need more time to absorb it and may need to do more work on their own after class to get fully up to speed.

Keep in mind that most concepts will be addressed in more than one class discussion, so not all students need to grasp the material completely in any given session. As a rule of thumb, most of the students should grasp most of the material in most of the classes. If nearly all the students are completely grasping everything, you should throttle up the level of rigor and intensity. How you fine-tune depends on the role of the course in the program. If you are teaching a course intended to weed out students ill-suited to a program, then leaving some in the dust is appropriate and perhaps merciful. On the other hand, if the course is required in the core curriculum, then teaching only to the strongest students would be misguided.

Asking for a Number at the Beginning

A simple poll at the beginning of class allows you to assess the variance in the answers in the classroom. You can also collect the answers from students the night before class via a learning management system or even email.

Once you have the responses, you can glean some critical information to help you structure the discussion:

- When there is a correct answer, are there students who got it? You might prefer to start with another, wrong answer, or go directly to a correct one. This also gives you a sense of how well students are doing.

- Did some fall into predictable traps? You might start with these to draw out a discussion of common errors.

- What are the lowest and highest numbers? Having these students justify their conclusions sets up a powerful debate. If you want to involve other students, have them pick one side or the other rather than defending their numbers in the middle.

Managing Math Phobia and Aversion to Numbers

Many students feel and express discomfort with working with numbers. Distinguish their reasons for aversion and treat them differently. Depending on your school and the nature of the interaction between faculty and students, you might make these adjustments individually or for all of the students during class time.

We typically encounter three types of challenging students: the phobic, those with shaky math skills, and those who may have the skills but don't like to run numbers in cases.

The phobic have genuine, palpable anxiety when working with numbers. Many have traumatic memories of previous quantitative courses, and their stress shows in class.

Even if you are lucky enough to have mathematics courses as prerequisites for your quantitative course, you are likely to have a significant number of students with little facility in the underlying mathematics, quantitative reasoning, problem solving, or formal logic. Bill still shudders when he recalls a joke based on a second derivative that he made early in his career in an undergraduate course with a calculus prerequisite. After making the joke, all he can remember is thirty-seven blank stares and the sound of a cricket chirping in the distance.

Some students may have the ability to run the numbers, but they hate doing it with a passion so abiding that it can override everything else. Overcoming these problems requires explicit effort on your part. We suggest the following four strategies.

Making the Value Clear

In every class, you have to reinforce the reasons quantitative skills are valuable and necessary. We find this necessary even in elective courses. All of the selling techniques described in chapter 3 apply.

Acknowledging the Phobic

While empathy can often help, it needs to come with a message that students need to work through their anxieties. Often you can improve their experience dramatically by acknowledging that they will be anxious during the course and advising them to accept this anxiety rather than fight it or self-flagellate over it. Let them know they are not alone; while everyone in the room may seem confident about his or her ability with numbers, many are actually quite nervous. If you are able to help them develop a greater sense of self-efficacy, their anxiety will abate.

Filling in the Holes

Provide resources for students to review material from prerequisite classes on which you are relying. Be sure to point to some resources that require little or no knowledge of the prerequisite classes, because some students may retain little or nothing from those courses. If you have the luxury, such as for a popular advanced elective, require a proficiency exam before your class starts. If that is not feasible, then start the course slowly in terms of the prior knowledge necessary to solve the problems; this gives students a chance to redevelop their fundamental skills. For the first few class sessions, consider distributing a summary of the key calculations after the class.

Fostering a Sense of Self-Efficacy

If students feel completely lost from the outset, many of them will be demoralized, and you will have a hard time getting them back. This does not mean that early discussions in the course need to be trivial or that all students need to get all of the analysis correct. But you do want to provide grounds for hope for all in the room.

Don't base all of the analysis required for a case early on in the semester on deep knowledge from prerequisites, for example. Provide opportunities for earnest but weak students to contribute to the discussion and complete part of the analysis even if they struggle with the more advanced aspects. During the course, increase that base-level requirement and remind students of the progress they have made.

Using the Board

Writing on the board in a quantitative case class can be intimidating. You may not have worked through all the numbers that are coming at you, and some of them are likely to be flawed. For faculty who never put anything incorrect on the board, this can be a monumental challenge. We suggest not being so doctrinaire about what to write on the board, but consider keeping one board with only final (correct) answers. Never knowingly put a wrong number there. You can then move something to that board as the standard for correctness (when answers are right or wrong).

Bill asks, "Does this go on that [correct answers only] board? Are we sure?" Use another board as work space for leading the class through its analysis. Show all or as much as you consider appropriate of each student's work on this board. If the students work through a subsection of the problem correctly, then transcribe it onto the board you reserved for correct work. This method works extremely well when you are working through a problem with many steps.

For more complex problems, you may prefer to use a computer when going over numbers. But rather than relying on a prefabricated PowerPoint presentation, build a spreadsheet dynamically. We discuss the use of in-class technology in chapter 10.

Turning Control Over to a Student

For most of the time in a case discussion class, students are speaking and in control of the room. But we have found that relatively few faculty are comfortable having a student come to the front of the room and take control of the boards or projection equipment. However, in a quantitative class, this may be the best way for students to convey their analysis. We encourage this technique and use it ourselves, but manage it carefully.

Here are some ways we have found to facilitate the process:

- Do whatever you can to smooth the transition to the student, such as having an empty board accessible or an easy way for the student to access necessary files and applications for projection.

- Take a seat to signal that you have yielded the floor.

- Ask guiding questions to keep the presenter from drifting.

- Wrap it up before the audience stops paying attention.

Making the Best Use of Students

Identifying the skills, knowledge, and level of preparation in the room is helpful. The more you can learn about the students before the course starts, the better. Look for any information that might indicate students who will do well with the material: undergraduate major, relevant skills, work experience, or interest in the topic. If nothing else, just knowing the generally high-performing and well-prepared students will help you calibrate the level of rigor for the group and for individuals and identify potential resources when you need them later (and you will).

If you are teaching a heterogeneous group with some students well versed in the concepts and others entirely new to the field, you need to find ways to keep the knowledgeable students engaged without losing the neophytes. To do this, you need to identify the students with relevant backgrounds, assess their skills (just because they've had course work, doesn't mean they know the material), and make sure they are both integrated into the class and periodically challenged.

Call on them when other students in the class are struggling with concepts (you might forewarn them with an email before class). This requires them to pay attention to what the students are saying, because they know they may be called on to correct or expand on comments that are made. But you need to resist the temptation to go too far into advanced concepts that are beyond the scope of the course and the students' ability to understand. You can generally keep students with extensive prior knowledge challenged by pushing on the application of the concepts rather than esoterica about the concepts themselves.

When Students Go Wrong

If a student has made an error, you have several options, each of which can prove useful in the right circumstances:

- Allow the student to continue. Here you run a great danger of leaving other students in the class confused about what the right answer is. If the error is minor and the student is otherwise doing well in terms of the quality and clarity of her analysis, then you can allow her to continue as long as you correct the error before the end of class.

- Move on to another student. Depending on the severity of the error, you might have the next student pick up where the prior one left off, go back to some earlier point in the analysis, or return to the very beginning.

- Ask clarifying questions to guide a student toward the correct answer. Your tone here can be supportive and encouraging, or more like an interrogation, depending on the signal you want to send. We reserve the harsh interrogation for groups where we are confident about their quantitative skills and in our relationship to the class. Singling out a student for harsh treatment, particularly when you are digging for a specific answer, can easily alienate you from the class if you have not established sufficient social capital.

- Get help from another student. This powerful technique is our favorite, if the student just needs a bit of help that you believe another student can provide.

- Correct the student yourself. You are likely to find this the most tempting option. But the more you directly correct students, the more you erode discussion. That does not mean it is inappropriate in all instances. Make the correction yourself if it is minor (a couple of digits transposed, a misplaced decimal point, a small omission), if the student has been providing a superb analysis for a while and presented a solitary error, or if you are pressed for time at the end of class.

When No One Has the Correct Analysis

Sometimes no student in the room has done the correct analysis. While relatively uncommon, particularly in classes with more than a couple of dozen students, it does happen. During class, you will have to decide how much value there is in chasing down a few blind alleys. If you have some slack in the course (and in quantitative courses, in particular, we urge you to build some in), then allowing the class to struggle with the problem can be a wonderful learning experience, assuming it is going in the right direction. If you think the students will not reach the correct analysis on their own, you may choose to guide them toward it during the class, as a homework assignment after the class supported by a supplemental reading, or in a subsequent session.

A key criterion for deciding whether to explore an incorrect analysis is how much can be learned from it. Is this a mistake many students in the class have made? Is this an error likely to recur in subsequent sessions?

If you want to explain the analysis during the class session, then the first step is to break the analysis down as much as possible so that you don't need to be heavy-handed in guiding the conversation in all aspects of the discussion. Perhaps you need to explain only a couple of fairly small but critical points and students can build the rest on their own.

Discussing a Quantitative Case with Subjective Numbers or Estimates

Quantitative analysis for business often requires subjective estimates or assumptions. For most cases, a thorough analysis does not yield a uniquely correct answer. In finance, the variance might come from how beta is calculated, assumptions about future growth, or the choice of market comparables. In operations management, assumptions about labor efficiency, logistics issues, and process complexity all drive differences. In marketing, different perceptions of consumer behavior, channel relationships, and marketing costs all affect the outcome. In many cases, there are myriad appropriate approaches to conducting the analysis as well. So how do we plan for and manage this in the class discussion?

You have two basic choices during the discussion: use your numbers or those of the students. There are positive and negative aspects to each. The more you use your numbers, the more certain you are that they are correct (although even faculty make mistakes). This reduces confusion for you and for the students, but it also risks becoming a game in which students try to guess what your analysis is. At the other extreme, you can have one or more students go through the steps of their analysis. This entails a great deal more risk. Students may make errors in logic or calculation that can be difficult to spot during the discussion. The group might become confused. Putting students on the spot this way can be uncomfortable for all involved.

If your primary goal for the class session is to understand the formal logic but not necessarily the minutia of the numbers, then having students provide the structure but substituting your numbers on the board for consistency can work well. You can involve multiple students in the discussion without introducing inconsistent numbers that would not yield a coherent solution. But we urge you to use the students' numbers whenever possible, even if it might be messy. When the analysis is subjective, the variance you get from the students' analysis is valuable for learning. If you encounter an error in logic, you can employ the strategies discussed earlier to correct it, or simply point it out and let the student continue if the rest of the analysis is sound.

Using Groups

Depending on admissions requirements to your program and prerequisites for your course, you might have students who struggle to learn the theoretical material on their own. Groups can be an invaluable support for these students. If logistics prevent requiring in-person meetings, you can still require online group discussions. By carefully phrasing questions for these discussions and requiring responses from each student, you can dramatically improve the understanding of theoretical concepts before the case discussion begins. If possible, seed each of the groups with a student or two with expertise in the topics so that they can provide support to struggling students. The same advice applies to work assigned after case discussions. You can also use group work in class to reinforce understanding of concepts. These can be brief or extended discussions of case topics or purely theoretical concepts.

Oddly enough, we have found that many students with excellent quantitative knowledge overlook the application of the appropriate skills when presented with a case rather than a problem set. For instance, Bill has taught master's students in finance who omit accounting for the time value of money (a very basic concept) when making a business decision in an information technology case. This alone is an excellent reason for using cases.

Teaching Technical Material

"Technology" is a scary word to many students (and quite a few faculty, too). We have had the experience of doubling the number of students signing up for a course simply by removing the word "technology" from the title. Nevertheless, neither students nor faculty can escape technology as a case topic, given that changes in technology drive much of business change, and responding to change, no matter what position one occupies or aspires to, is a priority for managers and leaders everywhere. We have to teach students about technology, but given that they tend to have little technical background, how can we do it?

To be effective, you must overcome the students' technology fear, but also deal with the legitimate difficulty in learning the complexities of the topic. The former you have to do with motivational techniques, the latter by teaching the students what each element means until they understand it, then putting the elements together and gradually developing a vocabulary of technology terms.

Motivating the Study of Technology

Just as you cannot motivate grade school students to like math by saying that it is easy and fun—it isn't—you can't motivate business students to like technology because it is fascinating. Instead, we recommend motivating students by underscoring the importance of technological understanding in business, by giving examples of how technological attributes influence business, and by emphasizing that knowing how the technology works and evolves helps you avoid costly mistakes (Andersen, 2005).

Espen once gave an assignment to a class of basic strategy students. He told them to pretend they worked for a producer of inkjet printers—HP, Canon, Epson, or Lexmark, for instance. In the inkjet business, the printers are very cheap, and companies make all their money on the ink cartridges, a strategy sometimes called the "razor and blade" strategy since it is used in that industry as well as in elevators, where you make your money on servicing them. The inkjet printer industry is challenged by producers of off-brand ink cartridges as well as companies that refill original cartridges or sell refill tools. The students were tasked with coming up with strategies for the inkjet printer companies to protect their business model.

When it came time to start the discussion, Espen started it by asking, "So, how does an inkjet printer work?"

The students were rather irritated and said so. They were business school students, their remit was marketing, sales, and profitability, and the details of how the product worked did not concern them. Espen pointed out that there is another market—laser printers— where the equipment is expensive and the ink relatively cheaper. Why so? The students suggested that laser printers were for businesses and inkjets for the home.

Espen proceeded to show that in inkjet printers, the print mechanism does not have any moving parts and, although expensive to develop, it is cheap to produce. It can be miniaturized and be on the cartridge, making the printer itself a relatively simple paper-moving device. A laser printer, on the other hand, has a very expensive light-sensitive roll, which (at least until 2008) could not be removed from the printer itself. Hence, the printer technologies themselves heavily influence the strategy of the companies selling them.

In other words, if you know the technology, you understand the business model.

Structuring the Teaching of Technology

Teaching technology through cases is less about teaching the technology itself than making the students understand the consequences of changes in technology. The practicalities of it are much like teaching quantitative cases as we described earlier. You make sure that students understand each part and maintain a pace that allows for reflection.

To facilitate understanding and reflection, we recommend these strategies:

- Provide notes and other material to explain how the technology works. These are available from many sources: case clearinghouses, articles in trade magazines or web sites, and Wikipedia (but be a bit careful; there can be too much information about technologies). Don't forget pointers to videos and presentations. There are also web sites dedicated to videos about how things work, but the quality can be uneven, from both technical and pedagogical perspectives. Provide pointers to material you think is correct.

- If at all possible, try to provide testing grounds, where the students can learn technology by using it. For most web-based technology, this is not very hard: you set up exercises that force the students to use the technology. If the discussion is about use of videoconferencing, teach the class or set up group exercises using desktop videoconferencing; if the topic is crowdsourcing, have the students edit Wikipedia (see the example in chapter 2); if the topic is about creating web sites, have the students set up blogs or mock company web sites using freely available tools and services.

- Use students as much as possible to explain how things work and to reflect on the nature of technological industries. You can do this by calling on them in the classroom or by putting together physical or virtual groups, making sure there are people with technical experience in each group.

- During the discussion, stop and explain (or, better, have someone else explain) what technologies mentioned are and what they do.

When diving into the case, take time to provide structure to the discussion and ensure students understand what difference technologies make. We have found that starting complicated cases by building a timeline can be useful, especially if you can refer to technology from earlier times. On the timeline, relate technologies to each other and tease out what they mean in terms of functionality, cost, maintenance, standards, and effect on business model, not to mention what factors encourage or discourage technology adoption. Use the timeline strategy sparingly, however. It can consume a large amount of discussion time.

A peculiar problem with technology-rich courses is that quite often the technology-savvy students do not do very well. We have both had students who come to classes on IT management or technology strategy and think that they will do very well because they have had long experience programming computers, configuring networks, or otherwise getting their hands dirty. Surprisingly often, these students don't ace the technology management classes.

There tend to be two reasons for this. Often, they think that because they know the technology, they can relax and not prepare well, which leads their analyses to be more colored by industry folklore and prejudices than solid thinking. At other times, they cannot articulate their thoughts about the technology because they know it too well, that is, their deep but often narrow expertise does not allow them to think in the abstract. Occasionally, their self-defined expertise turns out not to be so deep after all. Faking technical skill is not hard as long as your audience knows less than you.

In any case, be aware of this problem and think about how to manage it, especially the disappointment many of the technically minded students can feel when the grades come in. If they are particularly boastful about their background early in the course, have a careful word with them and explain that knowing the technology does not equate to knowing how to manage an organization and its strategy.

Conclusion

Teaching quantitative and technical material in a case class poses special challenges, but allows for contextualizing the numbers and the technology, questioning assumptions, and highlighting the importance of applying analysis to situations where numbers seem to be lacking. We strongly advocate using case teaching to teach the quantitative and the technological. You will teach *know-why* rather than *know-how,* which in our minds is infinitely more important.

References

Andersen, E. "The S-curves of Sinks, and Technology." *ACM Ubiquity* 6, no. 19 (2005). http://ubiquity.acm.org/article.cfm?id=1071926

Ellet, W. *The Case Study Handbook: How to Read, Discuss, and Write Persuasively About Cases.* Boston: Harvard Business School Press, 2007.

7

ADJUSTING FOR LANGUAGE AND CULTURE

Higher education is increasingly a global business. The number of students attending university outside their native countries is rising all over the world, many business schools are establishing campuses and joint programs in other countries, and the market for international teachers, especially in the executive market, is growing. Globalization increases the need for teachers—especially case teachers—to understand and be prepared for challenges arising from language and cultural differences.

English is the *lingua franca* of business higher education, so we will discuss this issue by assuming you teach in English. The challenges then come in three flavors:

- The *foreign student*—accommodating foreign students in your English-speaking classroom.

- The *foreign teacher*—the challenges you face as a teacher when English is not your first language and you need to teach in it.

- The English-speaking *teacher abroad*—issues when you do not speak the primary language of the country in which you are teaching and might not be familiar with the culture.

In our opinion, international differences are often overplayed, at least in a business school classroom setting. Business students often seem to us more similar to each other than they do to their compatriot students in other majors. Language, not culture, is often the main issue, but there are some cultural differences as well, such as expectations about teaching, the power relationship between teacher and student, and students' behavior when interacting with the teacher and each other. It is useful to know about these differences, but don't panic: most students get used to foreigners quickly and keep an open mind. After all, they will meet foreigners in their jobs after they finish—if they haven't already—so getting to understand them when studying is just good practice.

Language of Instruction

A recurring question at many schools in non-English-speaking countries is, "Should classes be taught in English or in the native language?" Opinions differ based on local customs, language proficiency of the teacher and students, students' ages and backgrounds, and school policy. Requiring English holds back some students, but makes "foreign" (exchange students, for instance) students more likely to participate, and can increase diversity of viewpoints and, in many cases, the level and quality of discussion. There is little reason to hold sessions in English if everyone in the class is more comfortable in the local language, but every reason to hold it in English if that is not the case.

A common rule, especially in European business schools, is that if at least one student in a class wants the language to be English, then it should be. Many faculty ask at the first class meeting; we recommend surveying the students before the first class to allow those who want English to indicate this without fear of hard stares from their less anglophile colleagues.

We begin with a caveat: we have had students from every corner of the world and have taught courses and facilitated discussions in more than fifteen countries. Still, we do not pretend to have anything approaching a complete overview of the topic. Neither does anyone else. And we write this chapter mostly from a European-American perspective because, well, that's what we are. Hence, take what we say here as a starting point based on experience (in some cases, falling flat on our faces) and make a conscious effort to learn from your own experience. This is not something you should panic over; most students are quite forgiving. Don't overthink it.

The Foreign Student

Having foreign students in your class adds valuable perspectives, but also raises challenges: the foreign student may not, for language or other reasons, be capable of participating with the same facility as the domestic ones. One or a few students are easy to deal with, but in many schools, the number of foreign students has increased well beyond that.

Your school may offer orientation for foreign students. This is likely to include some basic information about functioning in the country and local area as well as academic information, including standards and norms. Be sure to find out what students have learned in these sessions and supplement (or correct) as appropriate.

We often have foreign students request that we exempt them from speaking in class on account of their poor English. We never concede to this, telling them that the ability to speak English at an acceptable level is mandatory for acceptance in any business school program taught in the language. This attitude places the responsibility with the student and exempts you from making special considerations, but it does not solve the participation problem. In particular, a student who makes slow and incomprehensible comments can break up the flow of discussion quite badly and reduce energy in the classroom.

We advocate dealing with this in the same way you deal with students with speech impediments or other issues that make it hard to contribute. Group work or working in pairs may help, allowing students to discuss between themselves. Discreetly alerting a student with poor language skills that you will call on him to open the next class can give him time to prepare himself and find the right words, and perhaps script some of his remarks. Note that you don't want students to script everything. There is a danger that some students will script comments even when they don't know they will be called on and then either inject the comments when not relevant or fail to participate because they never found a slot where their canned comments would fit.

As you gain experience, you will develop your ability to understand bad English. But remember that this is not necessarily true for your English-speaking students, so you may have to go back and forth in the classroom discussion to make sure everyone understands what is meant.

Conversely, we sometimes see students with excellent English skills and a gregarious personality (in other words, stereotypically American students, but they can come from anywhere) dominate the classroom, even though their comments can be shallow. As a teacher, it can be tempting to lean on those students because they sustain tempo and energy in the classroom. Avoid this. Instead, keep them on reserve for tricky situations and make doubly sure that they direct their comments to the other students rather than at you and that their comments build on previous contributions. Be sure to ask follow-up questions to show that you know when students are giving superficial answers.

Even if a foreigner speaks excellent English, you need to understand that a foreign student, no matter how good, can face difficulties participating in a conversation. Until you have lived in a place for a year or two, you will have a hard time following a rapid discussion, simply because you have to translate everything you hear and then formulate an answer. For example, Espen's native language is Norwegian. He came to the United States as a graduate student speaking fluent English, but found that it took him two years to get up to speed on colloquialisms and language puns to the point to where he could participate in the rapid lunchtime repartee.

Be aware that foreign students can say things that sound outrageous and provocative but aren't necessarily meant that way. Many direct translations from a foreign language to English (and the other way) can have connotations that the students may be unaware of, especially with regard to race and gender.

For instance, a foreigner might characterize a woman of mature years as a "girl" by making a direct translation from his language into English, because in the foreign language, "girl" simply means "a lively and youthful woman," but in English, it can be pejorative or biased. Likewise, some languages (German and those spoken in Scandinavia) can seem almost confrontationally direct when translated literally to English, just as English literally translated sometimes can seem very rude to a Japanese person. Attitudes toward swearing, sexual jokes, and religion differ around the world—an Englishman swears and makes political jokes that would be offensive to many Americans. Some students pick up what they think is normal everyday language from music videos and comedy shows and might not understand that the incessant swearing and sexual innuendo in them is not permissible in everyday speech.

Verbal Faux Pas in the Classroom

If a student says something outrageous in the classroom, Espen prefers to move on and speak with the offending student during a break. Bill prefers to address it directly in the moment to signal that such comments are unacceptable. Depending on the context, his response might range from a lighthearted correction to a serious discussion.

Whatever you do, don't start a public confrontation based on gut reactions, unless the student says something that clearly is meant to be offensive, in which case you can make that a point of discussion. Make sure you also deal with offended students, lest you get an escalating situation on your hands.

Be aware that words sometimes do not have direct translations into other languages. Espen had trouble with words like "leverage," "ubiquitous," and "disruption" (in the technology sense) when he was a graduate student, simply because a whole sentence, if not paragraphs, is needed to convey the precise meaning in Norwegian. This goes both ways. In Norway, foreigners joke, a sharp intake of breath can constitute a fully formed sentence. A word like *kladdeføre*—meaning a specific set of snow conditions for cross-country skiing—would require at least a long paragraph to translate to an American, in both its literal and figurative uses. These issues are not limited to non-English speakers; Australian, Indian, and British English contain plenty of expressions that can cause grizzling when you really should be doing the needful and be chuffed to bits about it.

Making Adjustments for Foreign Students

To the extent possible, adapt your course, using cases and readings with a wide range of countries covered and with diverse protagonists. For the discussion to be effective, be conscious about some behaviors that you and your domestic students might have:

- Many foreign students originate from rote-learning cultures based on replication. They are unaccustomed to working with abstractions, "unreal" concepts, or theoretical frameworks. You can help them by being explicit and clear both in the syllabus and in the discussions, avoiding jumping between concepts without preparation, and giving explanations such as showing them how to do a (mini) case analysis.

- There are significant differences between cultures in what is discussable in a classroom. While it is perfectly OK to ask an American student about career goals and life ambitions, even in class, students in Europe and Asia see this as intrusive, even in a business school. Religion can be openly referred to (for example, as in commenting on going to church on Sundays) in the United States but is seen as intensely personal in Northern Europe and totally inappropriate in a Chinese classroom.

- Ensure that all idioms that arise in the discussions are defined. If possible, include the etymology, which can make the definitions more interesting to domestic students as well.

- Do not casually mention local companies, even if they are big names in your country, without explaining who they are. For instance, many well-known U.S. companies frequently used as management examples (Nordstrom, Verizon, Comcast, Best Buy, AT&T, USAA, Sears) do not operate outside the United States, at least not under their domestic brand names and with their standard offerings. This is even more important when referring to specific executives of these companies. Some references might work if the students have been in residence for most of a year at least.

- Have a broader view of the capabilities of local companies compared to foreign companies in the same industry. Glibly citing best practices from domestic firms can strain credibility, for instance, when referring to the U.S. banking, mobile communications, and airline industries, which substantially trail those in much of the world.

- Qualify statements about workplace norms. Long hours are common in some countries, even in spite of laws to the contrary, while rare in others. In some countries, notably the United States, firing is a viable and often acceptable option. In many other countries, it is either nearly impossible or prohibitively expensive for all but the most egregious cases.

- Avoid sports metaphors or at least explain them. Even terms you consider widely understood (*home run*, *offside*, and *slam dunk*) are likely to be lost on some foreign students and, in our experience, some domestic students as well.

- Explain your media references. Foreign students may be unfamiliar with even the most popular local personalities, programs, and widely visited web sites. Bill spent several semesters advising Chinese students to look things up or post videos on YouTube only to learn that the site is blocked in China.

- Job titles and organizational structures vary widely across the globe. Be sure to define such terms as *corporate, company, enterprise, division,* and *SBU,* and the responsibilities of jobs such as vice president and director.

- If you have a mix of U.S. and non-U.S. students, give distances and volumes in both metric and English units, but only when precision is relevant. It is rather annoying to hear people translate "about 100 yards" to "about 92 meters."

The Foreign Teacher

Many business schools around the world now have classes and even whole programs taught in English. This can be a challenge to faculty with less than stellar language chops. While they may speak understandable English, managing a discussion can seem like a formidable challenge, especially if they are mentally thumbing their way through a dictionary while doing it.

There are a number of ways to remedy this situation. First, you need to realize that linguistic perfection is not a requirement for a teacher, especially not in the United States. In fact, students tend to be quite forgiving about language details as long as you are knowledgeable about what you are teaching, are willing to listen, and are visibly making an effort. If the class has a number of non-native English speakers, you may actually be better off than the native-speaking teacher, simply because you are aware that your language—and that of the other speaker—might be imprecise.

Business negotiations tend to work well when both sides are imperfect English speakers, because they will keep going back and forth until they are sure they both understand what the other side means, whereas the perfect English speaker will deliver a carefully honed sentence and think the issue is understood and settled. (In one international company we know, a decision was made to have "broken English" as the official company language, something that quite scared the Oxford-educated CEO, who nervously mumbled that he had not the faintest idea of how to do that.)

One of our colleagues has a heavy Latin American accent and dresses with flamboyance and a lively color sense. Espen once invited him to Oslo to teach a quite complicated case he had written and watched with some anxiety as he scooted back and forth in front of the room, exhorting the Norwegian students (who looked austere in comparison) to opine on the case. Espen stole a glance at his co-teacher (an experienced American) and both thought, "He is way too Latin for this audience." We needn't have worried. In five minutes, he had the students hanging on every word, hands in the air to join a discussion far livelier than Espen ever had managed. Personality and knowledge always win, if you allow for a little setup and a few minutes for the audience to adjust.

Of course, you may have genuine language issues and lack the compensation of an exuberant personality. Our advice would be to acknowledge this, without making too much of a fuss about it, and work on simplifying your task as much as possible in order to have energy and attention to devote to understanding what people are saying. Though you do less talking when case teaching, the language requirements are at least as high as when lecturing; you need to process the input from the students in real time.

Acknowledging your language difficulties with students can go a long way. By sharing the fact that you are struggling with this (and you could not hide it for long anyway), you can gain empathy with students as long as they see you are working hard at it. Don't overdo this, though. What you consider a serious problem with language may not be seen that way by all students; and as with many other things, you don't want your acknowledgment to become the confirmation of a problem many students did not have.

Your language difficulties do not translate to an easier time for students: you can turn your language deficiencies into strength by keeping your own contributions to a minimum, moving from one student to the next without inserting your own comments. Couple this with careful follow-up questions to get students to clarify their comments, ostensibly to make things easier to understand for you (and other participants with language problems). You can create quite a challenge for the students. Being asked to explain something in simpler terms is a very good way to expose shoddy thinking and casually used jargon. Your quest for clarity and simple language may come off as an inquisitive and precise mind.

Simplification is a question of brain processing power. Since you will need your brain cycles to think in a foreign language, you should work on making everything else as simple as possible. When preparing the class, pay particular attention to structure, check your board language in advance if you can, and be meticulous about what goes where.

Try to avoid doing several things at once. If you are overwhelmed by writing on the board while simultaneously facilitating a discussion, consider appointing students to serve as scribes who will manage the board, allowing you to focus more on the conversation. Keep to your time plan, and make sure as you go that the students see the points clearly.

The Teacher Abroad

When you are teaching abroad, you are in effect a guest and can't impose your own rules to the same extent as you can at your home institution. You need to approach the situation with some politeness until you become familiar with the new environment. Spending some time and effort understanding the culture of where or whom you teach can be fruitful. Speak to people who have taught, studied, or lived in the country. Read guides about the culture and, if time permits, some literature as well. Consume some local media online. If you are pressed for time, at least skim a few web pages about the culture on your flight over.

But don't overestimate the differences. We have found that, generally, business school students are more alike than they are different. There is an international business culture, and you probably represent it (or would want to) and most students aspire to it. Differences aren't necessarily strongest between countries. Business school students from Shanghai and New York probably have more in common in attitudes and aspirations than students from Shanghai and a regional university in China, for instance.

Whenever possible, try to link the content to local behavior, but don't overdo it. Part of your value is your outside perspective. Be careful if you are tempted to joke about national stereotypes. You can make jokes, but you must unambiguously signal that you don't believe in stereotypes. Also, when making observations about the country you are teaching in, try not to repeat the same clichés everyone does; for instance, observing that Shanghai and Beijing have become modern cities in a remarkably short time is now trite. Treat the classroom as if you are visiting someone's home. As you get to know the students better, you can increase the breadth of issues discussed and the level of candor.

We have found that the issues you need to think about when teaching abroad fall in three categories:

- Differences in expectations for teaching

- Differences in the power between teacher and student

- Differences in expected student behavior in the classroom

Expectations for Teaching

Students' expectations of teaching and learning differ between countries. In general, students in northern Europe and the United States expect to interact with the teacher, both in and outside the classroom, to a much greater extent than those in most of Asia and southern and eastern Europe, where straight lecturing—even straight reading of manuscripts—is common. In many countries, a good student is a note-taking machine, accustomed to acing exams by repeating back what the teacher has said in class and what is written in books and articles. Students can have problems responding when asked to give their personal opinion because they lack training in discussion and quite often lack the presentation skills that many U.S. and European students get from their early school years. Language skills and contextual knowledge (for instance, about international economy or politics) can also be an issue. This is changing, and changing quite rapidly. Business school teachers in China, for instance, are increasingly educated in the United States or Europe and import a more interactive style.

Group preparation and presentations can be a useful way to overcome these varying expectations and also reduce personal risk of failure. In some Asian countries, being caught unprepared or otherwise lacking in the classroom is a very shameful event and a loss of face, and this personal shame extends beyond the classroom. An instructor who puts a student in such an embarrassing situation also loses face. The students can be very protective of each other.

Students who present as a group are much more willing to take chances and receive criticism, because there is much less danger of individuals losing face. Don't, however, overplay this. If you have been clear about expectations for preparation ahead of time—and all of our advice in previous chapters still applies—then you should hold the students to them. Be careful about criticizing an individual student in public, though. In many cultures, criticism is OK if it is done discreetly and the individual student is not publicly exposed. As your relationship with the class builds, you will have more latitude to engage individuals directly.

Teacher Power

The power differential between teacher and student is generally much larger in Asia than in Europe and the United States, but there are significant variations. In France, for instance, the teacher has very high positional authority. (A running joke is that though the standard grading system goes from 1 to 20, grades 20 and 19 are never used because "20 is reserved for God, and 19 for the teacher.") In the Nordic countries, there is little power distance, especially in executive classes. In India, the students will stand up to address the teacher if asked a question, a habit that can make you slightly nervous if you are not used to it. By all means, ask them to remain seated.

Deference to the teacher is shown in many ways. You are always addressed as "Professor" in China, for instance, but if you are a Western person, quite often as "Professor [first name]." This is not a token of familiarity, but happens because in China the family name comes before the common name. If you have lunch with students in

Germany and the Netherlands, they will invariably wait to start to eat until you, as the outside guest, do. European and Asian students are less likely to ask for advice in between classes and to complain about grading, unlike in the United States, where grades can seem merely a starting point for discussions.

How you choose to deal with this difference in power is up to you, but don't automatically assume that reducing it or behaving as you would in the United States or Europe is the way to go. Informality can sometime be seen as weakness and lack of structure, so be careful. The students may actually be more comfortable—and more willing to discuss—when a teacher observes some of the formalities. An insistence on equality can sometimes create problems: in some countries where underemployment is rife, for instance, a professor will be assigned an assistant or secretary whose job it is to get coffee and perform other small tasks. If that is their job, you should let them do it. By getting your own coffee, you could unwittingly imply that what they do isn't necessary or valuable.

Student Behavior

Student norms for behavior in the classroom (or in meetings, in general) can vary considerably around the world. A high-status participant in the class—say, a CEO or two—can stifle discussion until the authority figure says something, especially if the other participants belong to the same organization. We have observed this in China and France and have been told it is especially pronounced in Japan, whereas in India, it is almost the opposite. In India, you might have to work to slow down the discussion. There may be norms about how discussions should be conducted—in northern Europe, for instance, there is an implied rule that students should get the floor in the order they hold their hand up—so explicitly tell the students that you will violate that rule at the beginning of the course.

Norms for what is permissible behavior in classrooms can also differ. In countries where teachers drone on, reading from manuscripts, you can often see students openly sleeping in the classroom. In some places, taking cellphone calls while in class is quite normal, as is coming late to class.

Should you be in a situation where students behave in ways you think unacceptable, though seemingly accepted locally, explicitness works best, both in situations where you teach in a culture foreign to you or have foreign students in your class. Explain to the students concerned that you deem certain behaviors unacceptable and why (again, without berating an individual student) and ask them either not to do it or refrain from coming to class.

Similarly, never accept the "culture card"—which some students will play on you—as an excuse for not preparing, coming late, or not paying attention in class. Students live in a culture: it is your classroom, your course, and your responsibility to foster a culture of learning in the room. You just need to keep your rules simple, explicit, and grounded in a teaching strategy and make them legitimate by teaching well and knowing what you talk about.

Using Interpreters

You can be put in situations where you will need to use interpreters, either simultaneous interpreters, where the students have headphones, or traditional interpretation, where you say something and the interpreter repeats it in the local language. In the latter case, you will sometimes find that you get through your lectures *faster* than if you were lecturing directly, because you will try to formulate your sentences clearly, avoid anecdotes, and, of course, have fewer questions from the students.

Interpreters are a necessary evil—good ones are hard to find—and can be very tricky in an interactive context, especially if some students want to speak English and others demand interpretation. We have not taught case classes with interpreters, but we have run discussions inside traditional lecture classes. Getting a discussion going is possible (if the interpreters are good), and it helps a lot if at least some of the students speak your language. One compromise can be to have a native-speaking co-teacher, who can run a native-language discussion after your class, and then have the English speakers of the class refer some of the discussion back to you later.

The quality of interpreters varies widely and sometimes works only one way. Espen has had the experience of being simultaneously translated in Italy and not understanding a word of what the supposedly English-speaking interpreter was telling him when students had questions. The situation was solved by involving some of the English-speaking participants, but left Espen wondering how much the Italian-only speakers really had understood.

If you know you are going to have interpreters (simultaneous or not), try to have a meeting with them before the session starts, explain the outline of your session and some of the content, and be ready to answer questions. Find out how much of the content the interpreter knows. Espen once had an interpreter who worked for the stock exchange and had worked for stockbrokers, so he used examples from that industry to increase the richness of the description through the interpreter. If you have favorite jokes or anecdotes you are going to use, tell them to the interpreter before class, so he or she can work out a way to deliver the point.

During your session, try not to surprise the interpreter. Use straightforward language; do not jump between domains quickly, that is, don't use references to literature or movies when describing something; don't use sports metaphors or within-culture examples that require the interpreter to translate both context and language. Anyone speaking two languages will have seen the feeble attempts to translate, say, English TV game-show humor, and understand how difficult this is. Between sessions, be available, together with the interpreter, to answer questions from people who struggle with details.

An interpreter is a gateway between you and your audience, and you want that gateway to be as open and as flattering as possible.

A Teachers' Guide for Scandinavia

As an example of cultural differences, here are some pointers for U.S. teachers who want to avoid the most obvious pitfalls when visiting Scandinavia:

- Don't refer to Europe—or even Scandinavia—as a single country. There is much more variation among countries in Europe than among states in the United States—language, history, culture, attitudes, economics, and so on. Make sure you know which country you are in (and where your audience is from).

- Don't refer to going to church (for example, referring to someone as "we belong to the same church"). In Scandinavia, less than 10 percent of the population goes to church regularly, and religion is a very personal thing. Openly referring to church will make some people think you belong to a cult.

- In general, Europeans are less inhibited about off-color jokes than Americans—not that it takes much—but this apparent frivolity comes with subtle pitfalls. If you tell something that can be construed as demeaning to women, for instance, it will fall very flat even in an all-male audience. You should not attempt off-color jokes unless you really know your audience or possess an English accent more pronounced than Stephen Fry's.

- In general, Scandinavian businesspeople are less formally dressed than Americans during daytime, but dress up (or wear business suits) for dinner. So it is quite the opposite from the United States, so don't change into jeans for that after-work bash, unless you work in the software industry, which is thoroughly Americanized. (This is changing; if in doubt, ask. Precede it with, "In the U.S., we do this. What's the custom here?")

- Never suggest union-busting or de-unionization or stopping people from forming unions as a strategy. It is illegal, against the culture, and against anything considered good management by almost every Scandinavian manager. In most companies in Scandinavia, relations with unions are cordial, collaborative, and valued.

- Be careful about naming prominent people as "friends" and referring to them by their first names. In Scandinavia, "friend" implies a fairly high level of intimacy, usually reserved for the private sphere, and you probably wouldn't refer to them in a management speech. "Warren Buffett is a friend of mine, and ..." or "As Bill Gates said the last time we met ..." will tend to make you look boastful and leave people unimpressed, unless you can show that your conversation has made these grandees change their behavior and that you really have influence.

Trust the Locals

Local material helps, as does flexibility. The students like to have influence on the discussion and the teaching, and when they express wishes in that direction, pay attention. In 2005, Espen was teaching a class of sixty MBA students in China. The students were reasonably well prepared, but their English proficiency was uneven, so it was hard to get a wide-ranging discussion going. Espen was struggling, and the students thought the course rather theoretical and had difficulties connecting the reading to real companies.

Then, two days into the four-day program, Lenovo, China's largest PC producer, acquired IBM's PC division. The deal was on the front page of all the business papers, and the students wanted Espen's opinion on it. Rather than answer directly, he told the students that for the next day, they should all prepare for a class on Lenovo and IBM by reading all the articles they could find. Then the class would have a discussion on what this meant, strategically and technologically.

The students were hypermotivated. Many of them worked for Chinese technology companies, were proud of Lenovo, and were very knowledgeable about Chinese manufacturing. Espen contributed with some overview slides on the relationship between technology and market development. Two extremely interesting hours followed, during which both the students and the teacher learned a lot. Almost the whole class participated, some in barely understandable but very engaged English.

In other words, when you are abroad, there is no difference: trust the class.

8

PREPARING FOR THE NEXT TIME

When the course is finished, you tend to be rather finished yourself. All you want to do is avoid thinking about the course until it is time to teach it again. Yet, at the same time, it is seldom more important to be thoughtful and logical about your teaching. The reward will come when you need to teach the course again.

So, how can you be thoughtful and logical in order to improve your course?

Ambition gives you the motive. Every time you repeat a course, you should improve on the previous one. Practice gives you the routine to allow you to improve while you are teaching the first course. Taking time to review each course and organize your thoughts and materials during or shortly after you conduct the course pays great dividends for subsequent versions and for other courses. We'll show you a few tricks to make it happen.

Debriefing a Course

There is nothing mystical about debriefing a course. Go through your teaching plans and make notes to yourself as appropriate. Ideally, you should review each class shortly after you teach it. But in the window of time after class, just getting the participation grades recorded is often all you can manage.

The biggest problem is remembering which problems you needed to fix when the next course comes up. One good approach is creating the next course while you are teaching the current one. If you can, establish the next course instance in the learning management system (LMS), for instance. Immediately change presentations and course material where you need to adjust. Make notes about what to change next as contemporaneously as possible (and, we urge, electronically). Or write adjustments in red on your teaching plans and store them with your cases so that you will remember them the next time you teach. The same goes for the syllabus; write notes in red on the syllabus after each class, store it, and retrieve it next year. If you really want to be structured, figure out a good day to start preparing for the new course before the next semester starts, and post a link to your notes in your electronic calendar.

Review student performance on the exams and assignments and look for trends. If students were making similar mistakes or omissions, make note of them and consider how to change the course next time. If you had multiple exams during the semester, see if learning improved. Do a simple calculation in your grading spreadsheet to see how many students improved.

Consider the course as a whole:

- What went well or badly?

- Did you feel comfortable with it? Was it something you enjoyed? Did you like the students and the material?

- Does the course align with where you want to be as a faculty member?

- Are there aspects of the course that feel stale and could do with some revitalization?

- Have new things happened (or new cases been developed) that you could incorporate in the course next time?

- Can you use any of this year's students as guest lecturers or discussants in next year's course?

Interpreting and Using Student Feedback

Many faculty argue that student evaluations are not useful and should be ignored. While we acknowledge they should not be the only factors considered when evaluating faculty or classes, the data can be helpful. Many students are cynical about the feedback process because they believe faculty don't read the qualitative comments and that tenured faculty don't care about the numbers either. Many schools have moved to online collection of evaluations and have seen drops in response rates as a result. Where responses are required, they are often perfunctory. To combat student cynicism or indifference, be clear that you care about the feedback by explicitly requesting it. During the course, share the impact of previous feedback on the current course design. If appropriate, draw parallels to feedback mechanisms and continuous improvement you advocate in your course content.

Most university evaluation forms are geared to lecture classes, with the primary focus on the instructor's ability and willingness to present clearly and answer questions. This can leave case teachers at a disadvantage in terms of performance evaluation for their careers and with less actionable feedback for improvement.

You can ask students to include specific feedback in the standard evaluations or create your own survey in the LMS or elsewhere. We have found that most students will enthusiastically complete a separate evaluation if they believe that the feedback is valued and will have an impact. Be sure to ask about the dynamics of the discussion and have students evaluate the cases and other materials individually. If possible, create a forcing function to prevent students from giving vague feedback. For instance, ask them to name their two favorite and least favorite cases. Or if you have few enough cases, ask for a ranking (see online resource 15 for a sample).*

How to Read Student Feedback

Even for faculty who receive consistently high marks from students, reading student evaluations can be aversive. That should not keep

---

* To see this and other online resources for the book,
visit the web site: teachingwithcases.hbsp.harvard.edu.

you from reading your evaluations, but don't feel obligated to read them as soon as they are available. Wait until you have the time and inclination to be open and reflective about their feedback.

The numbers can be difficult to interpret without context, particularly for case teachers who demand more of the students than simply looking like they are paying attention during class. Look for current and historical averages and ranges, if available, for your course, department, and yourself.

There are a few common types of critical feedback that you are likely to see:

- Class participation is unfair or overemphasized.

- There is too much reading.

- There should be more lecture content.

- Cases are too old.

- Cases are not from a relevant industry (especially when teaching in-company sessions).

So what to do with these complaints? If you are seeing only a handful, ignore them. The point of feedback is not to eliminate student complaints. In fact, if you aren't getting any complaints that the course is too demanding, make it more demanding. If more than 10 percent of the respondents are making any one of these comments, then you should investigate to see if their concerns are justified. Perhaps you have underestimated the amount of work required, or you have not focused the course as well as you need to. And you should also consider whether you did enough to explain your rationale for the course and sell the value of it during the semester.

Beyond the usual responses, look for common themes and anything surprising. If you have the data, split the sample by interest, effort, or, if the surveys were not anonymous, grades. Knowing whether the complaints are coming from good or poor students can help you determine what actions to take. Keep in mind that you need to reach both groups, as well as the average students, but you may need to focus on different things to do so successfully.

Before deciding on what changes you will make, consider what might be idiosyncratic to this group of students. Were there issues or events that had a lasting impact, positive or negative, on the perception of the course (difficult students, running jokes, local and world events)? In addition to how that may skew the feedback, think about how you addressed the issues and what you could have done differently that might have improved the course.

Striving for High Evaluations

In many schools and countries, faculty commonly believe that "students here just circle the middle number (3 on a 5-item Likert scale or 4 out of 7)," and striving for or expecting better results would be futile. We have found this to be universally untrue. To challenge these assumptions, see if there are faculty that consistently score at the high end of the range or look at the evaluations for successful executive education programs, which are typically at the high end of the scale.

Higher evaluation numbers are not necessarily a result of catering to student whims. They can, and regularly do, result from good hard work on course development and delivery. With many schools now including questions about how difficult or challenging a course was or what grade a student expected to receive, it is harder for professors to buy grades with easy courses or high grades. That should help level the playing field for case teachers. Nevertheless, as a demanding case teacher, you may never be the most popular teacher in the school, especially if you are one of the few using cases, but you will make a deep impression on your students, and you can still achieve very high scores.

You may perform better in some classrooms or times of day than others, and with planning and a good rationale, you may have opportunities to schedule to your strengths. You may also be able to influence classroom design.

Reviewing Case Selection

The mix and order of cases in the course is a critical component of the success of the course. The next time you teach the course, conduct an abbreviated version of the case-selection process we describe in chapter 2, informed by what you learned from the just-completed course. If you repeat a course several times, you are likely to have cases you would like to replace, but cannot find anything better on the topics you want to cover. If you are not going to change the topic, then you need to either wait for another to be published or write one yourself. You will also have some older cases that work particularly well. You cannot keep very many of these, but having a few is fine. For each case, review your teaching plan to remind yourself of the energy level the discussion generated as well as how well the timing fit and the lessons you intended were covered. Again, make your notes now, and do not rely on your memory for when you set up the next course.

Debriefing with a Teaching Group

If several faculty were teaching the same course, be sure to debrief as a group. The sharing of multiple perspectives, best practices, and benchmarking opportunities is invaluable. When to do this depends on your school. Ideally, you have final grades and student evaluations ready, but in many schools, by the time all of that is available, crucial details are long since forgotten. Often, after exams, faculty vanish until the start of the next semester, so you are better off doing it right after classes end. In any event, at the beginning of the course, agree on a date for the debriefing. Beyond the working of the teaching group itself, the issues discussed are the same as for individuals.

Archiving Materials

In chapter 10, we advocate scanning all of your hard-copy notes. If you haven't had the tools or inclination to do so, we certainly advocate doing it now. If that's too much effort, at least create organized folders for each case with your related notes. If you have jotted any notes related to the course, gather them, and if you are not inclined to transcribe or scan them, at least read each to make sure they are very clear and will be clear to you months later when you revisit them. If you do put everything into electronic form, tag anything that isn't text with key words to make them more likely to be found later.

Evaluating Case Teachers, Including Yourself

Case teaching differs greatly from lecturing, yet most case teachers are evaluated as lecturers. The C. Roland Christensen Center for Teaching and Learning (2005) publishes "Guidelines for Observing Case Instructors" (http://www.hbs.edu/teaching/docs/Guidelines-for-Effective-Observation-of-Case-Instructors.pdf). It recommends a three-part process for faculty evaluating other faculty (before, during, and after class) that we have found helpful in our own teaching and when observing other teachers.

If the evaluations are tied to promotion or tenure decisions, faculty are likely to be more conservative in what they do and will prepare more thoroughly than they typically do. We encourage faculty to get the most from evaluations, whether they have career implications or not, because they are a scarce and valuable resource. This includes suggesting the guidelines to faculty who are doing the evaluating, especially if the evaluators are not case teachers themselves. In addition to the Christensen Center guidelines, we offer some advice for each step.

Before Class

If faculty are visiting a class for an evaluation, the faculty member being evaluated is generally notified in advance and will typically spend more time than usual developing the teaching plan and preparing. This is understandable, and even if not done deliberately, the Hawthorne effect, where simply being observed can change behavior, can lead to optimizing behavior. Keep this in mind when interpreting the results. To a degree slightly past your comfort level, share with the observer any issues on which you hope to improve.

During Class

Some simple metrics can be invaluable in evaluating a case teacher's calling patterns and the flow of the discussion. You can do this for yourself with one or two well-placed video cameras and some after-class analysis, or you can have someone gathering the data for you in real time. Start by drawing a seating chart or, even better, use an existing chart that has pictures of the students on it. In the simplest version of this evaluation, place marks next to the student each time he or she speaks, and place a mark next to the professor each time he or she speaks. This data will tell you the extent to which some students are dominating the discussion, whether the instructor is favoring sections of the classroom over others, and whether the instructor is dominating the discussion.

With a bit more effort, an observer can gather additional detail on the matters of interest such as the nature of the questions the instructor asks (open or closed, follow-up, retrospective, predictive, action-oriented), whether students are asking questions, whether students are referring to previous comments by other students, and the extent to which students are integrating theory into their comments.

After Class

You should meet with the evaluator as soon as possible once the evaluator has reviewed his or her notes. But as the Christensen Center guidelines point out, faculty are easily overwhelmed by the feedback. We agree with the advice to keep the evaluation focused, but we would also encourage faculty to revisit the report a month or two later and to set some small, specific changes to implement as a result. Then track your progress periodically and, if the evaluator is open to being a mentor over time, so much the better.

Managing Relationships with Alumni

You are not done with the students when they graduate. One of the best perquisites of teaching is the alumni network you can establish. This network can be invaluable to help guide the relevance of curricula, serve as guest speakers, support research agendas, and, if you are so inclined, provide you with lucrative consulting gigs and board positions.

But building and maintaining this network means you have to participate. We participate in our own universities' alumni arrangements if we can (not all, and not every time, of course, but this is an integral part of being a business school professor), invite and accept former students to our LinkedIn network, encourage them to follow our blogs, and otherwise stay in touch. We will write recommendation letters for those who ask and (in our opinion) deserve it. We try to connect our former students if they can help each other, if they are looking for someone with a specific competence, or if someone is looking for a job. This we see as a natural and important part of being a professor at a business school or, for that matter, at any school.

Your former students constitute a form of social capital that you have made an investment in creating. Don't waste your capital through neglect.

9

FOSTERING CASE TEACHING AT THE SCHOOL LEVEL

So far, this book has been about the practicalities of case teaching itself, from the perspective of the teacher. In this chapter, we shift gears and consider case teaching from the perspective of the business school administration: the deans, directors, or presidents, depending on where in the world the school is located.

Business schools are challenged by commoditization, partly due to technology. They struggle with being relevant to business and with integrating the many disciplines embodied within the term "business school." We—and an increasing number of well-known business schools—think an emphasis on discussion-based teaching can be a viable strategy to address these challenges. In this chapter, we discuss these issues and offer a few pointers for implementing such a strategy.

The Commoditized Business School

Business schools, compared to other academic disciplines, have traditionally had low production costs (no need for expensive lab equipment or one-on-one apprenticeships) and high demand for their students. This has made for many competitors and a tremendous growth in candidates. As a result, an undergraduate degree, even from a well-known institution, is now little more than a requirement for graduate studies, and only those with graduate education can statistically expect to be on a curve of increasing purchasing power (Autor and Dorn, 2013; Brynjolfsson and MacAfee, 2014). The diminished economic return of degrees has, of course, resulted in less willingness to pay for them.

This is not a problem for the top schools (which now are extending their reach electronically) or the low-cost, online competitors. However, the middle-ground business schools—decent performance, good faculty, but not a globally recognized brand—are increasingly facing a very difficult competitive situation, with geography and perhaps language as their main differentiators. What should a "regular" business school do to maintain its attractiveness?

We think the answer lies in addressing two perennial business study problems: lack of relevance and lack of integration. Both can be addressed by getting good at case teaching.

Relevance Is Relevant

The first business schools had a mixture of topics, some discipline-based (finance, accounting, leadership) and some industry-focused (production, agribusiness, railroad economics). Teachers were mostly former executives with pedagogical leanings and low salary demands. Now, most faculty members are PhDs with minimal business and leadership experience, hired for their ability to produce peer-reviewed articles, often in fields outside pure business, such as organizational psychology, sociology, economics, public administration, history, and psychology. Promotion is almost exclusively based on research and, though lip service is paid to teaching and citizenship as meritorious conduct, it is a practice more honored in the breach than the observation.

As a result, business schools struggle with market relevance and integration, and many students graduate with a deep knowledge of academic business research, but little ability to convert it into practice. This is reflected in our most common comment on student papers: "mentions theory, but doesn't use it." On exams, students often list theories and frameworks, before reverting to common sense and badly remembered consultant-speak when analyzing and discussing business problems.

The lack of relevance is also seen in the relationship between faculty and business. Few professors sit on company boards or consult to top management. Business schools are outliers, we think, in this aversion to practice among those who teach practitioners. A professor of medicine, unable to diagnose and treat patients, would seem absurd to any physician or medical researcher.

We think business schools should shift their emphasis from teaching the theory toward teaching its application. Case teaching, done right, is all about understanding problems and seeking solutions. This does not imply that case teaching is theory-free—far from it— but that cases are a way of teaching theory. This can be done inductively by teaching cases as examples, letting the students induct the theory from them, or deductively by teaching theory, then providing cases for application of same. With cases, you also let the students discover when the theory does *not* apply, something that is rarely done and should be done more.

Integration Is Integral

The increasing specialization into subfields in business schools is not necessarily a problem for research, but it is for teaching. Most business school programs now are a smorgasbord of subjects that have little connection to each other, leading to a situation where the students are, to quote John Quelch (2005), "left with the job of integrating the subjects since the faculty cannot." Management, especially top management, is a generalist's job, but how do you teach the integrative skills necessary to fill or at least understand the top management role?

Many MBA programs have some sort of integrative exercise toward the end, often in the form of a group consulting project in which the students work together to solve more or less real business problems. This is excellent, but hard to scale and can be quite specialized, depending on the projects.

We think most business programs would benefit from using case-based teaching to promote subject integration, both inside and between courses. In particular, we advocate having a *case-based capstone course*, team taught and with students from many different specialties in the same setting, as a final integrative exercise. Such a course is a great way to create a sense of community among the students, out of a class, to teach students to apply theory, see the interplay between various specialties (achieved by creating study groups composed of people with different expertise, just like real companies), and prepare for the messy and nondirective world of real business organizations. The creation of such a course can also institutionalize case teaching skills and integrative thinking by faculty members, since it will involve teachers from many different departments, learning from each other about how to teach the cases.

The key here is not that many faculty members teach the same course, but that they do it in parallel, teaching the same cases to different groups of students at the same time. The teaching group should consist of professors from many different fields, but every professor should teach every case. This means that finance professors teach strategy cases, and strategy professors teach accounting, and accounting professors teach leadership, and so on. This will be a source of anxiety for some and a surprising amount of learning for the rest, as the specialized professors teach each other how to teach the cases from their respective areas and in return learn how other perspectives can inform the analysis. In the end, you have created an integrative student experience and may have spawned all kinds of interesting teaching and research activities simply because smart professors—and you would try to cherry-pick the best to teach such a course—have had to collaborate about something important and interesting that forces them out of their fields.

Why Serial Team Teaching Doesn't Work Well

Some courses, particularly introductory overviews in the beginning of a program or capstone courses toward the end, are often taught by many professors who follow one another, each contributing with their specialty. Such courses are very hard to do well. The teachers rarely know in detail what the discussion was in the classes before them, leading to overlaps. They all have to introduce themselves and get to know the students, consuming time and energy. Frequently, teachers are allocated for such courses based less on their teaching and research prowess and more on distributing teaching hours and fulfilling teaching quotas.

The usual result is a fragmented course with wildly varying quality both in content and in presentation, with material missing or duplicated. Because nobody knows what has been said in class, students are largely evaluated based on the required readings, and the course ends up as a lottery where the winners are those who guess which literature is on the exam. There is little reason for the students to show up or, if they bother, to be prepared. The best they can hope for is that some of the teachers turn out to be entertaining or can correctly answer questions about the literature.

The solution is to have one faculty member responsible and present for the entire course so that at least one person knows which colleagues perform under which circumstances and can provide feedback about their performance, ways of teaching, and students' reactions. The role of evaluator and coordinator is hard to play, though, and doubling up for each class is expensive. It's better to broaden the scope of the course, use discussion-based teaching, divide the students into groups, and do the teaching in parallel. Teaching quality will vary, but you will be able to compare teachers across the same teaching material, giving the students a coherent experience.

Institutionalizing Case Teaching

During the last few years, we have seen a number of business schools—and graduate schools in non-business fields, such as nursing and public health—move to an increased use of participant-centered or case-based teaching methods. The main motivator seems to be a desire to access the executive education market, particularly the sought-after and highly profitable market for in-company top management development, a market currently dominated by consulting companies. The corporate executive education market demands knowledge that is applicable and integrated. A second motivator is the fear of digitization. New concepts such as Massively Open Online Courses (MOOCs) has led some (that is, Harden, 2013) to predict that many colleges and universities simply will be disrupted out of business by these MOOCs. Case teaching is resistant to digitization to a degree that lecturing is not. A third motivator may be the search for differentiation. With few exceptions, such as Babson College's focus on entrepreneurship or Simon's (University of Rochester) focus on financial technology, most business schools are hard-pressed to articulate how they are unique. Adopting a specific form of teaching, such as case-based or technology-assisted, is a form of differentiation that allows the school to keep the full breadth of subjects.

Regardless of motive, a transition to more use of discussion-based teaching is difficult. It requires changing how faculty behave, a task normally requiring the cunning of a Machiavelli or at least the full repertoire of university political techniques as described by Cohen and March (1986). At an instrumental level, it requires changes in recruitment policies, incentive structures, course design, and evaluation procedures, and perhaps also organization structures.

Recruiting, Incentives, and Promotion

Any discussion about promoting case teaching (or, for that matter, any kind of change in faculty behavior, such as more use of technology) inevitably turns to incentives. We have discussed this with a number of schools and have found that, though most schools have some form of incentives for case teaching (or, at least, case writing), those that really use case teaching do it mostly because it is in the culture of the school. Case teaching is integral to the school, required for tenure and promotion, and case production is regarded as a component of academic publishing.

These schools are few, however, and even they experience hiring difficulties because PhD candidates are increasingly specialized and focused on publishing academic, peer-reviewed articles in select publications rather than writing material (be it books or cases) for a wider audience.

At the outset, recruiting needs to change, shifting some focus from a candidate's publication list to his or her teaching skills and business network. Recruiting can become a general requirement, but we have also seen schools recruit teachers among retired business executives or experienced consultants. A word of warning: certain business executives want to leave the hustle and bustle of business and take on teaching as a more relaxing occupation as they get closer to full retirement. Many discover that teaching is hard, the academic competition at least as cutthroat as any business, and free time for deeper reflection neither free nor available. Those who survive, however, can be excellent.

Done right, recruiting from a wider faculty pool can help the PhDs stay relevant and the practitioners research-based. Done wrong and it can create two disjointed career systems, where teachers crave titles and researchers, money.

Most schools will consider direct incentives to increase case production. The most common incentives are financial rewards for case production, where the school pays a fixed fee for each case produced, after some form of quality review. If the school has a case repository and sells its cases via one of the case exchanges, there is often also a royalty fee. These financial rewards tend to be mostly symbolic; the faculty member who can produce quality cases and teach them tends to have alternative opportunities for consulting and other activities with relatively high remuneration. They are, however, an indication that the school takes case teaching seriously, and they are easy to implement.

A better incentive, in our opinion, is to increase the focus on teaching in decisions about tenure and remuneration. Academic hiring tends to be a rather slow and formal affair, often with committees of outside faculty that qualify and rank candidates according to their publications, but schools can then exercise judgment in who they select based on teaching ability and method. As schools more and more seek the executive education market, case teaching experience and ability becomes more desirable in a candidate.

Teaching-Related Procedures

Procedures for course design, support, and evaluation need to change. Case courses demand the grading of participation, for instance, which top management may need to publicly support against the opposition of student representative bodies and educational authorities. In Europe, students and authorities often oppose such grading for ideological reasons. What happens inside each classroom needs to become more transparent, both for training purposes, such as mentoring of younger faculty by experienced case teachers, and for evaluation. All procedures need to be designed to foster a quality culture around discussion-based teaching, where practice is shared between faculty, and both faculty and administration share the view of how good teaching is done.

Organizational responsibilities may need to change. For instance, if a business school is to focus on an executive or corporate market, the faculty need to be involved in the marketing and customization of course offerings, perhaps to the point where sales support becomes an integral part of a professor's job. Separate organizational units may need to be set up; for instance, several high-profile business schools have established case research centers aimed at producing teaching material unique to the school.

Getting Infrastructure Right

Changing the organizational culture—dealing with systems, people, incentives, and values—is by far the most important aspect of making a transition to case teaching. In any business school, nothing happens unless you involve the faculty and get them to change what they do and what they value. Administrations can, however, take quite a few practical actions relatively independently of the faculty transformation, in particular, configuring classrooms that work for case teaching and setting up the administrative support organization necessary to produce and use business cases.

Classroom Design

Business schools that focus on case teaching have specially designed classrooms, sometimes quite opulently tricked out with advanced technology (video cameras for recording student interactions, electronic boards, and so on). Lack of good classrooms is one of the most common obstacles to case teaching, and with good reason. Traditional classrooms and lecture halls are designed so that *many* students can listen to *one* teacher, not so that students can talk to one another. A good case classroom, on the other hand, works well as a regular lecture hall, if necessary.

Is investing heavily in specially built case classrooms necessary? Much can be achieved by retrofitting existing classrooms. The really expensive details have more to do with ceiling height and room shape that need consideration when the building is constructed.

There are, however, some mistakes that just should not be made. Here is our list of "must haves," in order of priority.

Good, Abundant Board Space

Case teaching demands lots of space, at least six good-sized boards, preferably set up so that they can all be visible at the same time. Case teaching requires lots of writing on boards and assists the students (and the teacher) in keeping track of the case discussion. Inadequate board space is one of the most frequent problems you encounter as a case teacher.

Blackboards Rather Than Whiteboards

Whiteboards seem to be the standard in almost all business schools, but writing with chalk on a good blackboard is actually much preferable to using markers on a whiteboard. The lines are thicker, and the increased friction improves the legibility of the handwriting. Arguments against blackboards tend to be administrative (nonstandard, different cleaning procedures) and cosmetic (some consider them old-fashioned). We love blackboards, however, and will take them over whiteboards any day.

Seating

Classrooms should have U-shaped, multilevel seating, with chairs that swivel. Ideally, the room should be close to square, but if it is rectangular, have the opening of the *U* face the long wall. This format brings the teacher close to the students and provides more wall space to hang boards on, at the price of students having slightly more difficulty seeing each other.

A common problem is insufficient rise in the seating rows. The rise is needed so that you can see the name cards of the students over the shoulders of the students sitting in front. If there is no rise, staggered seating will work, with each student sitting between two of the students in the row in front. Some additional requirements for seating are:

- Adequate desk space for students. In a case discussion, a student will require space for the case, notes, a laptop computer, and so on. Furthermore, bigger workspaces in front of the students give them more confidence to speak because it increases the share of the classroom over which they have control. Every seat should have a power outlet, of course.

- Slits for name cards. Each workspace should have a slit cut in its front to hold the name card. The workspace should also have a ridge in front to keep papers and coffee mugs from falling into the next row.

- Tables with front panels. They provide the students with a bit of privacy, making them feel more comfortable. For the teacher, panels quiet the visual image of the class, making each student easier to see. Room colors should be discreet. Don't choose the color scheme to be interesting in an empty room. The students, not the architect, should provide the color.

- No obstructions between teacher and students. For some reason, classroom designers put tables, sometimes even large, built-in sarcophaguslike monstrosities between teacher and student, maybe because some teachers are afraid of the class and want something to hide behind. For confident teachers, the only thing these tables provide is an obstacle they must pass to communicate with the students. There should be small tables on each side of the classroom to put notes and perhaps a computer.

- Maximum control over lighting: full lights on the blackboards and no light on the computer projector, for instance, preferably at the same time.

There are many other details, but these are the main ones. The keys are to remember that case teaching is not a presentation and the room should be a meeting place rather than a classroom, that case discussions involve long chains of reasoning requiring plenty of workspace for both teacher and student, and that the old technology works best. Fancy technology is not needed in the case classroom. And if you install new technology (smart boards, video cameras, buttons for access to a microphone), make sure that it both fits the purpose and does not occupy valuable classroom real estate when not in use.

Making Cases Easy to Use and Produce

A transition to participant-centered learning demands explicit administrative support, at least until a significant mass of experienced case teachers know what to ask for. Some of the more important forms of support are:

- Help in selecting and procuring cases. Some case clearinghouses have staff on hand that will help you, but make sure that ordering cases and payment for them are easy. Using cases should be as easy as using any other literature. Most case clearinghouses let teachers set up electronic case packages that students can buy, but at least in the beginning, schools should provide support to faculty. And case teachers need a budget for handout material, such as B cases.

- Organizational support for the necessary review and mentoring of teaching process and quality, including training of new hires in the case method.

- Systems to track the actual use of cases to make sure that the same case is not used for the same purpose in two courses by different teachers. Some schools have developed internal information systems to make cases from many sources available through their LMS, to track the use of cases vis-à-vis students, and even to facilitate the exchange of internally produced material between teachers.

Case Production

Writing and publishing cases is outside the purview of this book, but is an important part of any determined organizational push toward more case teaching. Almost all the case teachers we have met have eventually started to write their own cases, in more or less polished form. The students will demand it, for one thing, and instructors, having produced a few of the cases for a course, gain students' respect. Schools need to provide support for case production (some schools do this by recruiting staff dedicated to case production in low-cost countries). They should give credit for case production to case authors and develop a policy for sharing internally produced cases within the school. People can be surprisingly unwilling to share their teaching material unless they have some sort of control over its use. Using someone's case without his or her knowledge or assent should not be allowed.

Producing a case enhances the legitimacy of a teacher. Having local cases tailored to your courses and your students' situation is a valuable and hard-to-copy resource. After establishing a critical mass of cases, you can make case writing a part of every workday.

References

Autor, D. and D. Dorn. "The Growth of Low-Skill Service Jobs and the Polarization of the US Labor Market." *American Economic Review* 103, no. 5 (2013): 1553–1597.

Brynjolfsson, E., and A. McAfee. *The Second Machine Age: Work, Progress and Prosperity in a Time of Brilliant Technologies.* New York: W. W. Norton, 2014.

Cohen, M. D., and J. G. March. *Leadership and Ambiguity.* Boston: Harvard Business School Press, 1986.

Harden, N. "The End of the University as We Know It." *The American Interest,* January–February 2013. http://www.the-american-interest.com/article.cfm?piece=1352.

Quelch, J. "A New Agenda for Business Schools." *Chronicle of Higher Education*, December 2, 2005.

10

TECHNOLOGIES FOR
CASE TEACHING

In this chapter, we will discuss the use of all kinds of technology relevant to teaching with cases—from the personal technology teachers use to be productive to the various forms used to interact with students. We do not aim to be comprehensive, will avoid naming specific products (since today's cool tool rapidly becomes tomorrow's anachronism), and when we do, use them more as example than prescription.

Many of the tips here are not specific to case teaching, but we include them for completeness and because you may incorporate them in novel ways. We have also chosen to be quite detailed, because the devil is indeed in the details, and in case teaching, you will want to master details because technology screwups take more energy and attention away from the discussion and the content than in lecture-based teaching.

Case teaching is, like all teaching, increasingly moving online, to what we call asynchronous online teaching, where the dominant interface between the participants is an online discussion forum or interaction platform. We have devoted quite a bit of space to this form of teaching; though the technology is old, its use for case teaching is relatively new and will become prevalent in the not too distant future, and what is considered best practice is evolving quickly.

But, first, a word about who's in charge. We adamantly believe that two basic principles of technology must be fulfilled before you choose to use it: (1) you need to take control of it, and (2) you should never adopt a technology unless it makes either your job easier or the students' experience better and preferably both.

Take Control of the Technology

Back in our grade school days, whenever the teacher decided to reward the class with a movie on the 8mm film projector, the same thing happened: the teacher didn't know how to set up the projector and abdicated the responsibility to a student. By about seventh grade, we both got quite good at changing movies. We also thought to ourselves, these people are supposed to be our teachers. Why haven't they taken the time to learn how these things work?

This is still true for many instructors. Who hasn't seen teachers (or, for that matter, academics at conferences) fiddling with controls to get their computer to display a presentation or access a file from the net or some sort of portable storage. So, let's start with the most important advice we can give.

Take control of the technology; don't let it control you. There are many excellent tools to support courses and teaching, for presenting in the classroom, managing course material, and enabling students to do collaborative writing or videoconferences. Don't be slow in adopting these tools, don't use them only as an add-on, and don't think of them as another thing that can go wrong. Good carpenters know their tools; so should a good teacher.

But only adopt technology if it makes your job easier or the students' experience better. New tools are frequently seen as a bother because we don't use them as an essential component of our teaching. They are add-ons, frequently because technology use is inappropriately seen as a goal in itself. When a new technology comes along, it offers an opportunity to make work smarter and easier. Use new tools instead of old ways of doing things. For instance, the second you can distribute things electronically, distribute *everything* electronically.

Learning how technology works and thinking about how to apply it take time and interest. Technology gradually gets better, but if you are going to do something innovative, you will always have to learn at least some of it on your own. Learning how to use it takes practice and some foresight, such as making sure before class, not during it, that the material is available and the projector works. Learning how to use the technology takes patience and a willingness to understand what it provides. To someone who is just starting out, the task can look formidable, but like eating the proverbial elephant, this is something you do gradually, adding building blocks until you have something that gives you shelter and comfort.

Don't use technology for technology's sake. Use technology to make your classes better, and exercise choice so that you use only the parts of the technology that are genuinely useful to you and the students. Avoid becoming dependent on a single technology or a single instantiation of technology. Don't be afraid to experiment. You will have technology breakdowns, but you will learn from them and get better. Students don't mind technology problems if they see that you are pushing the envelope to make their experience better. They get irritated if you equate technology clumsiness with academic quality.

In the end, it is *your* course, *your* classroom—and *your* technology. Never forget that.

Technology for Teacher Productivity

Good technology use starts at home, with the technology you use for your own purposes: for designing and keeping track of teaching materials, evaluating and keeping track of students, automating repetitive tasks, and using the computer and the network as an extension of yourself.

We think it important to have a conscious strategy for personal information management; that is, that you think about how you are going to manage all the information you need to function as a good teacher (and academic) and make a conscious effort to make this process as reliable, easy, and rich as possible. Using active learning entails a variety of activities and that usually generates many documents. We will give examples of our own strategies, but keep in mind that this is something you need to design yourself.

We strongly advocate using paper only for display, not storage. Rather than having your information in file cabinets or binders, try to make it all electronic, to have only one electronic copy of each file, and to have the whole collection properly backed up. You need tools to do this, primarily some form of note and file storage, of which there is a good selection available, both online and as local software. These tools allow you to store documents and notes, tag them with keywords that make them easy to organize, and find and share material online.

To eliminate paper, you need a way to convert it to digital form. Most universities provide some sort of scanning service, often using shared printers or copiers as scanners, but if you deal with a lot of paper, we strongly advocate getting your own scanner and locating it right next to you on your desk. Get one that can scan in color, scan both sides of a page (duplex scanning), and connect to software that does optical character recognition (OCR) so that you can search and otherwise access the content of the documents you scan. You can also use smartphone scanner software.

The point is to make it easy to scan documents you want to keep, squirt them into your personal information manager, tag them with some key words, and then discard the originals. Combine this with a computer with enough internal storage (alternatively or in addition, a really good Internet connection and remote storage), and you will always have your notes and course material with you. Having it all electronically means that you will never have to go to your office to get something. It also makes it easy for you to be totally electronic in your communications with your students, and consistency in form is a good thing.

We also advocate that you assemble your own tool collection for information management, rather than blindly relying on what your institution provides. This is partly because tools work best when you choose and control them yourself and partly because you need to make sure that you own and control what you create. If you store all your course designs and material only on your university's online platforms, you risk losing them when you move to a different employer or the institution decides to change to a different system. Moreover, as a good teacher, you will frequently be asked to guest lecture or even run courses at other institutions—situations where you may be required to use different systems and where having access to and maintaining control over your own material are important.

To manage grades, creating a spreadsheet yourself makes it easier for you to implement your grading method. Most learning management systems allow you to upload grades if you format the columns consistently. Keeping first and last names in separate columns enables you to print out name tags and sort by first and last name, as well as organize the spreadsheet by creating individual columns for various partial evaluations, comments, and other information. This makes it easy to create customized reports for the students, with comments (see chapter 4 for an example), and gives you a well-organized repository of grades and notes, should a student ask for more feedback or complain about a grade. Some of our more technically astute colleagues use databases rather than spreadsheets to facilitate analysis across courses and make finding alumni information easy years later.

Teacher's Computer Use in Class

While the board and the spoken word remain the case teacher's main tools, there is room for technology use in the classroom as well. By this we don't mean just prepared presentations, but live demonstrations of computer use, audiovisual materials such as film clips or web sites, and tools to take notes or even do the board writing digitally for later distribution. In short, any kind of technology that enhances the student experience and makes your life easier.

As software has become an integral part of most jobs, using it can be appropriate and valuable in the classroom. Students appreciate seeing the tools used in practice. But if all you plan to do is a canned demo of a customer relationship management system in a marketing course or a general ledger system in an accounting course, consider not doing it live in class. Either locate a vendor-generated demo, or make one yourself using screen-capture software that allows you to record what is on your screen and a voice track to create a movie that serves as the demo. Have the class view that film clip before class or show it during class if you feel that the flow of the discussion requires it. But if you're going to spend hands-on time with software during class, make sure that it is interactive.

Perhaps you are using a tool (such as a mind mapping program) to draw a model students proposed during the discussion. Or you are using a statistics package to calculate a probability. Or you are running a simulation of the impact of a proposal a student made in class. In each of these cases, the software enhances the discussion by providing further analysis and representations that deepen understanding.

If you are going to use a spreadsheet in class to crunch numbers that arise during the discussion, be sure you are comfortable with how to show text and numbers on the screen in large format. You can do this by increasing the font size or zooming in, but either way you need to be comfortable navigating around the screen and legibly showing what you want on the display at any given time. Be thoughtful about which columns and rows to freeze or hide and what will happen if you navigate to other worksheets.

You can also use the computers that your students bring to class. You can ask the students to crunch numbers in real time, use social software of various kinds to create word clouds (see figure 10-1), polling students to report results of their calculations (for instance, into an online spreadsheet, which you then can use to project a graphical overview on the screen). If you are running a discussion or presentation that is simultaneously video-streamed, you can set up a session #hashtag and use your favorite social software, perhaps even projected onto the wall, to connect to remote participants who can write comments embedding the hashtag and thus have them streamed to you.

You can work around a lack of regular board space by writing on the screen of a tablet computer connected to the room projector. This works particularly well for quantitative cases where you need to show calculations. After class, you can distribute the digital notes to the students. If you have a large class—say, more than seventy students, especially if you are in a lecture hall—this solution may actually be better than a physical board, which can be hard to see from a distance unless you are writing with extra-thick markers. If you can set this

FIGURE 10-1

A word cloud for this chapter

The font size of a word indicates its relative frequency

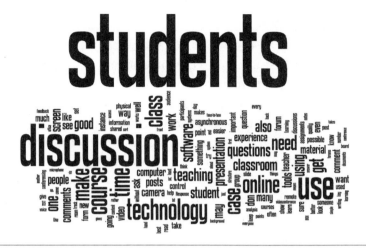

up with a wireless connection to the projector and walk around with the tablet computer in your hand, so much the better.

Presentation Software

Presentation software in a case teaching book? Well, chances are you will end up using it, so you might as well use it right. We don't subscribe to the renowned graphics designer Ed Tufte's (2003) admonition, "PowerPoint is evil." As with any tool, presentation software has its uses, even in a case class, where it should generate at least as much discussion as the time it takes to present.

There are two problems with using presentation software in teaching. The first is that the audience tends to read the presentation instead of listening and responding to you. The second is that a prepared presentation makes it hard to deviate from the prearranged slide order. Eventually, the presentation is running you rather than the other way around. Here are a few tricks to avoid this:

1. *Locate and learn to use the "black screen" key.* All presentation software has a key that, when pressed, will black out the screen (in PowerPoint, it is ".", that is, the period). If you use a remote

projection controller, it will normally have a "mute screen" key. Press this key frequently: every time you ask a question, every time someone in the audience says something, and so on. Press the key again, and you get the picture back.

2. *Always maintain control of your own presentation.* In some settings, you may be asked to load the presentation on a shared computer and use a remote control to advance the slides. In some instances, you may even have to say, "Next slide, please" to an assistant. We advocate using your own laptop or at least a computer you are comfortable with, and insisting on access to the keyboard. Maintaining full control allows you to skip slides without the audience noticing, to draw on the screen with your pen or finger (if you have a computer with that functionality), to switch over to other programs such as browsers or spreadsheets, or skip to another program if you want to demonstrate something. Don't tie yourself to your presentation. The audience may take you in another direction, and you should maintain the freedom to go there.

3. *Build continuous improvement into the presentation.* A smart trick is to create a hidden slide as the last slide in the presentation, on which you make notes about what you need to change after you have given the presentation. The next time you are using it, you can go to the last slide and immediately see what you need to improve.

4. *Don't use the presentation as an outline.* Bullet points *can* be evil. They can reduce you to a talking head, reading the text, which the audience can do much faster by itself. Instead, make two presentations—one with text, and one with just illustrations, diagrams, pictures, or, in a pinch, a few key words. Keep the comprehensive, textual presentation to yourself and show the pictorial one to the audience. Figure 10-2 illustrates why network airlines configure their networks in a hub-and-spoke configuration. Which slide allows for the best discussion? You should have access to the text version, but don't read from it; you probably won't need it, since you will remember what you will be saying when you see the pictures.

FIGURE 10-2

Picture versus text: Which slide enables the best discussion?

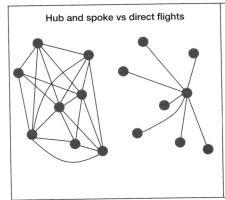

Hub and spoke vs direct flights	Hub and spoke vs direct flights
	• Passengers prefer direct routes, if possible, but also want high flight frequency • Reorganizing the route network from direct routes to a hub-and-spoke configuration allows more daily flights from all cities – Each plane takes traffic not just to the hub, but also to all the spokes – With more flights per day, your chance of finding a time slot that fits the customer increases • Hub airports are contested—dominating one is a competitive advantage • With increasing traffic, low-cost airlines can contest city-pairs, diverting traffic from the hub

You can hand out the textual presentation as documentation after class, if you want to. An added bonus is that slide decks with diagrams and pictures without text require a presenter, increasing your job security.

5. *Structured, terse slides work.* One way of thinking of slide design is to make the heading of each slide a declarative statement; the bottom line (if present), a conclusion of some sort; and the middle part, data, preferably in the form of a picture or diagram that supports the conclusion. Remember that each slide should have one—and only one—point. That is all you have room for.

6. *All rules can be broken.* We have met incredible presenters who show up with thick stacks of text-based slides and then engage the audience. One of them used to show up with more than forty text-based slides and on a good day would get through about five of them. He concentrated on having a good discussion with the audience and ended up giving the slide deck as documentation afterward.

7. *Dark classrooms induce sleepiness.* Dim the lights only as much as necessary. Modern projectors are bright enough that you can leave the lights at full brightness in most rooms.

8. *Consider going to the movies.* If you have a class involving a presentation you give often, consider having someone videotape you. Then you can show it to the audience (with or without you there) and then facilitate a discussion afterward (in person or via videoconference.) You don't have to repeat a presentation. You can follow the audience's reactions yourself and get to do the interesting part: the discussion.

Tools for Student-Teacher Interaction

There are many ways of using technology to interact with students and help them interact with each other. The key to using technology for interacting with students is to structure it so that you have less work while the students' experience is improved.

Learning Management Systems

Almost every university has a learning management system (LMS), a shared system through which teacher and students can interact, often the main (and mandated) information channel between you and the students. The systems keep track of which students are enrolled in a course and let you securely distribute material, information, and assignments. To varying degrees, they also provide plagiarism detection, discussion forums, and grading systems.

LMSs are easy to use and can automate many course management tasks, such as making sure students hand in assignments on time and get access to copyrighted material in electronic form. So, how can you make the best use of them?

Build a Sandbox

Give yourself a safe space to experiment by setting up a practice class with no students. If you can't do that yourself, get an administrator to do it. You need a place where you can fiddle around without anyone noticing, and then, when you are happy with what you have done, transfer the material to your regular courses.

Explore the System

Spend some time before your course to evaluate each of the options offered. That will help you decide whether to use them or adopt an external alternative. Learn what the various terms mean— document, assignment, posting, announcements. Each LMS uses these in different ways, and the meaning may not correspond to its analog version, at least not the way you think of it.

Maintain Communication Norms

For each course, decide on your main communication form and stick to it. Most systems let you make announcements that the students will see on the course front page with or without alerts sent out to the students. Some systems require you to send out messages by email; others have functionality for alerts via social media, an LMS smartphone app, or other channels. Decide what you will send in what form. Otherwise, students will claim not to have seen the front-page announcement because they were expecting an email, and so on. You may vary this from course to course, but be consistent within each course.

Create a FAQ Repository

Insist that students ask you questions outside class via email or public forum only and then answer them in a public forum. Thus, you avoid having to give the same answers many times.

Structure for Reuse

Write session descriptions, assignments, and other content blocks without dates, so that you can reuse them the next year without editing. You will need to differentiate between content that needs to be tailored for each class and content that can be held stable. This saves a lot of repetitive work and avoids students' complaints about incorrect dates on some material.

Facilitate Searching

When writing content, make sure it is consistently searchable, so if the students search for "assignment course XXX1234," they will get *all* the assignments, not miss the one that you decided to call "written quiz test" instead.

Consider the User's Experience

Give some thought to the aesthetics of the course page and the documents you upload there. Use consistent design elements such as fonts, colors, and heading sizes. Find one form you like and stick with it. Variation in layout without reason creates confusion.

Many LMSs also allow you to change the interface. Be careful when you do this, make only changes that you consider important, and be consistent. You are designing a system interface, not a document. If you can, remove student access to features you are not going to use. If you are not planning to use the in-system discussion forum, for instance, remove it. Otherwise, students may post questions that you don't see, giving the impression that you are unresponsive. Clean and simple is always the best option for any interface.

Maintain Structure

Give some thought to the organization of the course content. You can organize it chronologically, for instance, or you can keep all the session descriptions together, all reading material together, and so on. Whatever you choose, stick with it throughout the course.

Automate Availability

Most systems allow you to reveal things to the students at preset times. This powerful feature allows you to write assignments and material when you have time.

Explore the Analytics

LMSs have functionality to analyze what students are doing and by extension how the class is proceeding. This source is good for monitoring progress and grading, especially for remote students, assuming, of course, the students do most of their work inside the system. Often, teachers form opinions of students early in the course. Online analytics tools give a more dispassionate view of the whole class. Beyond metrics for postings and submissions, you can also see how many students have accessed materials.

Seek and Accept Help

Get to know your technical support people. They generally enjoy working with enthusiastic faculty. Ask them for examples of particularly good courses where you can find best practices.

Other Technologies to Support Student Interaction

There are many other tools you can use for student interaction besides those offered inside the LMSs or within the toolset your school offers. Since the pace of innovation is fierce in this field, we will limit ourselves to fairly generic advice here.

Social Media

You can use any form of social media to communicate with students, whether web-or app-based. They are not any worse or better than email, but as students move from email to these tools, you may want to move with them. You need to be careful about differentiating yourself as a professional and a private person, as well as the culture and technical attributes of each platform. Use what you feel comfortable with. If you are going to use the platforms properly, you need to spend time and energy on them. Having a presence on the Internet as a faculty member can be very useful, but it can also be a distraction. *Caveat emptor.*

In-Class Polling and Voting Tools

Polling and voting tools come in a number of incarnations, normally either as specially built hardware handed out to students or as software that students can access using smartphones, tablets, and laptops. You can use these tools to get quick answers to questions ("Which of these three strategies should we adopt?" "What should the price for the new product be?" "What word would you use to characterize this person?") and immediately produce graphs or word clouds to show the results. Though great for instilling some interaction in a presentation for a large class, for most case classes, these tools are probably overkill, unless the students are used to and like them. You can get the same result by asking the students questions and writing the results on the board. Some schools push these technologies on teachers in an effort to seem modern, but as always, you should not use technology for its own sake.

Questionnaires

Questionnaires are effective when you want to collect standardized information quickly. We use simple online questionnaire tools to get information from students, for instance, for the self-grading form mentioned in chapter 4. These tools probably work best when students answer the questions ahead of class—so you have some time to analyze the results and decide what you want to discuss—but you could use them for impromptu surveys if the students have laptops in class. However, you have to think carefully about what kind of data to ask for and the privacy implications of doing instant analysis on live data. A small tip: if you ask for student names, make separate fields for first name, surname, and, if relevant, student ID number to make sorting the results easy.

Shared Documents

Many people can edit shared documents at the same time online, eliminating version control issues and allowing participants to track who produced what. We have used this to solicit term paper suggestions (students enter their ideas and form groups in a shared document) and ask students to write in their own experiences with the topics of the course before the course starts, a great way to get to know the students in an executive class ahead of time. In some courses, we use shared documents for the syllabus, even letting the students edit so they can do their share of maintenance and development. They make their own Q&A pages, correct our errors (typically adding a new link when a link rot sets in), and give running feedback. This task can be fun and interesting for both students and teacher.

Analysis Tools

Because online students are doing their work with a computer, software can enhance the quality, efficiency, and presentation of their work. Drawing, mind mapping, and concept mapping tools can all be used or even required.

Online Simulations

Online simulations are available from a number of sources, including the well-known case dissemination services. Students have enthusiastically taken up the ones we have used, to the point where we sometimes must dampen their enthusiasm a bit and make them understand that the point is to learn something about a real-world situation, not play a game in which they try to figure out the underlying algorithm and score as many points as possible. If the simulation offers performance feedback, students can become very competitive, posting their point scores on social media platforms, so think carefully about how many times you are going to let them try the simulation before submitting a binding answer and be very clear about the learning goals.

Online Teaching

Many schools are moving curricula toward distance education. Teaching remote students requires forethought and new skills. We will discuss this in the context of teleconferences (where you use voice only, perhaps supported by a shared computer screen), videoconferences (where the students can see you and, perhaps, each other), and asynchronous online teaching (where we use discussion forums or a learning platform to teach via written comments and questions).

Teleconference Teaching

There is little difference between using teleconferences (conference calls) productively in an office setting and using them productively for teaching. Teleconferences involve getting the technology right and communicating in a way suited to the medium. Teleconferences free you from going to the office, and you can meet classes when you travel. Espen once had to lead a discussion standing at a payphone in Los Angeles International Airport, muting himself by holding his hand over the mouthpiece every time there was a flight announcement. It worked, sort of.

Get the Basic Technology Right

For a teleconference, getting the basics right means having a good headset and knowing how to mute it. If at all possible, avoid using a standard telephone or cellphone on speaker. If you can, get a wireless headset; standing up and walking around during a long teleconference keeps you energized. Unless you are lecturing, you will spend some time on mute, which everyone should do, unless they are speaking. It is very important that your headset has a way of quickly muting the microphone that does not leave you wondering whether you are muted or not. We have all heard stories of teachers leaving a portable microphone on in the bathroom.

One of our favorite headsets has a microphone boom that mutes by swinging it upright, so you are never in doubt about whether you are muted or not. If you really want to get technical, check that the headset has a low-latency return loop. That means some of your voice is sent from the microphone into the earphones. Hearing yourself in the headphones makes you lower your voice and speak naturally. The reason people holler when using cellphones and speak naturally when using an old-fashioned phone is that the latter has such a feedback loop.

You normally have a choice of using a regular telephone number or connecting to a teleconference using a computer. We prefer to use the computer, especially if it gives us added control of the teleconference, for instance, the ability to mute noisy lines.

Communicate in a Way Suited to the Medium

Good communication involves calling in early, keeping noise levels down (essentially, by having everyone mute as much as possible), having a very structured agenda, making sure everyone has his or her say, and being very conscious about time. If you are the leader of the conference, you should call in a few minutes ahead to welcome people, take note of participants, and give people the ground rules. If there are more than eight to ten students and any kind of lecturing is involved, try to have a colleague as the emcee. Unless you are very experienced, keeping track of the technicalities while also being responsible for the content is tricky. The emcee handles the introductory chitchat and turns the discussion over to the leader, manages question and comments, and keeps time.

When teaching with teleconference or videoconference software, be sure students know what is going on. Giving them a clear overview of the agenda at the beginning is essential, and you need to explain every transition from one element to another. You also need to narrate the mechanics of participation. For instance, state that you are going to ask a question, ask it, and then ask for students to use the agreed-on signal (such as pressing a button in the teleconferencing support software) for raising their hands, and then call on someone. You might even give the names of a series of students you are going to call on. After all, they won't know if you have seen their hands raise until you say you have. When students have finished their comments, remind them to mute their audio.

Communicate via Side Channel and Back Channel

A *side channel* in a teaching conference is an additional connection between teacher and students beyond the voice (or voice and video) itself, such as a shared presentation or the screen of the instructor or a student. Most software that supports sharing of material also supports interaction, allowing you to take written questions and communicate with the audience. If you don't use teleconferencing software, you can set this up with instant messaging software, a shared online document, or even text messages.

A *back channel* is a way to communicate with your co-teacher or emcee, if you have one. This is a place for messages such as, "Fred has a question. Can you take it?" "George has been droning on for too long. Can you cut in?" "If you want to discuss motivating salespeople, ask Roberta to open; she has experience." This is extremely useful and should be set up using either the conferencing software itself or some sort of messaging service, unbeknownst to the students.

One problem with teleconferencing is that it is a narrow medium, only communicating voice and perhaps a shared computer screen. You can't see students raise their hands unless you use software with that ability, and then you often find that most of the class doesn't know how to use it. You can't see which students are paying attention and which are doing their email or even are sneaking off to do something else. Asking open-ended questions does not work very well—students either don't say anything or start speaking at the same time—so you will need to keep careful track of who has said what and make sure you involve all the students. Cracking jokes works poorly. The students might be rolling on the floor laughing, but you won't know because they are on mute. When asking students a question, you need to give them some time to answer. They will have to unmute, and, if you are teaching an international class, there can be a lag of a few seconds between your question and the student's answer, simply because of the distance involved.

Get to Know the Students

If you are basing a course on tele- or videoconferencing, it really helps to have previously met the students face-to-face, so when planning the course, have some sort of physical get-together if possible, perhaps as a module at the beginning of the course.

If you can't meet the students in person, make sure you try to get to know them as much as possible by something other than their voices. Use social software (LinkedIn, for instance) to have them set up a professional profile, with pictures and background information. Use online tools to have them submit something that makes you understand them—why they are taking the course, what they hope to learn, and what their experience is with the topic—before the course starts. We like to use shared documents in which the students answer a question about their work situation in a context relevant to the course. Being something of a detective and keeping good notes can mitigate the energy-draining attributes of the technology.

Videoconferencing

Videoconferencing is essentially the same as teleconferencing, with the difference that the students can see you and, sometimes, each other. In the not-to-distant future, it may be possible to do videoconferencing classes where you can see twenty to thirty students' faces concurrently, but currently (2014) lack of bandwidth precludes this for all but the most deep-pocketed organizations. Consequently, you need to adapt the teaching to fit the technology.

Teaching Cases Online

With some technologies, you can have case discussions, student to student, that closely emulate a live classroom. From 1998 to 2005, we taught such a class, with one class in Oslo, Norway, and one in Waltham, Massachusetts. We started by using a regular videoconferencing room on each side of the Atlantic and eventually graduated to specialized case classrooms built at great expense with look-at-me cameras (each student had a button she pressed if she wanted to, turning the camera to her), ceiling-based microphones that picked up the students' voices from the classroom, and hugely complicated control consoles that left the teachers frantically pressing buttons to manage the situation.

The technology actually worked rather well and, over a decade later, the technology is more widely available, less expensive, and more widely used.

Doing a good videoconference is hard. If not quite as hard as giving a good performance on a TV talk show, it is in the same ballpark. You need to think about how you look, what you say, and how you say it. The problem is less the digital technology than the analog environment: lighting, acoustics, and how you use the camera.

Lighting and Background

Lights and background are the simplest problems to fix. Ceiling-mounted fluorescent lights make you look like a hung-over raccoon. Fix this with a small, soft light source on your face from each side of the camera. The light does not have to be strong (you don't want to squint), just strong enough to soften your face. Some screen-top videoconferencing cameras now come with LED lights.

The background is important. If you are doing the conference from your office or home office, position the camera so that the background is not distracting. Never do videoconferencing with a sunlit window in the background. It makes you look like a mafia informer—all black outline and no facial detail. If something distracting is in the background, consider hanging a curtain behind you, or get a roll-up stand-alone board from the marketing department of your institution.

Sound

Audio is just as important in videoconferences as in teleconferences, of course. You will have to make a decision about using a headset or an open microphone. We prefer open high-quality microphones if we are in locations that are quiet; otherwise, we use headsets. As we said earlier, consider investing in a proper microphone with a feedback loop. Some people think headsets look funny and unnatural—we agree—but they have the advantage of better sound and of signaling to your colleagues or family members that you are in a conference and are not to be disturbed.

The Video Camera

When you are talking to someone, you naturally look at his or her face—specifically, his or her eyes. A person who does not look you in the eye signals that he is not trustworthy or not interested. With videoconferencing, the camera is normally placed on top of the computer monitor. Consequently, when you are looking at the people you are talking to on the computer screen, you are not looking into the camera, and your audience's impression is that you aren't looking at them. This creates a stilted feeling and is one of the main reasons many people dislike videoconferences, thinking them less "personal" than face-to-face meetings.

There are several ways to fix this. You can train yourself to look into the camera when you speak, but that deprives you of the opportunity to read the faces of the people you're talking to. You can increase the distance between you and the camera—this typically works well if you are using specialized videoconferencing hardware—so that the angle between where you are looking on the screen and the camera becomes smaller. However, this requires a camera that zooms and very good lighting and can deprive you of access to your computer keyboard.

The easiest solution for a regular office setting is to have a webcam on top of the screen, not in front of it. Some webcams come with a pedestal, or you can improvise a way to hang the camera in front of the screen. Put the camera as close to the picture of the participants as possible.

Camera height is also an issue. Try to place it so that you are looking neither up nor down at it. If necessary, adjust your chair so your eyes are level with the camera. Having the camera too low means you are looking down on the participants, which gives authority but can stifle interaction, especially if you don't know the students. Having the camera too high gives the opposite effect, and it can even look comical. Of course, if you are very small or very tall, feel free to adjust the camera height to compensate.

If you are traveling or otherwise forced to use the built-in camera in your laptop or tablet computer, prop the laptop up in front of you at eye level. Not only will this help reduce the prominence of your double chins, but will also, almost automatically, improve lighting and background and make you look more like you are participating in a conversation rather than absentmindedly staring at something else.

What should your camera show the participants? Your face only? Head and shoulders? Or a seated figure against an office background? This depends on what kind of screen is at the other end. If the students are using PCs or mobile phones, they will typically have a picture of you that is small, ranging in size from a matchbox to a playing card. In these cases, you should zoom in as much as possible. As one videoconferencing expert told us, zoom in until it feels uncomfortable, then zoom in some more.

If you are addressing a group of students in a room where the video is projected on a screen, you should go with a TV host shot, showing your upper body and head. Don't fill up the screen with a high-definition face shot, allowing the students to examine your nasal hair and dermatological imperfections. The "professorial" picture (you seated in your office with bookcases in the background) should not be used, unless you want to get fancy and start the conference that way and zoom in later. You need to fill the picture up; the students need to see your facial movements and you need to communicate (see next point) nonverbally. If you are not willing to zoom in that far, you might as well just post a still picture of yourself.

Communicating with the camera can be a challenge. Videoconferencing is a medium that consumes energy. A person who would seem lively and energetic in a face-to-face meeting can come across as dull and monotonic in a videoconference. Consequently, you need to slightly exaggerate facial expressions and move more than you normally do in order to heighten the energy in the meeting. Study good interviewers and news anchors, and you will observe that they nod a lot when people are speaking and use very obvious facial expressions (smiles, frowns) to communicate that they are paying attention. Spending a lot of time training yourself to do this may be a bit over the top, but it is worth keeping in mind.

Signaling is important. In a classroom, students signal that they want to speak by looking at the teacher and raising their hand. In a videoconference, you can use that as long as you can see the participants. Just raising your hand is a bit blunt as a signal. We advocate using a protocol we have learned from formal political debates, where a raised hand means "I would like to make a statement" and two fingers held up means "I would like to give a short comment on the current statement," with no more than two short comments allowed for each statement. This protocol, which at first seems rather stultifying, goes a long way to help the students self-manage their interaction. Most course-based videoconferencing software has signaling functionality built in that can be adapted for the same purpose.

As always, learn to use the technology and test it. Modern videoconferencing software has lots of useful features. You can share your screen, show a presentation that has been uploaded to a server, communicate via side channels such as chat boards, poll the participants, and so on. Time spent learning these features is well spent. You should also learn about the most common sources of errors. For instance, some videoconferencing systems will, without warning, remove the video feed if the bandwidth is too low. Knowing about this in advance makes for a less stressful experience.

Video windows of students can enliven a class. Usually, when students speak, they should be asked to turn on their video. When students are speaking, you can turn off your video camera as a way of signaling that they own the discussion. You can ask students to turn off their video cameras after they finish or you can keep several students on the screen at once. When students offer differing viewpoints, you can have them turn on their video cameras and debate an issue.

Concurrently Teaching Face-to-Face and Remotely

Quite often we have some students face-to-face, while at the same time having someone—other students or the teacher—participate through tele- or videoconference. The main challenge here is ensuring that neither group dominates and both have a good experience.

Having a guest lecturer participate via videoconference is perhaps the most common variant and is relatively simple to manage. You need to make sure that the technology works, try to make the guest look into the camera, and do all the other things good videoconferencing entails. Your role is host and emcee, letting students ask questions, providing comments, and summarizing and guiding the discussion. In a classroom, you often have issues with getting students' questions and comments back to the speaker. We tend to paraphrase the students' questions to the speaker, but you could also pass around a wireless microphone.

If you do frequent guest lectures, record your presentation in advance and have the students watch it, preferably together and in the same room. Have the students discuss the presentation among themselves and then join the discussion via videoconference (or, for that matter, in person). Let's say the presentation takes an hour, the discussion among the students twenty minutes, and the discussion with you another hour. The experience for the students is two hours and twenty minutes with you. The experience for you is one hour of interesting discussion with prepared and engaged students. (A problem here is that many schools only pay for hours in front of students, not for delivering the material, so some negotiation may be required. But such is the life of the pioneer.)

Things can get a little trickier if you teach to a group of students in a classroom and another group of students participates via tele- or videoconference. Normally, the face-to-face group will dominate the discussion, simply because the remote students have fewer ways to signal that they want to speak. The face-to-face group has immediate nonverbal feedback from each other, allowing them to instantly jump in with a joke or a pertinent comment. The remote students need to ask for the floor in a more formal way, and when they get it, lacking the nonverbal cues, quite often drone on.

You can minimize the droning by asking well-crafted, specific questions and managing the discussion to set a norm establishing that responses should remain on point. Be careful to hold students in the classroom and students participating online to the same standard. Depending on the quality of your video stream, you may be able to use nonverbal cues to get the student to wrap up his or her point. We prefer to give the remote students some latitude rather than verbally interrupting them, particularly if such interruptions are uncommon in the physical classroom. Facilitating a case discussion is difficult if one group of students feels it's being treated more harshly than another.

Our ideal hybrid class is to have all students functioning as a cohesive whole. But both the instructor and the students need experience with hybrid courses. It takes a few sessions for a class to gel. At the outset, you should acknowledge the challenges and signal that you are explicitly managing the process to improve the experience for everyone. Pay careful attention to the distribution of airtime among people in the classroom and those who are remote. If several comments in a row have come from the physical classroom, say, "Let's hear from someone online." Use group exercises, and make sure that every group includes both local and remote students.

Teaching Asynchronously with Discussion Forums

In addition to individual and group assignments in traditional classroom courses, asynchronous discussion teaching typically involves some form of online discussion forum, such as the discussion facilities of an LMS, some other public or private discussion forum, or simply a shared document that everyone edits.

Asynchronous discussion teaching normally involves giving students a case or some other material to read and then, over a period of time, posting questions about the material for the students to address by responding directly to them or to each other's comments. In other words, the structure and process of an online asynchronous discussion course is broadly similar to case teaching as usual, except for time, geography, and the fact that everyone—not just the student you select—is speaking at once. Using discussion forums for case teaching is relatively new, and as is often the case with new technology, it is primarily used to replicate the structure and content of traditional teaching online.

The pace of a discussion forum is more measured and reflective than the more spontaneous case classroom. The intense back-and-forth in real time is replaced by interactions that take place over hours or days. The online discussions can be more intense, as students reticent to speak in live class find their voices and more students respond

Moderating a Successful Online Discussion

Running a good online asynchronous discussion class is very much like moderating a discussion forum on the open Internet—a dedicated Facebook page, say, or a mailing list. In the words of Peter G. Neumann, computer scientist, security expert, and moderator of the highly influential RISKS Forum discussion list since the early 1980s:

> The bottom line is that moderating a newsgroup wisely takes serious dedication to, familiarity with, and commitment to the subject matter and willingness to put oneself into an intrinsically sensitive position. It does not work well if someone is arbitrarily assigned to the task. (Neumann, 1996)

Neumann maintains the forum by setting the tone for the discussion; commenting on submissions in a terse, humorous way; linking submissions back to archived stuff; and occasionally submitting something himself. His personality comes through and is one of the major reasons the RISKS discussion list has a worldwide readership and has had submissions and discussion from international experts in the field.

In other words, you can make an online discussion sing, but it requires effort and personality. Just like a real-time case classroom.

to any point made. Without the rich signaling of physical presence—facial expressions, tone of voice, gestures—participants must be more conscious of the way they present their ideas and themselves. We remind students about these challenges and encourage them to consider these issues when posting and reading the posts of others. Making this explicit reduces misunderstandings and conflict. While it is hard to tell a joke in a tele- or videoconferencing class, it is even harder in a discussion forum. You need to exert greater effort to make your personality come through, and your charisma is needed more than ever.

Foundations: Designing the Course and Forming the Contract

An asynchronous online case course has to be structured in more detail than a face-to-face course. Things happen between sessions, and since the students can be in many time zones, you need to give them time to discover new material in the course pages and to react to it. A typical online case discussion takes three to five days and requires the students to visit the discussion forum every day.

An online case discussion begins when someone—usually the teacher or an assigned student group—starts a discussion thread (theme), and students comment. As in any Internet discussion forum, some of the comments spawn long discussions; others end with the first comment. One difference is that online, students don't face the immediacy requirement of the classroom. They have time to think about what they write, to look up online sources, and to consult the course material. Given that they are graded on participation, some may flood the discussion forum with material, possibly copied from the web, so you may need to institute some rules about comment length and enforce proper referencing.

If the course has room for physically meeting the students, try to set it up as early as possible, preferably before the online teaching starts. When the instructor meets the students, and, most importantly, the students meet each other, norms and a learning contract are more easily formed. In addition to an initial meeting at the beginning of the course, having one in the middle and one at the end is a good idea. The meeting midway through can be used to clear up misunderstandings, communicate things that don't transfer well online, and sort out any group work issues. The one at the end can help students mentally finish the course and celebrate with each other (doing wonders for your teaching evaluation scores).

If you can't do face-to-face meetings, try to have some informal videoconferencing discussions, again to let the students get to know each other. At the very least, get the students to answer some common questions in a public forum. It is important that the students create representations of themselves, for instance, by having profiles and a photograph that shows up with every comment they make. Not only is it easier for everyone, including you, to recognize who is commenting, but the standard of behavior goes up. It is hard to be rude or repetitive to someone who has a face and a recognized personality.

Use the tools in the discussion software to set up profiles. Having backgrounds on students helps you manage the usual problems of online forums: trolls (people who post deliberately provocative statements, then sit back to watch the sparks fly), lurkers (people who read everything but seldom comment), and spammers (people who post a lot of repetitive material, belaboring the same point). You can deal with trolls by challenging them in return, draw out lurkers with questions geared to something they should know about, and discreetly ask spammers to change their tune.

Crafting online assignments is the same as for a traditional classroom, but in an online course, you can easily require that assignments be posted for other students to see. This sharing can both elevate the quality of the discussion and allow the students to learn from each other, but be aware that some students can be uncomfortable showing their knowledge (or lack of it). Since the distinctions between an assignment and a posting will blur online, you need to clarify which assignments are individually graded and which count toward the participation grade.

Selection of cases remains critical in asynchronous courses. Cases with tricks or surprises don't work well. It is much harder to lead a class down a blind alley because you cannot control the revelation of the "right" answer. On the other hand, complicated cases can work well because students can consult their preparation materials during the discussion.

It is easier for students to skip preparing the entire case and perform analysis just in time based on questions asked. We prefer an opening question or assignment that requires broad knowledge of the case. Some instructors like to require that the students' answers to the case preparation questions are postings or assignments. Unless you plan to grade at least some of these or use the answers in another way such as a poll or word cloud, students will see this as busy work and resent it; no one will read other people's responses to these questions because they are not intended for discussion.

An Online Case Course Example

Our colleague, Idoia Olazar, is a very experienced online case teacher. Here is what she does when teaching an HR course for an MBA class:

The students are English-speaking executives, located all over the world. The course runs over five weeks, with one real-time videoconference lesson (Saturdays, with a lecture and group presentations) and one four-day online discussion (starting Monday, also with a case) every week. The thirty or so students are divided into six groups, and each session starts with a group case analysis. For the discussion part, Olazar typically starts two discussion threads per day except, since many of the students are in distant time zones, on the last day. She does not allow the students to start their own discussion threads and enforces a "five-five rule": each student must post at least five comments (but not more than two per day), each no longer than five lines. A typical session generates 150 to 225 posts over a week.

Her experience is that online case discussion can be a lot of work (and learning) both for the teacher, at least when you are new to it, and the students, who quickly learn that the longer the discussion, the smarter they have to get in their comments. Being tidy and disciplined—especially about in posting new discussion threads—is extremely important. The course structure works well with twenty-five to thirty students. More than thirty-five generate too many comments, and fewer than fifteen fail to get an interesting discussion going.

Flow: Running the Discussion

Just as in a physical case classroom, you want a discussion among participants, not a disjointed set of comments to your initial questions. To do this, you will have to use many of techniques from the physical classroom: call on students to comment (difficult if they only check in once a day), ask follow-up questions to probe deeper, make your presence known, and show enthusiasm.

There is no physical space, but still try to use the virtual space and be everywhere, albeit not all the time. You should pop into all of the groups and discussions during each case discussion, even if only briefly, to raise the level of student engagement. It can be a lot of work until you figure it out. You can easily spend three times as much time on the keyboard as you would in a normal class, just managing the discussion. Self-discipline is very important. On the other hand, some of the engagement is easier. For instance, if you organize your thoughts during an asynchronous discussion, you don't need to do it in real time in front of a room full of students.

In chapter 3, we emphasized the value of the board in case teaching. As Rollag (2010) notes, in an asynchronous discussion, there is no physical board, so you need to find substitutes. In discussion forums, people can contribute in the form of new posts (that is, first-level statements) and then by commenting on them, commenting on the comments and so on. The structure of a discussion can look something like this:

[Teacher]: Question 1 about the case

  [Student 1]: Response to question 1

  [Student 2]: Response to question 1

    [Student 3]: Response to [student 2]

      [Student 4]: Response to [student 3]

      [Student 2]: Response to [student 3]

    [Student 3]: Response to [student 2]

    [Student 5]: Response to [student 2]

[Teacher]: Question 2 about the case

[Student 4]: Response to question 2

[Student 6]: Response to [student 4]

[Teacher]: Interesting; please relate that to your response to Q1.

The structure of the discussion is very similar to how the discussion runs in a classroom, with one significant difference: instead of having only key concepts arranged on the board at the end of the discussion, you have *all* the comments and questions. Your job as a teacher is to ensure the concepts are linked together, preferably by the students. The way you structure the discussion questions corresponds to a board plan, but you lack the ability to filter and categorize comments as they come. This means that the implicit summary and linking that come from populating a board are missing, and students can get very frustrated because, for every good comment, they might have to wade through four or five mediocre ones making the same point.

Discussion forums on the Internet sometimes solve this with voting mechanisms, where people "like," "upvote," or "plus" a comment. For a teacher, "liking" comments is rather imprecise; instead, comment, ideally by explicitly linking a comment to other parts of the discussion, as the [Teacher] is doing in the example. You can also summarize discussions and move them on by asking directive questions (for instance, "So far you have all concentrated on the cost side of this decision. Any ideas on how to quantify the value side?").

Rollag (2010) notes that the lack of a board motivates many instructors to provide summaries at the end of cases, which are popular with students. We advise against them for precisely the same reasons we don't like to use them in the physical classroom. The students' frustration with ambiguity that arises when you don't provide a summary is an important part of the learning experience. Providing summaries, particularly in a recorded lecture format, sends a message that there was a correct answer and you are providing it. However, you can assign a student to briefly summarize the discussion of each question and then ask the class to improve the summary.

With no recourse to the more subtle techniques of facial expressions, intonation, and body language, we sometimes single out particularly good points in our posts, but we think it far more important to build a culture where students are actively evaluating the quality of the posts in the discussion themselves. Call on students directly, openly or privately, to challenge the ideas of others. If the issue is thin arguments or poor analysis, enable peer evaluation of posts. You could also publicly post the statistics about which posts are read or responded to.

Just as in the physical classroom, some students will dominate the discussion if left unchecked. The problem is amplified in online discussions when students with more flexibility in their schedules are able to respond immediately to newly posted questions and take up a virtually unlimited amount of space. To control them, you can set limits on the number of comments per day or in total, or you can send a private message asking them to tone it down a bit.

Guidelines for Students

There are great benefits to pithy posts, and it is tempting to impose a maximum length on them. But doing so can obviate depth, nuanced analysis, and rigor, the equivalent of allowing students to speak for less than a minute each during the class discussion. While you could probe in-depth understanding through the use of assignments, forcing all posts to be short risks a superficial discussion.

Standards for quality of writing pose a challenge; do you want polished prose or impromptu conversation? Is text-messaging-type writing acceptable? We prefer to frame the standards as the level of a blog you would be happy to have a prospective employer read—grammatically correct but informal and punchy. Without such a standard, the discussion can quickly degenerate, much like the comments sections of most popular blogs.

One strategy is to limit the number of posts per student, which has the added bonus of lowering your grading burden. But this rules out some interesting potential debates and discussions and may demotivate some of your best contributors. If you do set a limit, make sure students are allocated enough posts to reply occasionally within a question. Deciding who answers each question first can also help, similar to the use of openers in a traditional case discussion. No matter what, set and maintain quality standards to avoid the forums filling up with low-value posts.

All of the types of questions continue to work online, but the opportunities to ask them differ. Unlike in the classroom, opportunities to ask follow-up questions and redirect the discussion come and go without you being there. Do not be as doctrinaire about the flow of the discussion as in a physical classroom. Remember that asynchronous discussion is discontinuous for participants anyway. Capitalize on interesting points by using them as the basis for new questions, even if the point was made much earlier.

Unlike in the physical classroom, we have found great value in letting students know how long a discussion will be open online, typically one to three days, and closing it exactly as scheduled. Students have enough time to read and participate in the discussion, and the case discussion will move along with the introduction of new questions. But we cheat. The forum indeed ends right on time, but if the discussion is still going well, we open a new question derived from the discussion immediately afterward. Deciding when to do this is the same as for a topic in a traditional case discussion.

We appoint student moderators for the discussions and evaluate them based on the quality of the discussion for the time they are running it. These moderators can rotate weekly and, if the discussions are done within groups, all students have the opportunity to moderate during the course, perhaps more than once.

You can have students generate the questions for the discussion, but this often leads to relatively low-quality discussions. We've had more success by requiring all students to submit potential discussion questions and then have them vote on the ones to be discussed. In some instances, we pick them. After all, students have no training in leading discussion, and we shouldn't expect them to be well equipped to craft good discussion questions. You might need to train them. But we do encourage students to include focused questions within their posts to prompt responses when appropriate, for example, "Have you seen other examples of this? Would this work in your company?"

Role-playing is different in asynchronous discussion because of the time lags. A good role-play requires several exchanges to develop, and that could take days in asynchronous mode. Rather than abandoning role-playing, assign it as a group exercise, in pairs or small groups, to be done synchronously or during a short period of time, such as one day. Alternatively, you can conduct the role-playing directly with students with shorter lags between responses.

Debrief the process of the discussion after each case, at least in the beginning of the course, pointing out what went well and what can be improved. You might consider doing this in a brief video. We have found that people often don't pick up cues in the discussion, get overwhelmed reading a great deal of instructor feedback, and don't absorb much of it. You can craft a magnificent manifesto about how to participate online, but the people you most need to read it are the ones who won't. Boil it down to some simple rules and highlight them clearly. Then discuss how things are progressing after each case.

Reading through discussion forums can be incredibly tedious, particularly given the way many software products structure the flow. You can reduce this by breaking the class into groups so that thirty or more people aren't simultaneously joining one discussion. Setting limits on the length of any given post can also help, but remember our earlier caution that word limits can work against in-depth analysis and rigor. We prefer to advise students to keep posts concise and to exceed one hundred words only when their content demands it.

Feedback: Evaluating and Closing the Loop

Grading and feedback in online asynchronous settings is easy in the sense that you have the students' comments, analyses, and postings in a digital format. The quantitative aspect of grading is relatively simple. Most learning management systems produce a report on participation by student, for instance. However, judging the quality—that is, assessing whether conversations are leading to learning—can be a lot of work. You can get some indication of comment quality in a quantitative format. In most software, you can track the number of times each post has been visited, for instance, but it may have been opened but not read. Using the number of replies to a post to judge quality undervalues excellent comments that may not lend themselves to replies. But you should emphasize the value of posts that provoke discussion as well as the importance of building on previous points.

For your own productivity, it helps to employ the same tools as with a class session: do the grading after each discussion, divide the students into relatively simple groups: one point, unremarkable; two points, OK; three points, very good. Tally up the students' points toward the end of the course. Using the "standard comment" technique mentioned in chapter 4 also helps cut down the workload. As with any grading system with a quantitative component, it can be subject to gaming. A student can easily flood a discussion forum with lots of posts, writing "Great point!" as a reply to some other student's comment. Listing comments per participant quickly lets you see when someone attempts that strategy.

Many students in online courses ask how many times they must post during a given week and simply keep track of that. They also tend to slam in their posts at the last possible moment to still be eligible to receive points toward their grade. You can partially address this by having relatively tight deadlines of only a day or two for participation in the discussion of any given question. You can judge student posts by the number of other students who read them or comment on them. You can also have students explicitly evaluate posts. In fact, some emerging discussion systems have peer grading as an option, even on video input.

Academic honesty can be difficult to manage thoroughly in asynchronous classes. For one thing, you have no idea who is really at the keyboard, making student collusion difficult to spot. We are familiar with liquid markets for ghostwriting assignments, and those for taking entire courses are likely emerging. Synchronous sessions can be useful for probing individual students, but if that is not an option, watch for incongruously similar styles in posts by different students, and for disproportionately positive feedback on posts. One advantage, of course, is that the dialogue is preserved, making plagiarism searches much easier.

Managing the Inevitable Technical Failures

Even the best academic infrastructures have failures, and if you are going to use technology innovatively, you will experience the occasional disaster. For instance, while writing this chapter, Bill inadvertently plugged a 110V wireless display receiver into a 220V socket in Finland, producing an impressive amount of smoke and shorting out every device in the classroom. Espen still remembers, as a twenty-four-year-old, crashing a mainframe computer in front of the entire staff of his university, an experience that hardened him for life. A certain lack of self-importance is essential for the technology-enthusiastic teacher; rest assured that it will come naturally as you get older and more battle-scarred.

You can do a lot to avoid technical failures, chiefly by testing things ahead of time, bringing redundant technology, and being ready to teach without the technology if necessary. If possible, get to the classroom early to check the room setup and make sure the technology works as you expect. If the room is occupied immediately before your presentation, get in earlier that day or the night before or try a similar room down the hall. Even with your best preparation, you're likely to encounter some technology glitches. Ask for help and do your best to calmly assess the situation. If possible, turn over responsibility for debugging the situation to someone else and start your session on time. Perhaps use one of the students' machines if possible. Once the technology is up and running, transition to using it or take a break and resume with the technology at that point.

Preempting Tech Failures

To minimize the impact of technology failures, plan ahead and manage calmly and rationally in real time. Planning ahead involves some basic risk analysis. You need to decide what might go wrong, how likely that is, and what impact such a failure would have. This allows you to make good choices about how much to mitigate your risk.

These measures, from the simple to the truly paranoid, mitigate risk:

- Carry your own computer.

- Put all of your necessary files on one or more flash drives.

- Store your files on a cloud server.

- Learn a web-based alternative to the application you plan to use.

- Create a working copy on your mobile phone.

- Email the documents to yourself or others as appropriate.

- Load files into your learning management system.

- Bring hard copy.

- Record a demo ahead of time that you can play if the technology fails or the network is not working.

- Purchase and configure your own wireless network connection.

- Bring your own projector.

- Carry a wide range of adapters for various types of video connections, and be sure you know how to change settings for connecting to an external projector or monitor.

Conclusion

Technology is here to stay. You may as well command it for your own purposes and become comfortable with it. The key is to experiment, to fail (often and early), and to learn. Not knowing how to use teaching technology is bad teaching, pure and simple. Don't *ever* see technological incompetence as a sign of academic eminence. It simply isn't.

To reiterate: use technology to make your students' experience and your own life easier, never for its own sake.

References

Neumann, P.G. Personal communication, 1996.

Rollag, K. "Teaching Business Cases Online Through Discussion Boards: Strategies and Best Practices." *Journal of Management Education* 34, no 4 (2010): 499–526.

Tufte, E. "PowerPoint is Evil." *Wired* 11.09, September 2003, http://archive.wired.com/wired/archive/11.09/ppt2.html.

Index

About the Authors

Espen Andersen is an Associate Professor with the Department of Strategy and Logistics at the Norwegian Business School (www.bi.no), where he leads the Technology Strategy Research Center. Based in Oslo, Norway, he has done research on topics such as technology disruption, information access technologies, technology strategy, technology in the airline industry, mobile business, e-commerce, learning technologies, digital business strategy, and CIO-CEO interaction. He has worked as a researcher with Computer Sciences Corporation Research Services and for ten years as the European research director for The Concours Group.

Andersen holds an M.Sc. in Business and Economics from BI Norwegian Business School and a DBA in management information systems from Harvard Business School. He has consulted on technology and strategy issues for a wide range of large organizations in the United States, Europe, and Australia, and is a frequent speaker on technology and strategic management topics. He has published academic and practitioner-oriented articles and is an enthusiastic participant in debates about technology and society. Professor Andersen has been a visiting scholar at Bentley University and MIT Sloan School of Management's Center for Information Systems Research and has given guest lectures and courses at many universities. Since 1994 he has had his own website at www.espen.com and writes the blog www.appliedabstractions.com.

Bill Schiano is Professor of Computer Information Systems at Bentley University, where he has developed and taught graduate courses in software project management, enterprise architecture, design for business, information systems management, and e-commerce, as well as undergraduate courses in risk management, web development, and e-commerce. He is a former director of Bentley's Master of Science in Information Technology program. Professor Schiano has also taught at Aalto University, TIAS School for Business and Society, the Norwegian Business School, Hult International Business School, and the Asian Institute of Management. He teaches both managerial and technical courses, exclusively using discussion and the case method, and has done so in traditional classrooms, in online courses, and in hybrid formats. Professor Schiano is an avid experimenter with technology that supports case teaching.

During 2000, Professor Schiano served as president of Thoughtbubble Productions, a New York–based new media company founded in 1995, helping secure an investment from The Formula Group. Before becoming president, he was a senior consultant with Thoughtbubble. He was also a research affiliate at CSC Index Research and Advisory Services.

Professor Schiano's research, consulting, and teaching of executive education courses all focus on the role and management of information systems in organizations. He has authored several Harvard Business School cases on information systems and finance. He has also published numerous academic journal articles on topics including information systems security, architecture, and cyber ethics, and was a coauthor of *CyberLaw: Text and Cases*. He holds an AB in economics from Williams College and a doctorate in Information Systems from Harvard Business School.